THE MAJESTY THAT WAS ISLAM

Great Civilizations Series

General Editors: A. L. Basham and Christopher Brooke

THE GREATNESS THAT WAS BABYLON
H. W. F. Saggs

THE GLORY THAT WAS GREECE
J. C. Stobart

THE GRANDEUR THAT WAS ROME
J. C. Stobart

THE SPLENDOUR THAT WAS EGYPT
Margaret A. Murray

THE MAJESTY THAT WAS
ISLAM

The Islamic World
661-1100

W. Montgomery Watt

PRAEGER PUBLISHERS
New York · Washington

Published in the United States of America in 1974
by Praeger Publishers, Inc.
111 Fourth Avenue, New York, N.Y. 10003

Library of Congress Cataloging in Publication Data

Watt, William Montgomery.
The majesty that was Islam.

(Great civilizations series)
Bibliography: p.
1. Civilization, Islamic. 2. Islamic Empire - History. I. Title.
DS36.85.W37 910'.031'7671 74-331
ISBN 0-275-51870-1

Printed in Great Britain

Contents

THE MAJESTY THAT WAS ISLAM

Introduction

The aim of this book is to give an account of the experiences and adventures of a large part of the human race over a period of four and a half centuries. In itself the subject is clearly defined by dates and by the peoples involved; but it is difficult to name. One may speak simply of the 'caliphate', and it is true that for about a century there is a single empire to which this distinctive name may be given. After A.D. 750, however, this empire began to disintegrate, and for a time there were at least three independent rulers each claiming to be a caliph, besides several other virtually autonomous rulers. On the other hand, despite the administrative disintegration the group of peoples concerned remained in some sense a unity. Many, perhaps most, still felt that they belonged together. All had entered into the heritage of Muḥammad, the Messenger of God, had come to see the world in terms of an intellectual scheme based on the Qur'ān, and were at least professing to direct their lives by the Book of God and the Sunna (practice) of his Messenger. The term for this cultural unity is 'Islamic', and the subject may thus be briefly described as 'the prime of Islamic civilization'.

One of the more particular concerns of this book is to try to make clear the relationship between religion and politics in the events described. Religion is important, and in naming the period the term 'Islamic' is more adequate than 'Arab'. Yet when a university colleague suggested that Islamic history should be regarded as a branch of ecclesiastical history, one could only laugh. The history to be studied is no more and no less religious than that of medieval Europe; but religion enters into it in a different way, since there is no papacy, no ecclesiastical hierarchy, and no priestly class in the strict sense, though there are religious intellectuals and what may be called a religious institution.

Another particular concern is to show how the Christian culture of Egypt, Syria and Iraq was transformed into Islamic culture. This change is one of the great failures of Christianity, though it has received little attention from Christian historians. This neglect may indeed be due to the very fact that it is a failure and that Christians would like to forget it; but for the same reason it is a historical process whose analysis should be of value for Christians. The transformation, of course, was far from being an absolute change. In the early seventh century before the Muslim conquests the culture of these heartlands of Christianity was Christian in the sense that it found its focus in a central core of ideas derived from Christianity; but at the same time it had incorporated much of the age-old wisdom of the Middle East. In the process of transformation most of the ancient heritage was preserved, but it was now given an Islamic focus, or set within a framework of Islamic ideas. Although the change is thus less than the description might at first suggest, it meant that what had once been part of the organism of Christendom now became part of the organism of Islam.

In the study of this process of transformation there is a special difficulty to be overcome. The main sources are Muslim historians, and these tend to neglect Christian matters. One of their basic assumptions was that practically everything Islamic came exclusively from Islamic sources. They were not prepared to admit Christian influences of the type so dear to nineteenth-century historians. The conception of influence connoted dependence, and dependence implied weakness; and to admit weakness was something Arab pride could not stomach. In respect of the Qur'ān the matter was abundantly clear for the Muslim historian, since according to Islamic dogma the Qur'ān was the very speech of God himself, and it was blasphemous to suppose that God could be 'influenced' by what Jews or Christians had written. So it came about that in many places where to the eye of the modern scholar Judaeo-Christian influence is obvious, the Muslim saw an idea or practice which was essentially Arabic or Islamic. At certain periods the practice of inventing stories was rife, and among the inventions were many tending to confirm an Arabic or Islamic origin for matters previously held by Jews or

Christians. For example, there is an anecdote (in several variant forms) in which Muḥammad is described as commending to his followers a prayer containing most of the clauses of the Lord's Prayer of the Christians. The pious Muslim of today will argue that there is no impossibility in supposing such a prayer to have occurred independently (perhaps by divine inspiration) to Muḥammad; but the modern occidental scholar considers this suggestion as being so improbable as not to be worth entertaining.

Another difficulty for the modern historian is created by the fact that Muslim historians tended to assume that Islamic society had a static character, and that what was practised by Muslims in later times had been practised by Muslims from the first. The Arabs of the desert had always been suspicious of change, and the Arabic word for 'heresy' (*bidʿa*) properly means no more than 'innovation'. Apart from this general assumption there were deliberate attempts by holders of distinctive views at a later date to show that their views had been held by unimpeachable authorities of the first and second generation of Muslims. The Shīʿites seem to have been specially prone to rewrite history to make it support their political claims. Because of this we find that in the ninth century there were bitter arguments about what happened in 632 (at Muḥammad's death) and in 656 (at the murder of ʿUthmān); but the motive for these arguments was not an objective interest in history but a contemporary political concern. Various modern scholars have written well-documented works calling attention to these anachronisms and as far as possible rectifying them. Such works will in general be followed here, and will be mentioned in the Bibliography.

* * *

The story to be told here begins after the death of ʿAlī on 24 January 661. This date marks the end of the period of the four Rāshidūn or 'rightly guided caliphs', and the beginning of the Umayyad caliphate. The period of the Rāshidūn had run from the death of Muḥammad on 8 June 632. Muḥammad's public career had begun only about 610, but the half-century between his 'call to be a prophet' and the death of ʿAlī had seen outstanding changes.

Conditions in Arabia round about the year 600 had been much affected by the great struggle between the Byzantine and Persian empires. These two empires had been at war, one might say, since 527 with some brief intervals of peace, and the war was to continue until 628. Though Arabia was distant from the main area of confrontation, both sides made efforts to improve their position there. The Persians supported ruling minorities at various points on the Persian Gulf, and about 570 had sent a force which had expelled the Abyssinians from the Yemen and had continued to maintain itself there, though without much support from the mother-country. The Byzantines maintained good relations with their fellow-Christians the Abyssinians despite doctrinal differences, and had made at least one attempt to bring Mecca under their control. While this war ran its course, and perhaps as a result of its making travel difficult between Iraq and northern Syria, the commercial centre of Mecca was experiencing great prosperity. It had gained monopoly control of the trade by the caravan route up the west coast of Arabia, and it would appear that this route was now being used by most of the goods passing between the Indian Ocean (including East Africa) and the Mediterranean area.

The appearance of the religion of Islam in Mecca about the year 610 is to be connected with the various tensions which had developed in Mecca as a result of its sudden prosperity. Muḥammad came to believe that he had been called by God to convey messages to his fellow-Meccans, messages which were subsequently written down and which constitute the Qur'ān as we now have it. The earliest passages of the Qur'ān may be said to have insisted that the root of the social malaise at Mecca was the individualistic materialism of most of the Meccans, especially the pride of the great merchants at what they had achieved through their wealth and expertise. Niggardliness with one's wealth and lack of consideration for the poor and unfortunate were the points chiefly criticized. Even the theological assertions of these early passages had a relevance to the Meccan situation. It is thus not surprising that Muḥammad's proclamation of the messages found a response among many of his fellow-citizens, not only among the poorer and less influential but also among the sons and younger brothers of the wealthiest merchants. It is also not surprising that in due course the success of Muḥammad's preaching roused the hostility of the great merchants and their henchmen. By about 616 life in Mecca had become difficult for Muḥammad and his followers, and in 622 he emigrated to the oasis settlement of Medina, some two hundred miles to the north.

The inhabitants of Medina were chiefly dependent on agriculture, especially the cultivation of dates and cereals, but there was a little local manufacture and trade and perhaps also some caravan trade. A year or two before Muḥammad's migration or Hijra a long-standing feud which had come to involve most inhabitants of the oasis had culminated in a bloody battle, after which there had been an armistice but no real peace. Muḥammad's invitation to Medina by a majority of the inhabitants doubtless came about in part through the hope that as an impartial arbiter he would help them to maintain internal peace and secure a reconciliation between the opposing parties. It may also be that the Arabs of Medina had become attracted to belief in God by the presence among them of some Jewish groups. Whatever their reasons may have been, most of the clans of Medina (other than the Jewish clans) accepted Muḥammad as Messenger of God or Prophet, and became Muslims at least in name. Along with this religious conversion, however, if it may be so called, went a political agreement with Muḥammad embodied in a document which has been preserved and is usually known as the 'Constitution of Medina'. The present form of the document is probably not the original form, but it makes its essential nature clear. By it there was brought into being a federation of clans according to the principles generally accepted in Arabia. The Emigrants from Mecca, with Muḥammad as their chief, were reckoned as one clan, and there are also named eight clans of the Arabs of Medina. There was nothing specifically Islamic in this federation except that the main parties to it were all Muslims. Muḥammad was recognized as prophet, and it was stated that disputes were to be referred to him, but otherwise he was only one clan chief among nine (the other eight clans being the main Arab groups in Medina).

It is not clear how Muḥammad expected the Emigrants to earn their living in Medina, though he had presumably considered the question. They could not remain indefinitely as guests of the Muslims of Medina, and it is unlikely that they were planning to take up agriculture. That left trading and raiding, and either alternative was liable to bring them into conflict with the pagans of Mecca. It was in fact through raiding that the conflict developed. The raid or razzia was a normal feature of Arab life, and could almost be described as the national sport of the nomads. The aim was to drive off the camels or other animals of the hostile tribe, or sometimes to capture the women. The razzia was carried out in such a way that there was little or no loss of life. After Muḥammad had been some months in Medina small groups of Emigrants tried to intercept Meccan caravans on the route to Syria. The Meccans seem to have received information about their movements, and all the raids were unsuccessful until Muḥammad sent out a small party with sealed orders, which were not to be opened until they were a day's journey from Medina. This party managed to capture a caravan in the neighbourhood of Mecca itself, while one Meccan was killed.

This incident roused the Meccans to action, and at the same time encouraged the Muslims of Medina to join the Emigrants in razzias. In March 624 Muḥammad led a force of 86 Emigrants and 238 Medinan Muslims to a place called Badr to intercept a rich Meccan caravan returning from Syria. The caravan eluded the raiders, but a relief force of 800 men from Mecca ran into Muḥammad and the Muslims and was severely defeated, several of the leading men of Mecca being killed. To avenge the defeat of Badr the Meccans invaded the oasis of Medina the following year with 3,000 men. A battle took place near the hill of Uḥud. The Muslims repelled the Meccan infantry but were thrown into disarray by a cavalry charge and only with difficulty regained the security of the hill slopes. The Meccans were so shaken that they could not follow up their success, and so the battle may be considered drawn. The Muslims, however, were full of dismay, since they regarded the victory of Badr as due to God's help and now wondered if he had deserted them; but Muḥammad eventually revived their spirits.

In the military struggle with Mecca there were no major incidents for two years. In 627 the Meccans made a supreme effort to dislodge Muḥammad but failed. When he tried to make the pilgrimage to Mecca in 628 the Meccans blocked his way, but after negotiations an agreement was reached in which Muḥammad was treated as an equal. The ensuing peace lasted for a year and a half, but in January 630, after the terms had been infringed by allies of the Meccans, Muḥammad marched on Mecca itself with 10,000 men and the city surrendered with virtually no resistance. The growth of Muḥammad's religious movement at Medina and among several nomadic tribes, together with his disruption of their trade, had left theMeccans with no will to continue the struggle. Indeed, a week or two after his entry into the city some 2,000 Meccans fought on his side at the battle of Ḥunayn against a concentration of nomads which threatened both Muḥammad and Mecca.

Muḥammad was now the almost unchallenged ruler of Medina and likewise the strongest man in Arabia. Tribes or sections of tribes from most parts of Arabia came asking for alliance. Apart from any religious considerations, alliance with Muḥammad meant that one was free from being raided by Muḥammad or his allies. Soon after going to Medina Muḥammad had entered into pacts of non-aggression with various tribes in the neighbourhood. As he grew stronger the circle of pacts widened and their character changed, and they came to involve mutual assistance in fighting. Eventually Muḥammad was able to demand that would-be allies should become Muslims, the two practical points which were insisted on being that they should perform the public worship or prayer and should hand over in money or in kind the contribution known as 'alms' or *zakāt*. By the time of Muḥammad's death most of his allies appear to have become Muslims, but some of the strong tribes on the route to Iraq may have been exempted from this requirement.

It is difficult to estimate exactly the extent at Muḥammad's death of the body politic he had thus created. Probably at least two-thirds of the tribes of Arabia had in some way entered into alliance with Muḥammad and become Muslims. The chief exceptions were the partly Christianized tribes on the route to Syria, which were still attached to the Byzantine empire. Of the tribes which later claimed to have been in full alliance with Muḥammad, however, it is difficult to know whether the whole tribe was involved in the alliance. Many tribes had deep internal divisions, and frequently the alliance seems to have been made by one section which was trying to get the better of another section of its own tribe. In a somewhat similar position were those minorities at certain localities in the Persian Gulf and South Arabia which had maintained themselves in power through the backing of the Persian empire. When that collapsed in 629, they turned to Muḥammad instead for support, but of course their adhesion to Islam did not commit the less powerful majority. It is our ignorance of the internal situation in each nomadic tribe or settled community which makes it impossible to state the precise extent of Muḥammad's power.

Muḥammad died on 8 June 632. He had, perhaps wisely, made no plans for the maintenance of his administrative functions except that he had appointed his chief lieutenant Abū-Bakr to conduct the prayers when he became too weak to do so. The Muslims of Medina wanted one of their number to succeed Muḥammad, both because Medina was the centre of administration and because they had made an essential contribution to the growth of Muḥammad's power. At length, however, they yielded to the argument that a man from Medina would be less able to hold the federation of tribes together than one from Mecca. Abū-Bakr was then appointed 'caliph [deputy or successor] of the Messenger of God'. It was of course only Muḥammad's temporal power to which he succeeded, since his function of 'Messenger of God' (or Prophet) depended on a divine initiative and could not be transferred by any human arrangement.

Abū-Bakr's caliphate lasted only two years until his death in 634. Most of this time was taken up with the so-called wars of the Ridda or 'apostasy'. These were revolts against rule from Medina by various tribes or groups of tribes in different parts of Arabia. Because entry into Muḥammad's alliance or body politic involved acceptance of Islam, withdrawal from it involved repudiation of Islam, and hence the name of 'apostasy'. The motives behind the revolts were mainly political or economic, but the outward form was necessarily religious. It is a curious fact, however, that the various leaders of the revolts felt they had to support their military activities with a basis of religious ideas. They claimed prophethood for themselves, and even produced 'revelations' resembling parts of the Qur'ān. The most notable of these 'false prophets' was Musaylima, who was supported by most of the tribe of Ḥanīfa in central Arabia, and who had begun his revolt before Muḥammad's death. The risings were all eventually quelled by the superior generalship and strategy of the Muslims; but at the same time the Muslim leadership removed the causes of discontent by showing great clemency to those who submitted and accepting them back as brother Muslims. Doubtless a factor contributing to the settlement was that on submission the former rebels had an opportunity of taking part in the lucrative razzias of the Arab expansion.

Abū-Bakr was succeeded by 'Umar I (ibn-al-Khaṭṭāb). His reign of ten years (634–44) saw the first phase of the phenomenal expansion of the Islamic state. Some expansion – though not of course the details – had almost certainly been foreseen by Muḥammad, since expansion was in a sense implicit in the conjunction of the practice of the razzia with the idea of the Islamic federation. Muḥammad had shown special interest in the route to Syria – one of the main exits from Arabia – and an expedition along this route was ready to set out at the time of Muḥammad's death. The fact that Abū-Bakr despatched this expedition, despite the threatening situation nearer home as news of the revolts came in, shows that this route for expansion had a prominent place in the strategic thinking of the Muslim leaders. As soon as the wars of the 'apostasy' were at an end, large raiding forces burst out of Arabia north-westwards into Syria and north-eastwards into Iraq; and before long these had also made their way from Syria to Egypt.

Once out of Arabia the Muslims found themselves in a power vacuum. The Persian and Byzantine empires were exhausted after their long series of wars. In Iraq the Arab victory against the Persian army at Qādisiyya (probably in 637) led to the fall of the capital Seleucia-Ctesiphon, and indeed marked the end of organized resistance by the Persian empire as a whole. The Arabs were now able to occupy Iraq and Persia as soon as they could find sufficient man-power to deal with the situation in each fresh locality, while maintaining their hold on the territory already occupied. Mosul in the north of Iraq was reached in 641, and by the same date two other armies were on the central Persian plateau. In Syria the Byzantines put up a stiffer resistance, but after several minor battles were so decisively defeated at the river Yarmūk in 636 that the Arabs were able to advance to the Taurus without much difficulty. After the surrender of Jerusalem in 638 and Caesarea in 641 the whole of Syria and Palestine was in Arab hands. Meanwhile another Arab army had entered Egypt and reached Heliopolis, and before the end of 641 the Byzantine governor had signed a treaty handing over the whole province to the Arabs, including the capital Alexandria.

Thus by the end of the reign of 'Umar in 644 the Islamic state extended to western Persia, the whole of Iraq, Syria and Lower Egypt and some of the North African coast towards Cyrenaica. It is a measure of the achievement of the Arabs that only twenty years earlier Muḥammad had won his first important victory with just over three hundred men. The organizational and administrative procedures which made it possible to hold together these vast territories had been initiated by Muḥammad and further developed by

ʿUmar; they will be described more fully in the account of the Umayyad state.

In November 644, aged sixty or a little less, ʿUmar was stabbed and killed in the mosque at Medina by a Persian slave with a personal grievance. A committee of the six senior Companions or associates of Muḥammad selected as his successor ʿUthmān (ibn-ʿAffān), a son-in-law of the Prophet and a member of the important Meccan clan of Umayya. The general character of ʿUthmān's rule has been a matter of controversy since early times. It is usually agreed that the first six years of his reign were a period of prosperity and good government. During these years the Arab expansion continued. In the west the Byzantines recaptured Alexandria, but soon lost it again. The Muslims built up a fleet from the seafaring populations of Syria and Egypt, and before long had conquered Cyprus and driven the Byzantines from the western Mediterranean. In their move along the North African coast they reached Tripoli. Northwards from Iraq they occupied much of Armenia and penetrated the Caucasus region, stationing a garrison at Tiflis. In the east they had practically reached the Oxus, they were at Herat in modern Afghanistan, and they were passing through Mukran in south-east Persia and into Sind.

This process of expansion continued for a year or two after 650, but 650 is usually taken to be the date at which a change for the worse manifested itself in ʿUthmān's policies. Certainly discontent made its appearance among various groups of Muslims. The reasons for this discontent are to be found in the general situation. In the course of some twenty years the nomadic Arabs from the desert, who constituted the bulk of the armies, had experienced a revolutionary change in their manner of life. Formerly they had spent their time herding camels and occasionally going on a razzia, but now they had become what was really a professional army. While the summer campaign (which was the norm) might be described as a long-distance razzia, they returned from it to spend the winter in a garrison-city. It was usually out of the question to attempt to go back to Arabia. Thus the political unrest of the years from 650 to 661 can be regarded as part of the process of readjustment to greatly changed circumstances. By 650, too, the distances to the frontiers were so enormous that the effort and fatigue of campaigning were much greater and the rewards rather less. One of the particular grievances alleged by the dissidents was that ʿUthmān had put members of his own clan of Umayya in the most lucrative governorships and similar posts. While it is true that there was an undue percentage of men from Umayya in the higher echelons, virtually every appointment could have been justified by the efficiency and trustworthiness of the individual in question; and so it is reasonable to see the main source of trouble as lying in the general malaise resulting from rapid social change.

The ruler of what was now a vast empire still lived a very simple life in Medina, and had not so much as a bodyguard. When in 656 malcontents from the provinces besieged him in his house, they had little difficulty in overcoming the young men of Medina sent to help in its defence and then killing the caliph. As will be seen later, the rights and wrongs of this matter were debated for centuries. Since some sort of arrangements had to be made for the administration of the empire, the Muslims present in Medina appointed as caliph 'Alī ibn-Abī-Ṭālib of the Meccan clan of Hāshim, Muḥammad's cousin and son-in-law. 'Alī, however, was never universally recognized as caliph, and what western historians have called the First Civil War continued for the whole of his reign. The first phase was a revolt based on Basra and led by three representatives of the lesser Meccan clans: 'Ā'isha, daughter of Abū-Bakr and Muḥammad's favourite wife; her kinsman Ṭalḥa; and another prominent Companion, az-Zubayr. 'Alī defeated the rebels without much difficulty at the battle of the Camel, so called because the fiercest fighting was round the camel bearing 'Ā'isha's litter which was eventually captured. She was released on condition that she withdrew from politics, while the two male leaders had fallen in the fighting.

A more serious challenge to 'Alī came from Syria. The governor there, Mu'āwiya ibn-Abī-Sufyān, was related to 'Uthmān, though he received his appointment from 'Umar. He refused to acknowledge 'Alī's election as caliph, and, when 'Alī took no steps to punish the murderers of 'Uthmān (with whom he had perhaps been in sympathy), he claimed to be the avenger of 'Uthmān's blood and *ipso facto* his heir. There was an armed confrontation between the two men at Ṣiffīn on the border between Syria and Iraq; but before there had been any serious fighting certain groups in the two armies, dismayed at the prospect of Muslims fighting Muslims, persuaded or forced the leaders to put the matter to arbitration. What happened next is very obscure, since at a later date propagandists of various political groups rewrote the account of events to suit their own claims. It seems that the decision of the two arbiters was against ʿAlī and that he refused to accept their decision. He was kept fully occupied, however, in maintaining peace in those parts of the empire which acknowledged him, and was not in a position to engage Muʿāwiya in battle. Meanwhile Muʿāwiya was able to expel ʿAlī's governor from Egypt and to send raiding parties into Iraq. In May 660 he had himself proclaimed caliph in Jerusalem. Before ʿAlī could take any steps to meet this challenge to his authority, he was assassinated by a political opponent in an act of blood-revenge.

The death of ʿAlī in January 661 led to the acknowledgement of Muʿāwiya as caliph throughout the empire. ʿAlī's son al-Ḥasan at first claimed to succeed his father, but he was weak in character. When he was threatened by the advance of Muʿāwiya's army, he agreed to negotiate, and gave up all claim to the caliphate in return for a large sum of money which enabled him to retire to a life of luxury in Medina. There was no further large-scale resistance to Muʿāwiya, though there were some small insurrections. The year 661 may thus be taken as the beginning of the caliphate of the house of Umayya or, as they have come to be called, the Umayyads.

I

The Umayyad Period

661 – 750

THE UMAYYAD CALIPHS

Sufyānids:	661	Muʿāwiya I
	680	Yazīd I (son of Muʿāwiya I)
	683	Muʿāwiya II (son of Yazīd)
Marwānids:	684	Marwān I
	685	ʿAbd-al-Malik (son of Marwān I)
	705	al-Walīd I (son of ʿAbd-al-Malik)
	715	Sulaymān (son of ʿAbd-al-Malik)
	717	ʿUmar II (nephew of ʿAbd-al-Malik)
	720	Yazīd II (son of ʿAbd-al-Malik)
	724	Hishām (son of ʿAbd-al-Malik)
	743	al-Walīd II (son of Yazīd II)
	744	Yazīd III (son of al-Walīd I)
	744	Ibrāhīm (son of al-Walīd I)
	744	Marwān II (nephew of ʿAbd-al-Malik)
	750	fall of the Umayyads of Damascus

THE UMAYYAD DYNASTY

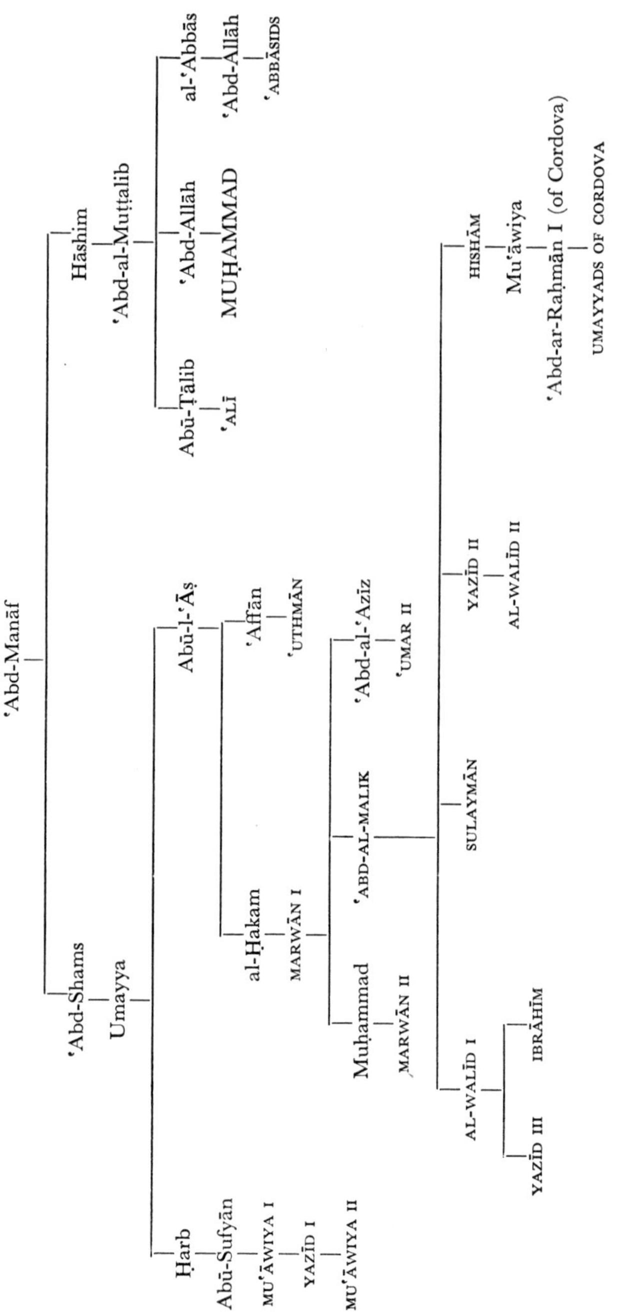

Note: Names of caliphs are in small capitals.

1

THE INTERNAL STRUGGLE FOR POWER

The basis of Muʿāwiya's strength

The success of Muʿāwiya in the First Civil War and his establishment of the rule of the Umayyads was not due solely to the accident of ʿAlī's assassination. From the beginning the governor of Syria had certain advantages denied to his rival, and these might well have given him the victory had the question been decided on the field of battle. For an understanding of these matters and of subsequent events it is helpful to consider the main contestants for power from 656 onwards, and also the groups supporting them.

First there was ʿAlī, who managed to get himself elected caliph on the death of ʿUthmān. He belonged to Muḥammad's own clan of Hāshim, and had married Muḥammad's daughter Fāṭima. Because of this some of his contemporaries may have believed that he had inherited certain charismatic qualities from Muḥammad. Later Shīʿism made much of this charisma, some branches even developing it into near-divinity; and it was claimed that Muḥammad had designated ʿAlī as his immediate successor, so that Abū-Bakr was a usurper. Despite these claims and the later rewriting of history it would appear that the charisma did not count for much during Alī's lifetime. He seems, too, to have been somewhat lacking in political skill, at least as compared with a man like Muʿāwiya. He was a stout fighting man, though the accounts of his prowess with the sword at the battle of Badr, for example, are probably exaggerated. Muḥammad made him leader in one or two small razzias, and gave him one or two administrative posts. Our main historical sources, then – which of course are Sunnite and anti-Shīʿite – have nothing to show either that Muḥammad designated him or that he had any outstanding gifts of leadership.

In seeking the caliphate in 656 ʿAlī was promoting his own personal interests and also those of the clan of Hāshim. Among nomadic tribes it was common for the office of shaykh or chief of the tribe to be given to the most competent individual in a particular family; and for this reason it might have been expected that the succession to Muḥammad would remain in the clan of Hāshim; but some of the best men of the clan had been killed in Muḥammad's battles, and in 632 ʿAlī was probably felt to be rather young and inexperienced. In 656 the members of Hāshim supported ʿAlī, especially when they saw how members of other Meccan clans who had long opposed Muḥammad were now far wealthier and more important than the Hāshimites.

ʿAlī seems to have had the support of most of the original Muslims of Medina. Their bid for power on Muḥammad's death had come to nothing. Now as they saw the growing power of Umayya and other clans which had opposed Muḥammad till shortly before his death, they could not but remember that without their support Muḥammad could not have won his first critical battles. Along with ʿAlī they held that priority in Islam should confer special rights and privileges. Despite their great service in the creation of the Islamic state, however, few of the men of Medina attained any prominence in the Umayyad empire, so that it must be presumed that they lacked any notable gifts for administration or leadership.

ʿAlī also had support from members of former nomadic tribes now living in Iraq. In particular the town of Kufa contained many zealous supporters of ʿAlī, chief among whom was Mālik al-Ashtar. In the army with which he confronted Muʿāwiya at Ṣiffīn, however, ʿAlī had other former nomads whose support was not so whole-hearted. It was a group of the latter who brought pressure to bear on him to submit the question of the caliphate to arbitration, and to nominate Abū-Mūsā al-Ashʿarī as one of the arbiters. They are commonly reckoned as the first of the Khārijite sect, and had as their slogan 'no decision but God's' (*lā ḥukm illā li-llāh*); by this they meant that the policies of the Islamic state, including the succession to the office of caliph, were to be decided on the basis of God's word, the Qur'ān. The men who killed ʿUthmān had justified their action on similar grounds, and ʿAlī was sufficiently in sympathy with them not to take any steps to punish them. The nomads who constituted the bulk of ʿAlī's army were thus by no means homogeneous; and many of them still showed a good measure of nomadic individualism.

The leaders of the army which was defeated at the battle of the Camel formed a second group of contestants for power. This group did not cease to exist after that defeat, since the son of one of them, az-Zubayr, was the chief anti-establishment figure in the Second Civil War. The chief members of this group came from some of the less important Meccan clans, and, though they had been Muslims at an early date, made little of their 'priority in Islam' and instead seemed to favour traditional Arab methods of conducting affairs. Their main supporters in 656 were apparently the former nomads settled in Basra. In the Second Civil War, while they continued to have many sympathizers in Basra, their strongest following was probably in Mecca and Arabia. They do not appear to have had any clear and distinctive set of ideas as a basis for their claim to the caliphate.

Thirdly there was Muʿāwiya and his supporters. Muʿāwiya was the son of Abū-Sufyān (from whom the first three Umayyad caliphs are called Sufyānids). Like one or two other members of the clan of Umayya during the earlier part of Muḥammad's life, Abū-Sufyān was a wealthy merchant, with hardly any equals in Mecca for sheer intelligence and business acumen. It was he who led the caravan which escaped from the Muslims just before the battle of Badr, and it was he who rallied the Meccans after that defeat and guided their policies for the next three years. After the failure against Medina of the great coalition which he brought together in 627, he seems to have lost heart. He did not become a Muslim until after the fall of Mecca, but it was largely through his conciliatory activities that Muḥammad was able to enter Mecca in 630 without fighting. At a later date Muḥammad made him governor of a region in south-west Arabia, and he lived on till about 652.

In his leadership of the pagan Meccans Abū-Sufyān was also

acting in the interests of the clan of Umayya, of which he was chief. There were several other wealthy and successful merchants in the clan and they co-operated well with one another. After they had all become Muslims they still held together. The third caliph ʿUthmān also belonged to the clan, and it will be recalled that one of the charges against him was that he had filled many important posts with his fellow-clansmen. Though ʿUthmān himself was one of the earliest Muslims (and probably not outstandingly successful in commerce), the others had mostly been opponents of Muḥammad until after the fall of Mecca; and their prominence under ʿUthmān and later was particularly galling to anyone who had fought for Muḥammad while they were fighting against him.

When Muʿāwiya refused to acknowledge ʿAlī as caliph and then claimed the office for himself, he represented the interests of the clan of Umayya, and indeed of most of those who had the administrative skills which were much in demand in the rapidly expanding empire. He was also supported by the Arabs of Syria who for many years had experienced good government under him. Most of these Arabs were not men straight from the desert, but came from families settled in Syria for a generation or two. They were thus much more stable and reliable than the ex-nomads on whom ʿAlī depended. The quality of these Syrian Arabs was an important factor in Muʿāwiya's favour.

Muʿāwiya himself had outstanding gifts as a ruler. He is reported to have had in an unusual degree the virtue of *ḥilm* for which the Meccans were famed. Many translations are given for this word, of which some are a little misleading. The nearest English word is perhaps 'steadiness', but the conception is best understood by looking at the contrasting defects. It is the opposite of being hasty and hot-headed and acting in the heat of a momentary emotion. It means not becoming flustered, but looking at the consequences and implications of a course of action before committing oneself to it. In one aspect it is the virtue of the shrewd businessman, but in another aspect it suggests genuine maturity of character. Muʿāwiya had all this, and at the same time he had great practical skill in handling men. He was therefore able to cope with the growing-pains of the empire of which he had become head, and to solve the problems which had baffled ʿUthmān and ʿAlī.

He was also wise in the choice of subordinates for important positions. Three men are of special note. ʿAmr ibn-al-ʿĀṣ was a

Meccan of comparable status to Abū-Sufyān, but younger and from a different clan. He became a Muslim only a few months before the fall of Mecca, but Muḥammad at once made use of his abilities as military leader and diplomat. He is mainly remembered as the conqueror of Egypt in ʿUmar's reign. In 656 he supported Muʿāwiya, was his nominee as arbiter, and became governor of Egypt under him.

The second man was al-Mughīra ibn-Shuʿba, a member of the tribe of Thaqīf which inhabited aṭ-Ṭā'if, a town not far from Mecca and once its commercial rival, but since before 600 subordinate to it. Al-Mughīra had acted rashly and forfeited the support of his tribe (which in any case was less influential than the Meccan clans), and this meant that he could never aim at supreme power for himself or even an independent kingship. Muʿāwiya recognized his great political skills and made him governor of Kufa, a post which he had held for a year or two under ʿUmar, and which carried with it oversight of the northern half of Persia. Al-Mughīra was successful both in the wider sphere and also in the lesser matter of maintaining peace in Kufa where a large proportion of the inhabitants had favoured ʿAlī.

The third man was even more devoid of family and clan influence. He was Ziyād ibn-Abī-hi, that is, 'Ziyād son of his father', indicating doubt about his paternity. His mother was a slave from aṭ-Ṭā'if who had belonged to Abū-Sufyān but had passed into another man's possession before the birth of Ziyād. ʿAlī had made him deputy governor of Basra with a special commission in southern Persia, and he did not acknowledge Muʿāwiya as caliph until 662. Muʿāwiya attached him to himself by publicly accepting him as the son of Abū-Sufyān (and so his own half-brother), and made him governor of Basra and the southern Persian provinces. He ruled with severity but was essentially just and fair, and the provinces under him were relatively peaceful and prosperous. His speech to the people of Basra on his arrival there has been preserved and has become famous. After enumerating the types of conduct he will not permit, he concludes roughly as follows:

> Hatred towards myself I do not punish, but only crime. Many who are downcast at my coming will become glad of it, and many who are glad will become downcast. I have come to you with the

> authority of God to rule you and to watch over your welfare. It is your duty to heed and obey me in what I think best, and your right that I should be just in my sphere of responsibility. In whatever else I may fall short, there are three things in which, I am resolved, I shall never fall short: I shall listen to your requests for help, even if a man comes to me by night; I shall not withhold your rations and pensions beyond the due time; and I shall not send you on distant lengthy campaigns. Pray for the welfare of your leaders, for they are your rulers who correct you and the refuge where you seek shelter. Do not let your hearts be filled with hatred and anger against them; for then it will go ill with you. If you see me managing your affairs competently, make a fitting response. I see among you many corpses; let each man see that he does not become one of them.

Though Muʿāwiya's reign was free from major troubles, there were many minor disturbances. Several of these were due to small groups of men labelled Khārijites, whose views were similar to those of the group which had criticized and opposed ʿAlī. In some respects their policies might be described as anarchism, but for them they had a religious basis which influenced the further development of Islam (as will be seen in a later section). Although there had been widespread support for ʿAlī during his lifetime, this feeling apparently led to only one revolt against Muʿāwiya. That happened in Kufa in 671, and was rapidly quelled.

Of the internal affairs of the caliphate under Muʿāwiya only one small point remains to be mentioned, namely, the question of succession. In pre-Islamic Arabia there was no law of primogeniture. In a polygamous society it may be difficult to remember who is a man's first-born, and besides, descent in the female line seems often to have been more important. Much property was held in common, too, and even when this was not so the obvious way of dealing with property in the form of camels was to divide them up among the heirs. In the case of a position such as that of chief of a tribe, a common practice was to appoint as a man's successor the best-qualified male in a certain family. The Muslims had no other political model than the practice of the pre-Islamic Arabs. The appointment of Abū-Bakr as caliph may be said to have implied two decisions; first, that the head of the Islamic state should come from the 'tribe' or 'clan' of Emigrants (Meccan Muslims who had gone to Medina with Muḥammad); and second, that Abū-Bakr was the best-qualified person among the Emigrants. The next three caliphs had reached that dignity by different routes. There was thus no clear Islamic precedent to determine what should happen on Muʿāwiya's death; and, if no steps were taken before his death, it was likely that there would be turmoil comparable to that on the death of ʿUthmān. Muʿāwiya therefore tried to secure a peaceful transfer of power by arranging a few years before his death to have homage paid to his son Yazīd. Most men seem to have agreed to do this, but one or two leading men refused. When Muʿāwiya in fact died in 680, some of these – notably ʿAbd-Allāh ibn-ʿUmar, often reckoned head of a middle or neutral party – reluctantly acceded; but two, another son of ʿAlī called al-Ḥusayn and ʿAbd-Allāh ibn-az-Zubayr, persisted in their refusal and left Medina. This may be regarded as the beginning of the Second Civil War.

The Second Civil War (680–92) and the reign of ʿAbd-al-Malik (685–705)

Al-Ḥusayn went first to Mecca, but then, following appeals from the people of Kufa, decided to make a bid for supreme power and set out for Iraq. Everything went wrong for him, however. Even as he set out the governor ʿUbayd-Allāh ibn-Ziyād, son of the previous governor, was executing the agent he had sent ahead. He got no farther than Kerbela, some fifty miles north-west of Kufa. There he and the small band accompanying him, mostly members of 'the family', found their progress barred by an Umayyad army. When those still with al-Ḥusayn refused to surrender, they were cut down to a man. The historian al-Masʿūdī gives the figure of eighty-seven dead, but notes that they had killed eighty-eight of the Umayyad troops; and this is perhaps as near the truth as we can now get. All Shīʿite Islam and many Sunnites came to regard al-Ḥusayn as a martyr, so that the day of Kerbela has acquired great religious significance. The nearest parallel would be the place of Good Friday in Christian devotion. Shīʿites now celebrate the tenth of the month of Muḥarram each year with 'passion plays' and long processions in which the worshippers beat their breasts or shoulders with hands or whips, even to the extent of drawing blood. In Shīʿite tradition the story of the martyrdom has been expanded to include countless harrowing details which have little or no historical foundation, while the Umayyads appear as villains of the blackest dye. The repercussions of Kerbela have thus been out of all proportion to its minimal importance in contemporary politics.

Much more serious for the Umayyads was the revolt of ʿAbd-Allāh ibn-az-Zubayr. He too went to Mecca, but there he began to organize opposition to the Umayyads. He even managed to extend his activity northwards and to build up support for himself in Medina. The events of 681 and 682 are confused, for there were many comings and goings behind the scenes; but in 683 most of the people of Medina threw off their allegiance to Yazīd and besieged the thousand or so members of the clan of Umayya resident in Medina. Though the besieged were at length allowed to withdraw, the men of Medina were soon confronted by an Umayyad army on the Ḥarra or lava-field outside the city and were defeated (August 683). Because many of the persons who suffered were descendants of the earliest Muslims, anti-Umayyad propaganda made much of this incident and exaggerated the harshness of the Umayyads. The alleged plundering of the town for three days by rough soldiery is probably an invention. Certainly Medina was sufficiently quiet for the army to move on southwards and besiege Mecca. In the course of the siege they are alleged to have set the Kaʿba on fire. In November 683, however, they received word of the death of Yazīd, and in the uncertain situation the general at once abandoned the siege and withdrew northwards.

Yazīd left a son called Muʿāwiya who was recognized as caliph by the leading Muslims in Damascus, but he was only a child and obviously incapable of exercising authority. In this vacuum almost anything might have happened, but after a few months Muʿāwiya also died (684). In these critical circumstances the members of the clan of Umayya met to decide on a policy at a place called Jābiya in Syria (June 684). Realizing the seriousness of the situation – for in Damascus, Homs and elsewhere in Syria many were going over to Ibn-az-Zubayr – they all gave allegiance to Marwān as caliph. He was one of the senior members of the clan, cousin of ʿUthmān and second-cousin of Muʿāwiya, who had held various administrative appointments, but had not been specially sympathetic to the Sufyānids. A few weeks later the Umayyads had collected sufficient men to offer battle at Marj Rāhiṭ, north of Damascus, to those Syrian Arabs who favoured Ibn-az-Zubayr, or at least opposed the Umayyads. The result was a victory for Marwān, and in August he received formal homage as caplih in Damascus. The victory of Marj Rāhiṭ also meant that for the Umayyads the worst of the crisis was over, and that they were gradually able to build up their strength once more. Marwān himself died about April 685, and the programme for recovery was therefore directed by his extremely competent son ʿAbd-al-Malik.

Although Ibn-az-Zubayr was nominally in control of all Arabia and Iraq and the northern part of Syria – Marwān before his death had recovered Egypt – things did not go smoothly for him. In 685 his brother Muṣʿab, who governed Iraq for him, had to deal with a Shīʿite rising in Kufa. This was led by al-Mukhtār, a man from aṭ-Ṭā'if, who for a time had supported Ibn-az-Zubayr, but now claimed that he was acting as the agent of another son of ʿAlī, Muḥammad ibn-al-Ḥanafiyya (that is, son of the woman of the tribe of Ḥanīfa). There was still much devotion for 'the family' (really the clan of Hāshim) in Kufa, and al-Mukhtār was able to defy Muṣʿab, and even, at the battle of the river Khāzir in August 686, to defeat an Umayyad army from Syria. To begin with, the followers of al-Mukhtār were mainly Arabs, but they also included *mawālī*, 'clients' or non-Arab Muslims. When the Arabs caused difficulties, al-Mukhtār found himself relying more and more on the *mawālī*. This is significant as marking the emergence of a new factor in the politics of the Umayyad period. At length Muṣʿab brought a stronger army, besieged Kufa, and in April 687 defeated and killed al-Mukhtār. Meanwhile the Zubayrid party also had another insurrection to deal with, that of the Azraqites, a sect of the Khārijites, who for several years from 684 terrorized Basra and the region to the south-east, but were eventually driven off eastwards.

By 689 ʿAbd-al-Malik was able to increase his pressure on Iraq, and in October 691 Muṣʿab was killed in battle and the whole province passed into the hands of ʿAbd-al-Malik. Al-Ḥajjāj ibn-Yūsuf, a trusted subordinate, who was also from the Thaqīf of aṭ-Ṭā'if, was now put in charge of the operations against Ibn-az-Zubayr in Mecca. After aṭ-Ṭā'if and Medina had been recovered Mecca itself was besieged, though not without scruples being raised about the violation of its sanctity. The defenders held out for seven months, but towards the end of this period most of them lost heart, went over to the enemy and were pardoned. Ibn-az-Zubayr, left practically alone, met his death fighting in October 692. This was the end of the Second Civil War, though some of the Azraqites held out in the east until nearly 700. It was also in a sense the last attempt of Arab secularism to dominate the empire. The Umayyads were later accused of setting up a secular Arab kingdom, but, as will be seen later, they were far less purely secular than the movement under Ibn-az-Zubayr.

The remaining dozen years or so of the reign of ʿAbd-al-Malik were a time of prosperity and internal peace. The whole of the eastern empire was in the charge of al-Ḥajjāj, the iron-handed conqueror of Mecca, while other provincial appointments were given to relatives of the caliph. This meant a concentration of power in the hands of ʿAbd-al-Malik. His control of the details of administration was strengthened by his insistence on the use of the Arabic language everywhere. When the Arabs first conquered the various provinces, they retained the existing provincial and local officials, and allowed them to continue to employ Greek, Syriac or whatever language they had previously used. This was now changed, but the same officials continued in office and were not required to become Muslims. In course of time, however, an increasing number of Muslims had the necessary secretarial skills, and the non-Muslims either accepted Islam or were squeezed out.

ʿAbd-al-Malik and al-Ḥajjāj also introduced the first purely Arabic coins. In the first flush of conquest the Arabs had no time to think about coining money, and were content to use the coins, mostly Byzantine and Persian, already circulating in Arabia and the conquered lands. Later certain Qur'ānic phrases were superimposed, but ʿAbd-al-Malik was the first caliph to mint coins with only Arabic and Islamic inscriptions. The coinage was bimetallic, consisting of the gold dīnār and the silver dirham (the Arabic words being derived from Latin *denarius* and Greek *drachma*). The standard rate of exchange was supposed to be ten or twelve dirhams to one dinar, but the actual rate was subject to market fluctuations and so varied at different times and places, the dirham often being much less in value. The Arabs had likewise taken over the previous systems of taxation, mainly taxes on land and *per capita*; but about the same time changes began to be made in the system of taxation to bring it more into line with Islamic precepts. (This will be discussed more fully later.)

The period of relative stability

ʿAbd-al-Malik was succeeded by four sons and a nephew. First came two sons, al-Walīd I and Sulaymān, then the nephew, ʿUmar II, then the other two sons, Yazīd II and Hishām. The three in the middle had short reigns, but that of the nephew had a special significance.

The reign of al-Walīd (705–15) reaped the harvest of the stability and prosperity achieved by ʿAbd-al-Malik, and was the beginning of a fresh period of expansion. In the west the advance through North Africa continued to the Atlantic and across the Straits of Gibraltar into Spain. On the northern part of the easterly front the Oxus was crossed and on the southerly part forces penetrated into Sind. This expansion will be described more fully in the next section. Al-Walīd appointed his cousin, the later caliph ʿUmar II, as governor of Arabia, and under him the mosque at Medina was enlarged and many other improvements made in the holy cities for the sake of the pilgrims. In Iraq al-Walīd retained al-Ḥajjāj as governor and gave him the fullest support. He was in supreme control of all the eastern provinces and was chiefly responsible for the expansion just mentioned. He died in 714, aged only fifty-two, and left a somewhat mixed reputation. While he could be stern and pitiless in carrying out what he believed to be his duty to God and the community of Muslims, it is now generally accepted that the stories implying wanton cruelty and sadistic tendencies are inventions of his enemies, notably the ʿAbbāsids. Julius Wellhausen (in *The Arab Kingdom and its Fall*) compared him with Ziyād ibn-Abīhi and gave as his judgement: 'They both regarded themselves not as holders of a lucrative sinecure, but as representatives of public order and of the Sultan (the caliph); they were granted great authority and left in office to the end of their lives, and they repaid the trust placed in them by their sovereigns by faithfully fulfilling their duties regardless of whether they found favour with public opinion.'

The brief reign of Sulaymān was similar to that of his predecessor. Expansion continued in east and west, but some considerable effort was also expended in an unsuccessful attack on Constantinople.

Some of the administrators trusted by al-Walīd and al-Ḥajjāj found themselves out of favour when power was given to their rivals, notably to Yazīd ibn-al-Muhallab.

When 'Umar II (ibn-'Abd-al-'Azīz) came to the throne affairs were in a critical state. There had been great losses of men and equipment in the attack on Constantinople; but even more serious was the fall in tax revenue owing to the extension of two old practices, namely, the exemption from the poll tax of non-Muslims who became Muslims, and the granting of lands to Muslims for a reduced amount of land-tax. 'Umar worked out a compromise which removed most of the discontent among the Muslims, but the regulations against the protected minorities were more strictly enforced to their disadvantage. 'Umar's policy, however, did not solve the financial problem, and, had he reigned longer than three years, he would probably have had to modify it. It is perhaps in part because of the shortness of his reign that he is regarded by later Muslim historians as something of a saint, in sharp contrast to all the other Umayyad caliphs. The main reason for such a reputation, however, is that he had been brought up in Medina among members of what will be described below as 'the general religious movement' and retained his sympathy for their views. This meant that he based his policies on Islamic principles more explicitly than the other Umayyads.

The reign of Yazīd II, another son of 'Abd-al-Malik, began with the rising of Yazīd ibn-al-Muhallab, son of the general who had conquered the Khārijites in the east. This rising well illustrates the confusion between tribal and family feeling on the one hand and religious principle on the other. The caliph Yazīd had married a niece of al-Ḥajjāj, whereas Yazīd ibn-al-Muhallab in the reign of Sulaymān had made life difficult for the friends and relatives of al-Ḥajjāj and was now afraid of reprisals. He collected a considerable force in Basra from his own and friendly tribes, and also had the support of some neighbouring Persian provinces. So far this is a description of an Arab family and tribal feud. He went on, however, to claim that he was summoning men to follow the Book of God and the Sunna (practice) of his Prophet and to take part in the Holy War, thus implying that the Umayyads and their Syrian troops were unbelievers. At this the much respected and saintly al-Ḥasan al-Baṣrī spoke against his claim; and later some of his followers criticized him because aspects of his conduct were not in accordance with his lofty claim. Once the caliph's army had reached southern Iraq it had little difficulty in defeating the insurgents. The leader was killed in battle, and his relatives pursued and put to death without mercy. Little else of moment occurred during this reign.

Yazīd was succeeded by his brother Hishām, who reigned for nearly twenty years. At the beginning of his reign the empire was in a relatively settled condition, and some further advances and consolidation were effected on the frontiers. Hishām had a competent governor in Iraq, Khālid ibn-ʿAbd-Allāh al-Qasrī. He was removed from office in 738 on being accused of having speculated in grain in such a way as to violate the cardinal Islamic principle of no usury. The removal of his strong hand was followed by a rising led by the ʿAlid Zayd ibn-ʿAlī ibn-al-Ḥusayn, which was quickly put down and was perhaps mainly an indication of the general deterioration of Umayyad rule. Hishām managed the finances of the empire with care and prudence, but he had not an attractive personality and acquired the reputation of being stingy.

The fall of the Umayyads

Of the remaining Umayyad caliphs only Marwān II (ibn-Muḥammad), another nephew of ʿAbd-al-Malik, had a reign of any length. The period of about two years between Hishām's death and Marwān's entry into Damascus was marked above all by quarrels within the Umayyad family. Even if the family had held together, however, it is doubtful whether they would have been able to retrieve the situation. There were too many adverse factors.

The most important of these factors was probably the discontent of the large numbers of non-Arabs who had become Muslims, especially in Iraq and the eastern provinces. These were known as *mawālī* or clients, since in practice it was necessary for all non-Arab Muslims to become clients of Arab tribes. This was not a principle of the religion of Islam, but, as will be seen later, was something implicit in the nature of Arab political thinking. In itself the status of client conveyed a suggestion of inferiority, and this suggestion was strengthened by the arrogance of the Arabs. Not merely did their attitudes express their sense of superiority, but they expected this superiority to be recognized in a material way, namely, that the annual stipends paid to the clients by the state, if any, should be less than those paid to full-blooded Arabs. Indeed, the Arabs supporting al-Mukhtār in his rising in Kufa in 685 are said to have objected to the *mawālī* receiving any share at all of the spoils; and a contemporary, criticizing al-Mukhtār for the encouragement he gave to the *mawālī*, is reported to have described them as part of 'the booty which God has given us' along with the conquered territories. Under these circumstances it is not surprising that there was widespread discontent among the *mawālī*. They had had a full share in the fighting on the eastern frontiers, and in Iraq particularly some had attained a level of scholarship far above that of even well-educated Arabs.

A second important factor was the increasing disunity among the Arab tribes. Gradually most of the Arabs in the garrison towns and throughout the empire came to be attached to one or other of two great groups of tribes, usually referred to as Qays and Kalb, from their leading members. The Arabs of the period regarded these two tribal groupings as constituted by genealogical affinity. The name of a tribe is normally in the form of 'the sons of X', and so the tribes were fitted into genealogical trees. Every Arab tribe had its place in the genealogical lists, and there was wide agreement about these, though a few points were disputed. The tribes associated with Qays are also known as the northern tribes and were all supposed to be descended from ʿAdnān. The tribes associated with Kalb are also known as the southern or Yemenite tribes, because they had for a time lived in the Yemen as agriculturalists before taking to a nomadic life. Their supposed common ancestor was Qaḥṭān. Most western historians doubt the authenticity of the genealogies. The extreme view is that the genealogies were invented in the Umayyad period to give a basis for the alliances between tribes which had in fact been formed in the garrison towns, where each tribe was quartered together. Arab historians accept the genealogies as authentic and as known to the Arabs in the century before Islam. The truth is probably between the two extremes but nearer to a moderate western view.

The growth of the political influence of the two tribal groups certainly seems to have taken place in the garrison towns and to have been a side-effect of the rapid transformation of nomads into professional soldiers and town-dwellers. When for any reason they felt insecure, it would be natural to link themselves with other men who also felt insecure, and an element of kinship would strengthen the tie. There was probably more to it than this, however. The Kalb group included most of those Arabs who had abandoned nomadism and settled in Syria before the coming of Islam and who wanted a stable and secure empire, whereas the Qays group consisted almost exclusively of men who had first left Arabia in the Islamic armies, and who wanted further expansion and the plunder it brought. The Umayyads had at first the support of the Kalb. In the Second Civil War the Qays of Syria went over for a time to the side of Ibn-az-Zubayr; and the battle of Marj Rāhiṭ was largely one between Qays and Kalb which, because of the number of deaths involved, deepened the feud between the two groups. For a time the caliphs themselves managed to maintain an uneasy balance, but as the eighth century proceeded this became increasingly difficult. A provincial governor might find himself powerless unless both the main part of his army and his chief subordinates were all of the same tribal group. Especially in Khurasan the struggle for power between the two groups became so intense that they failed to realize the growing threat to Arab supremacy from the *mawālī*.

A third adverse factor was the disaffection of many men of genuine religious concern. Most Muslims, both Arabs and others, accepted the world-view presented in the Qur'ān, and indeed could think in no other terms, but only a small proportion had a deep concern about religious matters. It is these last who are here being referred to as the general religious movement. In discussions of the Umayyad period they are sometimes called the 'pious opposition'; but they were not all opposed to the Umayyads, and in some cases 'piety' is not the best description of the religious attitude. The Umayyad dynasty was far from being as irreligious as the ʿAbbāsids alleged it was and had the support of scholars who could give a religious defence of its position. Nevertheless many, perhaps a majority, of the members of the general religious movement came to be out of sympathy with the Umayyads and ready to support the ʿAbbāsids. This was not a primary factor in the change of dynasty, but it contributed something. The general religious movement was interested in Islamic principles, and Islamic principles implied the treatment of the *mawālī* as brothers and not as inferior beings. In this way the general religious movement linked up with the ʿAbbāsid claim to be seeking justice for the *mawālī*.

Fourthly, there was also a vaguer form of religious feeling which was found in most provinces of the caliphate. This was the desire for a saviour or deliverer, coupled with a readiness to follow with complete loyalty and devotion anyone who looked like filling the role. There were various types of this feeling, some emphasizing more the political aspects, others the religious. The wide spectrum of feelings and attitudes associated with the idea of a deliverer were at a later date brought under the heading of Shīʿism, and will be described as part of the religious conditions of the Umayyad period. There existed in many quarters the feeling that a member of 'the family' (the clan of Hāshim) would be the best person to guide the empire out of the mess in which it was; and with great skill the ʿAbbāsids were able to harness this feeling to their military effort. Zayd ibn-ʿAlī in 740 had also tried to use this feeling, but he had not made sufficiently careful preparations.

The ʿAbbāsid family which led the successful rising against the Umayyads was descended from al-ʿAbbās, an uncle of the Prophet who opposed him nearly to the end, and from his son ʿAbd-Allāh, who was regarded as the chief early authority on the interpretation (*tafsīr*) of the Qur'ān. The grandson and great-grandson of this ʿAbd-Allāh, Muḥammad and Ibrāhīm, are said to have begun to plan for the seizure of supreme power as early as 718, but this does not seem very likely, though they had probably begun active operations before 735. In 743 Muḥammad died and activity was intensified under the leadership of Ibrāhīm. Various emissaries were sent to the Persian province of Khurasan, the most important being Abū-Muslim, probably of Persian origin and at one time a slave. There had been long and careful preparations, and in June 747 Abū-Muslim was able to unfurl the black banners of the ʿAbbāsids. Some of the Yemenite section of the opposing Umayyad army was won over, and Abū-Muslim was able to drive the Umayyad governor and his troops slowly westwards. Merv was occupied about the end of 747 and Nishapur six months later. After the defeat of a relief army from Syria in March 749 an ʿAbbāsid force was able to enter Iraq and occupy Kufa, which had always been a centre of enthusiasm for 'the family'. This was about the end of August.

The next three months were critical for the Islamic empire. In his propaganda, in order to attract to his army as many as possible of those who looked to 'the family' for guidance, Abū-Muslim had not said he was acting in the name of any specific person but had called on men to support the cause of 'him of the family of Muḥammad who shall be approved'. Unfortunately Ibrāhīm the ʿAbbāsid was somehow captured by Marwān II in 748, and died in 749, perhaps from plague. This left it uncertain which of the family of the Prophet should be chosen. Meanwhile affairs in Kufa were under the control of another ʿAbbāsid agent, likewise a non-Arab, Abū-Salama. It is said he might have chosen someone other than an ʿAbbāsid, but the presence in Kufa of a dozen members of the ʿAbbāsid family and the arrival of Abū-Muslim forced him to select Ibrāhīm's brother. On 28 November 749 Abū-l-ʿAbbās received the oath of allegiance as caliph in the mosque of Kufa.

A large part of the empire still supported the Umayyads at least nominally. In January 750, however, Marwān II himself was decisively defeated at the battle of the Greater or Upper Zab, a tributary of the Tigris east of Mosul. He then fled to Egypt, while the ʿAbbāsid forces gradually occupied the main cities of the Asian provinces of the empire and assumed control of affairs. They put to death all the members of the Umayyad family on whom they could lay hands. Finally, when they reached Egypt, a detachment found and killed Marwān II (August 750). So ended the Umayyad caliphate of Damascus.

2

THE EXPANSION OF THE EMPIRE

The character of Arab expansion

To understand the rapid expansion of the Arab polity from a primitive state to a vast empire it is important to realize that the military expeditions which won the empire were in a sense an extension of the nomadic practice of the razzia. A razzia (as explained above) was undertaken in a light-hearted spirit, the usual objective being the animals of the tribe raided, though sometimes women and children might be seized. A common plan was to swoop suddenly with greatly superior force on a small group of the hostile tribe in charge of camels. In these circumstances it was no disgrace for the herdsmen to make their escape, and thus the camels could be driven away without any loss of life. Occasionally, where there was a serious difference between two groups, there could be bloodier fighting, but in the razzia proper this was not the case. The military expeditions of the caliphate were on a much larger scale, of course, but a main part of the objective was still plunder, now in the form of movable booty.

A subtle change was brought about in the razzia through the influence of Qur'ānic ideas. It was not that it was given a religious objective. It is conceivable that such a verse as 73.20 – 'some travel about in the earth seeking the bounty of God' – refers to nothing more or less than a razzia; and many of the 'expeditions' of

Muḥammad's Companions, which were described as 'fighting in the way of God', had at least as part of their aim the seizure of camels or movable goods. The change came about because through a combination of Arab and Islamic ideas restrictions were placed on the groups against whom a Muslim might make a razzia. Just as an Arab could not raid his own tribe or a friendly tribe, so the Muslim could not raid other Muslims or any groups in alliance with Muḥammad. By the time of Muḥammad's death there was already a sizeable Islamic federation within which mutual raiding was impossible. In other words, raids had always to be directed outwards against non-Muslims, or at least groups not members of the federation.

As the empire grew, this last phrase came to cover a large section of its population. According to the Qur'ān Muḥammad was the last of a long series of prophets, all of whom had proclaimed in essentials the same message. Moses was taken to be the prophet of the Jews and Jesus of the Christians. Whereas pagans could not enter the Islamic federation without becoming Muslims, it was open to groups of Jews, Christians, Zoroastrians and other monotheists to enter the federation as 'protected minorities'. At first most of the inhabitants of Iraq, Syria and Egypt had this status. Once a group had gained this status, it could no longer be raided, and therefore any raiding parties had to travel still further afield.

The Islamic military expeditions are referred to as the Jihād or 'holy war', but it should be clear from what has just been said that there was no specifically religious objective. The accusation that Islam was spread by force of arms and that men were given a choice of 'Islam or the sword' is true only to a limited extent. It is true in that in dealing with idol-worshippers within Arabia the Muslims insisted that, if they wanted to escape raids by entering the federation, they had to become Muslims. Outside Arabia, however, nearly everyone was treated as belonging to 'the People of the Book', that is, as having a written scripture equivalent in principle to the Qur'ān and so being able to enter the federation as a 'protected minority'. There was no suggestion of forced conversion here, and for the most part it was only gradually that members of the minorities went over to Islam, usually because of some form of social pressure. The Arabic word *jihād*, which like the corresponding verb is found in the Qur'ān, has no primary reference to religion or warfare, but means 'the expenditure of effort' or 'striving', the full phrase being 'striving in the way of God'. For the ordinary Muslim in the ranks the chief implication of the phrase was that, if he died fighting thus, he would be a martyr and receive a rich heavenly reward. Though there is some superficial similarity with the idea of the Crusade, the similarity vanishes on closer examination and the Christian conception of the Crusade is seen to have grown from roots within the Christian tradition and to be independent of Islamic ideas.

Thus the Arab practice of the razzia, coupled with the idea of a federation in which raiding was forbidden, gave the Islamic state an outward thrust which continued until it found obstacles sufficient to halt it. The thrust was strengthened by the degree of unification of the Arab tribes achieved within the federation. What halted the thrust was probably not simply the military force opposing the Arabs, but a combination of increasingly severe opposition with a decreasing expectation of plunder. In other words, the expansion ceased when the booty to be obtained was no longer worth the effort expended in obtaining it.

The failure to expand northwards

Though there was a certain amount of seafaring round the coasts of Arabia, which is reflected in Qur'ānic descriptions of storms at sea, there was never any question of expansion by sea. The general outlook of the Islamic federation was that of Arab nomadism, and so the only form of expansion contemplated was that of the extended razzia or land expedition. Even when the Muslims had acquired a fleet in the Mediterranean, its role was mostly one of supporting the land forces. Such enterprises as the conquest of the island of Cyprus (649, 653) were felt to be exceptional. Since maritime expansion was thus excluded, geographical conditions severely restricted the directions in which the Arabs might expand. The primary directions of expansion were north-westwards into Syria and north-eastwards into Iraq. From Syria one could go south into Egypt and then either continue south up the Nile (which was difficult and not very profitable) or go westwards to Morocco; or else one could go north into Asia Minor. Since northern Syria and northern Iraq were adjacent, from the latter one could go north into the eastern parts of Asia

Minor, as well as into Armenia and Transcaucasia. The main directions of expansion from Iraq, however, were through Persia; but, because of the great desert and other obstacles in the centre of that land, the routes were mostly either north-eastwards towards the Caspian Sea and across the Oxus to Russian Central Asia or else south-eastwards parallel to the Persian Gulf, though branches of this southern route went northwards into Afghanistan.

It was in the eastern half of the northern front that in the period up to the death of ʿUthmān the Muslims had made most progress, for they had occupied Azerbaijan, much of Armenia, Transcaucasia and parts of Georgia, besides moving half-way up the west shore of the Caspian. Under the Umayyads there were no further advances in this region, but great efforts were expended in attempts to penetrate western Asia Minor and capture Constantinople. After the death of ʿAlī it became the practice of Muʿāwiya to send a raiding expedition into Asia Minor each summer to harry the Byzantines. The growing power of his fleet, however – it had already defeated the Byzantine fleet off Lycia in 655 – encouraged him about 670 to attempt the siege of Constantinople. His fleet penetrated through the Dardanelles into the Sea of Marmora and landed troops on the European shore not far from Constantinople. The precise dates of events after this are uncertain. Pressure is said to have been maintained for seven years. At one point a second Muslim army was on the Asian shore opposite Constantinople. The Byzantines, however, fighting for their lives and within sight of their capital, were too strong for the Muslims at such a distance from their base. Though the latter established winter quarters on the island of Cyzicus in the Sea of Marmora, and had virtual command of the seas for bringing reinforcements, they were unable to penetrate the fortifications of Constantinople. About 677 after severe losses Muʿāwiya decided to abandon the whole enterprise and make peace with the Byzantines.

During the Second Civil War the energies of the caliphate were directed inwards, but by 692 ʿAbd-al-Malik was able to take the offensive again, and it was apparently in the reign of al-Walīd I that the Muslims finally established their authority in the territory immediately south and east of the Taurus and Anti-Taurus. The caliph Sulaymān felt himself strong enough to make another attempt to capture Constantinople. It is said that an army of 80,000 men accompanied by 1,800 ships besieged the enemy capital for a whole year from August 716 to August 717. Once again, however, the city proved too strong for the besiegers. To losses in the fighting were added losses of ships by storm. It is usually said that it was 'Umar II rather than Sulaymān himself who realized that the caliphate was being placed in a critical state by the financial strain and material loss and who gave orders for the withdrawal of the expedition. This was the last major expedition of the Umayyads against the Byzantines, though there continued to be minor activity across the frontiers.

The failure of the Muslims to advance further towards the north, although Constantinople was a glittering prize, was due first and foremost to the strength of Constantinople. Its fortifications were formidable, and it could call on the services of great armies. The Arabs now had the usual siege-equipment of the time, but their mentality was perhaps not yet wholly adapted to sieges. The Byzantines were technically superior, too, in one point, namely, in the possession of a flame-throwing device known as 'Greek fire'. The Muslims found this particularly devastating, apparently both by land and sea. A further advantage of the Byzantines was that the peoples of Asia Minor were not disaffected towards Byzantine rule as were the peoples of Syria and Egypt. The Arabs too seem to have disliked the climate of Asia Minor, especially the severity of its winters.

The Arab failure to defeat the Byzantines in the two sieges of Constantinople is among the more significant events of world history. Positively it meant that Arab energies were channelled westwards into North Africa and eastwards into Persia, Central Asia and north-west India. Negatively it meant that eastern Europe did not at this period come under Muslim rule. Even if Constantinople had fallen, of course, the Muslim advance into Europe at this point might have petered out as did the advance into France. On the other hand it is possible that much of the Greek heritage would have been lost before it could be transmitted either to the Muslims themselves or directly to western Europe.

The expansion eastwards

In the first wave of expansion under the caliphates of 'Umar I and 'Uthmān the Arabs had practically reached the Oxus or Amu-Darya, though the territory was not firmly held. They had also reached Herat in the west of modern Afghanistan. The First Civil War interrupted the expansion, and no further appreciable advance was made until after the Second Civil War. Once Mecca had been recovered and the war ended, the viceroy in the east, al-Ḥajjāj, was able to assert his rule over the eastern provinces and to prepare the ground for further advances. His subordinate governor in Khurasan, Qutayba ibn-Muslim, eventually crossed the Oxus and in campaigns lasting from 706 to 709 subdued Bukhara and then from 710 to 712 Samarkand. In 713 he went still further eastwards into the region of Fergana – the valley of the middle Jaxartes or Syr-Darya – and remained there until the death of al-Ḥajjāj in 714 led to further uncertainties. These places are mostly in the Soviet Socialist Republic of Uzbekistan. About the same time the subordinate governor in Basra, Muḥammad ibn-Qāsim, advanced through southern Persia and Baluchistan, reaching Sind in 711 and Multan in the southern Punjab in 713.

In Central Asia the next twenty years were mostly a period of retrogression. The chief reason for this was probably the appearance in the vicinity of the Arab outposts of a strong Turkish power, the Türgesh, with large mobile bodies of cavalry and apparently some support from the Chinese. At the same time the local populations and their princes had become hostile to the Arabs as a result of much harsh and cruel treatment and the breaking of agreements. The Arab tribal feuds, too, to which reference has already been made, were showing themselves in the armies in this region and reducing their military effectiveness. A change came about, however, after the assassination of the Türgesh king, because the removal of this one outstanding personality led to a complete disintegration of the Türgesh polity. Meanwhile the Arab governors had been showing increased respect for the local populations and cultivating the friendship of the leading men among them. This made some further slight expansion possible from about 737 until the internal troubles of the empire put an end to external expeditions.

It seems probable, however, that apart from the break-up of Umayyad power the Islamic empire had reached the furthest region that could be effectively governed from Syria or Iraq. Indeed the province of Fergana, with its neighbours Shash (now Tashkent) and Ushrusana, were the outposts of the Islamic world for centuries, while Bukhara and Samarkand were important bastions of Islamic culture and centres of learning. When conquered by the Arabs these regions were mostly inhabited by Iranian peoples, whereas the steppes to the north and the mountainous lands to the east were mainly occupied by various Turkish (or Turanian) tribes. In general the Turks were more warlike than the Iranians; and this was probably one factor in halting Arab expansion. Another factor was lack of manpower. The Arabs were far from their homeland and scattered throughout a vast empire, and, even with a high birth-rate, could not meet all the demands upon them. They used Muslims of Iranian origin in their armies, but these were less effective as fighters, it would seem, than, for example, the Berbers in the far west.

In Central Asia, then, the Umayyads seem to have reached limits set by geographical and ethnic factors, but what they conquered remained solidly Muslim, even though at times it passed under non-Muslim Turkish or Mongol rulers. There was from time to time an influx of Turkish groups into the Islamic lands, but these almost all became Muslims and usually also sedentary. Over the centuries the religion of Islam spread to the north and east among the Turkish tribes, and even gained a foothold in China (which is still thought to have over ten million Muslims).

In the Indian sub-continent, on the other hand, the expansion of the Muslims had by no means reached its limits, as later centuries were to show. In the later eleventh century Maḥmūd of Ghazna raided down the Ganges as far as Benares, and the capital of the dynasty he founded was latterly at Lahore. A further advance in the late twelfth century by the Ghūrid dynasty was followed by the establishment of various sultanates and eventually of the Mogul empire, which under the Great Moguls from Akbar to Awrangzeb (1556–1707) ruled most of India. And even this was not the end of the expansion, for the religion of Islam has come to dominate Malaysia and Indonesia, though there it was spread by merchants and holy men before generals came on the scene.

The interesting question at this point, then, is why the Muslims, after reaching the line of the Indus during the lifetime of al-Ḥajjāj (d. 714), made no further advances for another three centuries. Clearly Umayyad weakness could not have been the basic reason. Much weight must be attached to the factor already noticed with regard to Central Asia, namely, shortage of manpower. In north-west

India, however, even more weight should probably be given to another factor, the difficulty of communications in the mountainous territory between Persia and India. All this territory including eastern Afghanistan was now nominally under Muslim rule, but for a time effective control can have been exercised only over the main routes and the main towns. The distance from the centre of the caliphate and the precariousness of communications through the mountains must have made advance beyond the Indus hazardous. When the advance did come about, Islamic rule had been much more firmly established in the mountainous territories, and the actual base of operations was itself in eastern Afghanistan.

This eastward expansion of the Islamic state under the Umayyads is an event of profound significance in world history. It brought together under a single rule most of the provinces which had once been grouped together in the Achaemenian Persian empire of Cyrus and Darius, which had been overrun by Alexander the Great, and which then had been partly regrouped under the Parthians and Sasanians. If Asia Minor of the Persian domains was excluded from the caliphate, this was amply made up for by the conquests westwards into Africa and Spain. The area of the former Persian empire was one of the earliest seed-beds of human civilization. Here was carried forward the wisdom and the insight garnered from millennia of the experience of living in community. This vast area was also contiguous with two other great and largely independent cultural regions, India and China. Communications were not good, but the Islamic world thus became to some extent open to cultural influences from south and east Asia. Paper-making was learnt from China and various artistic techniques from both India and China.

The expansion westwards

In the reign of ʿUthmān the Arabs had reached Tripoli in Libya. As soon as things had settled down after the First Civil War the advance westwards was resumed, now under the leadership of ʿUqba ibn-Nāfiʿ. With Berber support he defeated the Byzantines in what is now Tunisia (but to the Arabs Ifrīqiya), and in 670 established Cairouan (Qayrawān) as a permanent camp. Its position, far from the sea and near the desert, shows that the Arabs regarded their strength as being primarily in their land forces, although during the reign of Muʿāwiya their fleet raided Crete and Sicily. The Berbers of Tunisia were still far from subdued, however. In 681, after a period of disgrace, ʿUqba was restored to office and led a great expedition westwards which is said to have reached the Atlantic; but on the way back, while accompanied by only a small detachment, he was ambushed and killed by a Berber chief called Kusayla.

While the Arabs were distracted by the Second Civil War and had temporarily loosed their hold on North Africa, the Berbers resumed control of much of the region, first under Kusayla and then under a woman known as the Kāhina or priestess. The accounts of this period are confused, and the precise sequence of events has not been determined. The Arabs seem to have profited from the dissensions among the Berbers to break up the coalition of tribes supporting the Kāhina, who was defeated and killed in 702. Meanwhile in 698 Ḥassān ibn-an-Nuʿmān had finally driven the Byzantine garrison from Carthage. Many of the Berbers now seem to have become Muslims and to have joined in the advance. Consequently between 705 and 708 Mūsā ibn-Nuṣayr, the new governor of the province of Ifrīqiya, was able to reach the Atlantic with a considerable force and to establish Islamic rule over the territories traversed.

This success was soon overshadowed by another, the conquest of Spain. Spain was at this time controlled by a small aristocracy of Visigoths under their king Roderick. There is a story, or perhaps rather legend, of how the beautiful daughter of a certain count Julian was seduced by Roderick, and how Julian to gain his revenge induced the Muslims to invade Spain. It is indeed likely that dissentient Visigoths interested the Muslims in the booty to be obtained in Spain. In July 710 a party of 400 made a reconnaissance in force which showed that reliance could be placed on the reports of excellent booty and weak resistance. In the following year, therefore, a Berber lieutenant of Mūsā called Ṭāriq (who has given his name to Gibraltar – Jabal Ṭāriq, the mountain of Ṭāriq) crossed the straits with 7,000 men, mostly Berbers. While King Roderick was absent in the north of the country, the Muslims were able to establish themselves in Algeciras. When Roderick eventually marched south to confront the Muslims, who were now reinforced by a further 5,000 men, he was defeated and apparently killed, for no more is heard of him (July 711).

The whole of Spain was now open to the Muslims. The remaining Visigoths were scattered, and the ordinary people were in any case disaffected towards them. Here and there the chief men in a district would organize some resistance, but in most cases this was overcome after only a short delay. Visigothic Spain had included the province of Narbonne (in what is now southern France), and that was also occupied by the Muslims in 715 or a little later. There are stories of rivalry between Ṭāriq and his superior, Mūsā ibn-Nuṣayr (who had crossed into Spain with 18,000 men in 712), and then of how Mūsā was suspected by the caliph in Damascus of attaining undue power. It is not clear to what extent, if any, these stories are true. What is certain is that Mūsā and Ṭāriq were both recalled. The story continues that Mūsā made a slow triumphal progress back to Damascus, but was harshly treated after his arrival there.

For the period from the conquest until the fall of the Umayyads in 750 Spain was a province of the caliphate, ruled by a series of governors, subordinate to the governor of Ifrīqiya in Cairouan. The province was organized on the usual lines, with the bulk of the inhabitants having the status of *dhimmīs* or 'protected persons'. Some of the local rulers, such as Theodemir prince of Murcia, made treaties with the Muslims and retained at least some of their rights. Beyond the region brought into the *pax Islamica* by conquest or treaty the probing raids and expeditions continued. One party is said to have reached Autun on the Saône. The best-known expedition is one up the west coast, apparently making for Tours; in October 732 between Tours and Poitiers this was met and defeated by Charles Martel, prince of the Franks, who had been building up a position of strength in central France. There were one or two further Muslim raids up the valley of the Rhône, but nothing much was achieved. A year or two after the fall of the Umayyads the successor of Charles Martel took advantage of the distraction of the Arabs to recover Narbonne.

The battle of Tours (or, as the French call it, Poitiers) has been claimed as one of the decisive battles of the world. Whether this is so depends on what exactly is meant. Tours was not like Waterloo, for Waterloo marked the final end of the political structure created by Napoleon. The defeat at Tours brought virtually no diminution of Muslim power in Spain. Its significance was that this was the furthest northward penetration of the Muslims into France. It marked the turning of the tide. The Muslims were chiefly concerned with plunder, and the resistance of Charles Martel showed them that there was no more easily gained plunder to be had in this direction. A few years later another victory of his made it clear that the Rhône valley route was equally unprofitable. This certainly meant a diminution of the Muslim will to advance. Other factors, however, contributed to the ending of the raids into France. Manpower, both Arab and Berber, must have been fully stretched, and by about 740 the leading men may have been aware of the dangers threatening the Umayyad caliphate at the centre, and so more inclined to harbour their resources. The climate of France, too, may have made the Arabs feel that this was not a place in which they would ever want to settle.

There may also have been a turning of the tide at this period in the north-west corner of Spain. Traditionally, either in 718 or between 721 and 726, a Muslim force was defeated at Covadonga (near Oviedo in the Asturias) by prince Pelayo; and the importance of this event has been magnified by regarding it as the first step in the Christian *Reconquista*. From the somewhat legendary accounts it is difficult to know how serious the defeat was for the Muslims. The probability is that it was a trifling affair. The most important factor was doubtless the disinclination of the Arabs to occupy this inhospitable and mountainous corner of Spain. Lands in the north-west were allotted to Berbers, but after a famine which began in 750 many of these left their lands and returned to Africa. It seems to have been Arab policy to withdraw from a vast area in the north-west and to see that most of this remained uninhabited as a 'march'. Certainly the son-in-law of Pelayo, Alfonso I, was able to create the small kingdom of the Asturias among the mountains and to rule over it from 739 to 757. The existence of this kingdom weakened the position of the Arabs in Spain, but not to such an extent as to make the loss of all Spain inevitable. That came about only through a growth of Christian power in Spain over the centuries and a corresponding decline in the power of the Muslims.

In view of western Europe's leading part on the stage of world history during recent centuries the occupation of Spain by the Arabs in the eighth century is of profound significance. It was chiefly through Spain that the superior culture of the Islamic world made its impact on Europe. At the time of the conquest most of the Arabs were rough men from the desert with little culture beyond their traditional poetry, and the Berbers were perhaps even rougher. Yet within a couple of centuries the Arabic language had become the vehicle of all the inherited culture of the Middle East, including its Hellenistic elements (as will be seen in later chapters); and the western European response to the Arab presence is an important factor in the rise of Europe.

The Arab occupation of Spain and North Africa also led to, or at least contributed to, the break-up of the unity of the Mediterranean. There had already been a loss of unity in the western Mediterranean, though the eastern Mediterranean was controlled by the Byzantines when the Arab conquests began. Though the Arabs eventually controlled most of the sea, on its northern shores, apart from Spain, they had only slender and temporary footholds. One of the results of this, according to Henri Pirenne, was that European commerce began to look northwards rather than to the Mediterranean.

* * *

In whatever way one looks at it, there is something phenomenal about the expansion of Arab political power in the period between 632 and 750. One can mention various factors involved in the expansion – the exhaustion of the Byzantine and Persian empires and the consequent power vacuum; the superior fighting qualities of the Arabs from the desert, and perhaps also of the Berbers; the unification of the Arabs through the Islamic faith; the administrative skills of the merchants from Mecca and elsewhere. Yet, when all this has been said, there remains something mysterious. For instance, how could men with the ability to organize camel caravans adapt themselves so quickly to the much more complex task of organizing a vast empire? How could they maintain communications over enormous distances? How could they place so much trust in subordinates? In a process which seems so largely secular, had religion an essential part to play? Or was the main thing the qualities of character produced by the experience of life in the desert? The expansion of the Arab empire is certainly something to be pondered.

3

THE FORMS OF GOVERNMENT

Before describing more fully the political institutions or forms of government which have already been mentioned incidentally, it is important to emphasize that, at least in the first place, the political conceptions of the Muslims developed out of the previous experience of the Arabs. They were familiar with tribes and federations of tribes, with the relationship between the chief and the ordinary members of the tribe, with the protection of weak tribes and groups by strong tribes. It was inevitable that the political structure of the empire they won so quickly should be worked out in terms of the familiar. The Arabs had had some contacts with the Byzantine, Persian and Ethiopian empires, but they had no insight into their political functioning. When they describe what are really imaginary scenes at the emperor's court (to show, for example, that the emperor was sympathetic to the Islamic religion), the emperor becomes a slightly grandiose version of an Arab chief. It was only towards 750 that they began to realize that politically they had something to learn from the Persian tradition of government.

The state as a federation of tribes

The Islamic state in the time of Muḥammad and until the end of the Umayyad period was basically a federation of Arab tribes. This is shown by the fact that in the document preserved by Ibn-Hishām and known as 'the Constitution of Medina' the primary parties to the agreement are eight clans of the Arabs of Medina and the 'clan' of the Emigrants of Quraysh from Mecca. Though there are many difficulties in the interpretation of the document, there is no uncertainty about this point. The document also mentions several Jewish groups, but these appear to be in a subordinate or dependent position, since they are mostly referred to as 'the Jews of such and such an Arab clan'. While it is implied that the primary parties to the agreement are all Muslims and is stated that whoever supports a dissident individual will be exposed to 'the curse and wrath of God on the day of resurrection', many of the clauses deal with such traditional matters as the paying of blood-wits, the ransoming of captives, the granting of 'neighbourly protection' (*ijāra*) and the like.

The traditional character of the practical provisions of the Constitution is to be emphasized, since it has sometimes been supposed that Muḥammad had brought into being a community of a new kind, for which there was the special name of *umma*. Indeed the first article of the Constitution states that the groups involved in the agreement 'are a single *umma* distinct from other people'. To discuss this matter fully here would lead too far afield, but the following summary of conclusions may be given. In many verses of the Qur'ān the *umma* is an ethnic or linguistic community regarded as an object of the divine plan of salvation. In several passages, however, the *umma* is a community which has rejected the prophet sent to it and is therefore consigned to Hell. The common Arabic word for 'tribe' or 'people', *qawm*, is actually used more frequently than *umma* in the Qur'ān, and is sometimes applied to the group to which a prophet is sent. For reasons which are not obvious *umma* does not appear to be used in the Qur'ān after about the year 625, whereas *qawm* is found in later passages. Mostly the community of Muḥammad's followers had no special name but was known simply as 'the believers'. In all this there seem to be no grounds for thinking that an *umma* was differently constituted from a *qawm*; rather it was a *qawm* to which a prophet had been sent. Perhaps it was felt that *umma* was more appropriate to a body of the complexity of that based on the Constitution of Medina, whereas after 625 with even greater complexity *umma* was felt to be no longer appropriate. In later periods the word *umma* has been used in different ways, normally with a religious connotation.

The body politic at Medina, then, though the primary parties were Muslims, committed to believing in God and obeying his commands, was conceived politically as a federation of Arab clans or tribes. As the years passed tribes outside Medina became allies of Muḥammad and the Muslims. Perhaps at first Muḥammad did not make conversion to Islam a condition of alliance, but after a time conversion was insisted on. Thus gradually Muḥammad came to be at the centre of a complex system of tribes and smaller groups all in alliance with him and therefore restrained from fighting one another. This is essentially a federation, but there is no common Arabic word for that conception, although *jamā'a*, which is found in some of Muḥammad's treaties, comes close to it.

After the conquest of Mecca and victory of Ḥunayn in January 630 there followed what is known as 'the Year of Deputations'. Muḥammad's power was so much in the ascendant that nearly every tribe in Arabia wanted to be in alliance with him. A section of the collection of historical material relating to Muḥammad made by Ibn-Sa'd (d. 845) consists of accounts of these 'deputations'. The importance of the accounts is that they are the basis of the claim of the tribes in question to have been members of the federation during the lifetime of Muḥammad. Some of the stories gave but a slender basis for the claim. The worst was that of Ghassān. In this case the 'deputation' consisted of three unnamed members of the tribe who came to Muḥammad in December 631, were convinced of the truth of his prophethood, but went home and did nothing about it, though one lived to make a public profession of Islam in 635. It is not surprising that this was the best story Ghassān could produce, for they were allies of the Byzantines until the Muslims showed themselves clearly superior. However large or small the section of a tribe in alliance with Muḥammad at the time of his death – or even if a tribe was in the position of Ghassān – all Arab tribes which were Muslims belonged to the federation, and their members might be said to have the status of full citizens.

The 'protected' groups of non-Muslims

The position of the Jews in the Constitution of Medina was that of weak groups dependent on strong groups for protection. Before

Muḥammad's death a similar status was given to Christian and Jewish communities on the Gulf of Aqaba. When provinces of the great empires were occupied, the Christian and other religious communities found there were treated in the same way. These 'protected minorities', as they may be termed, were known collectively in Arabic as *ahl adh-dhimma*, 'people receiving protection', while an individual belonging to such a community was a *dhimmī*. In Ottoman Turkish one of these 'protected minorities' was known as a 'millet', and the system of millets persisted in the Ottoman empire until 1922.

This system of 'protected minorities' is sometimes said to have precedents in the Sasanian Persian empire, but it is more likely to be an extension of the desert practice by which a strong tribe, in return for a consideration, gave 'protection' to a weaker tribe or group, that is, was ready to come to its aid if attacked and to help it to avenge any hurt or loss of life. When a strong tribe had given an undertaking of this kind, it was a matter of honour for it to see that its 'protection' was effective. In the light of this fact it is not surprising that Islamic states have on the whole had an excellent record in respect of the treatment of non-Muslim minorities – it was a matter of honour for them to treat them well! In the case of the 'protected minorities' under the early caliphs the idea of protection had a central place. Each minority community paid the Muslim treasury an annual tribute in money or kind according to the agreement made with each. It also had to pay a poll-tax of so much per head. In return for this it received protection from external enemies and was entitled to the same protection from 'internal' crime as was given to Muslims. In a province containing minorities the governor was concerned only to see that they paid the appropriate sums of money, etc., and to settle disputes between Muslims and *dhimmīs*. In its internal affairs a protected minority was autonomous. The religious head of the community was responsible for the payment of the tribute and poll-tax and also for all the internal affairs of the minority, including the provision of law-courts to administer the particular (religious) laws of each community.

The status of 'protected minority' was open only to *ahl al-kitāb* or 'the People of the Book'. By these were understood believers in God who had a written scripture. In the first place Jews and Christians were intended, but the privilege was eventually extended to Zoroastrians, Buddhists and indeed most of the religions in the conquered lands, even to Hinduism. On the other hand, pagan tribes in Arabia could not have this status; but in practice most of them were so keen to join Muḥammad's federation that they were ready to accept Islam; and certainly long before the Umayyads came to power all the Arab tribes had become Muslims. In the agreements of Muḥammad's lifetime it had been explicitly stated that each 'protected minority' was free to practice its religion, and this freedom was continued. The Christians retained their churches and the Jews their synagogues. The later theory was that they had no permission to build new ones, but this rule, like many of the other petty rules about *dhimmīs*, was probably not always observed. Rather exceptionally the cathedral of St John the Baptist in Damascus was shared by Muslims and Christians until the reign of al-Walīd I (705–715) when on some pretext the whole was transformed into a mosque.

On the whole the *dhimmīs* had a tolerable life, though in some regions there was a deterioration after about the thirteenth century. It was not impossible for them to have high administrative positions in the state, though as time went on this became exceptional in practice. Even the conservative theorist al-Māwardī (d. 1058) allowed that the 'executive vizier' (*wazīr at-tanfīdh*) might be a *dhimmī*. At first most of the physicians, including those in attendance on the caliph himself, were Christians, and for centuries we hear of Christian and Jewish physicians in various Islamic countries. On the other hand, there were some minor disabilities. Whereas a Muslim man could marry a woman from one of the protected minorities, a male *dhimmī* could not marry a Muslim woman. 'Umar II is credited with introducing discriminatory legislation against Christians and Jews, such as requiring them to wear special clothes. In general this discriminatory legislation seems to have lapsed and fallen into abeyance until the practices in question were revived by some pious reformer. In the Islamic heartlands the normal practice was that *dhimmīs* did not serve in the army. In any case the town-dwellers of the region were probably unaccustomed to fighting; but there may also have been some idea that, since they paid for protection, they did not need to share in the work of protecting the country. In Spain, however, the Christians under Muslim rule seem to have continued to have arms and to use them both in self-defence and in other ways. Thus the position of the *dhimmīs* was moderately satisfactory, but they remained a kind of second-class citizen; and this disadvantage may have contributed to the steady trickle of conversions to Islam.

The Arab Muslims

The corollary of the system of protected minorities was that the Arab Muslims became, as it were, a military aristocracy. In the heartlands, as just noted, service in the army was restricted to Muslims, who at first were all Arabs. Correspondingly, participation in the Jihād was an obligation on all able-bodied male Muslims at first, though in practice universal participation soon became unnecessary. In the early Umayyad period the nomadic tribes sent only a proportion of their manpower for service in the army.

What made it possible for so many Arabs to spend so much of their time in military service was an institution commonly known as the Dīwān of ʿUmar, since the second caliph had a hand in setting it up. On the one hand, it was implied that the conquered lands would not be divided up among the victorious army, as was done with movable booty, but would be left to the existing cultivators on condition that the rents were paid into the treasury of the Islamic state. On the other hand, there were elaborate arrangements for disbursing the money in the form of annual stipends. The principle was adopted that a man's stipend should vary in accordance with the extent of his services to the Islamic state, measured by the date at which he had become a Muslim – sometimes called the principle of 'priority' (*sābiqa*). Several different forms of the list of categories have been preserved, presumably coming from different dates. As an example the following list of categories and stipends may be given:

Those who fought at Badr	(dirhams) 5,000
Those who were Muslims before al-Ḥudaybiya (628)	4,000
Muslims by the reign of Abū-Bakr (634)	3,000
Fighters at Qādisiyya and in Syria	2,000
Muslims after Qādisiyya and the Yarmūk	1,000
Various minor groups	500, 300, 250, 200
Muḥammad's widows	10,000
Wives of men at Badr	500
Wives of next three classes	400, 300, 200
Wives of others, and children	100

The actual statements in our sources are all idealizations of early events made by later jurists to suit their theories. All we can be certain about is that something of this sort was initiated by ʿUmar. It is also clear that in the course of time a distinction came to be made between stipends paid to civilians and the pay of the actual fighting men. There is no record of the system of stipends ever being cancelled, and some were still being paid at the end of the Umayyad period; but the system gradually faded away. This fading seems to have happened in two ways. Whereas originally stipends seem to have been paid to all those Arab Muslims who went to live in the conquered lands, and doubtless also to those in Medina and Mecca, in the course of time various categories were removed from the list until in the ʿAbbāsid period only some members of the clan of Hāshim seem to have been left. At the same time the actual stipend, while not necessarily less in nominal value, became a less significant part of the recipient's income.

Muslims who took part in military expeditions had always received a share of the booty, usually expressed in money terms. For a time this may have been sufficient to encourage men to go on compaign; but when most of the fighting took place in distant frontier areas, further inducements were required. These were primarily financial rewards, but the supply of provisions is also mentioned. In Syria under the Umayyads a system of what are called *junds* was tried out. Men were settled in particular districts and apparently given a little property in addition to the stipend, on condition that they would serve as soldiers when required to do so. Despite the successes of the Arabs they had something to learn from various opponents by way of military techniques, and as technology became more complex the army had to become more professional. Things were moving in this direction under the Umayyads, but it was the ʿAbbāsids who made the main support of their rule a professional army.

Administration and taxes

The word *dīwān* has many meanings, being the source of both the English 'divan' and the French *douane*. The Dīwān of al-Mutanabbī is his collected poems. The Dīwān of ʿUmar was in the first place the list or register of persons entitled to stipends. Later the word was used of an office or bureau of government. The Dīwān al-Jund was the bureau which dealt with the army register and related questions. In the central administration at Damascus there were also a Dīwān al-Kharāj (taxes, especially land-tax), a Dīwān ar-Rasā'il (correspondence), a Dīwān al-Khātam (which sealed and despatched letters and kept copies) and some other probably minor ones. Mu-'āwiya introduced a Dīwān al-Barīd to organize the service of posts throughout the empire, and this was developed by 'Abd-al-Malik. To begin with these bureaus were largely manned by Christians, since they alone had the necessary qualifications and training. The Christian theologian John of Damascus succeeded his father and grandfather in a high financial post, possibly the headship of the Dīwān an-Nafaqāt, which dealt with expenditure, retiring from this during the caliphate of Hishām. In the provincial capitals there were always at least Dīwāns for the Jund, for Kharāj and for Rasā'il.

The early history of the Islamic tax system is very obscure. When the matter came to be codified by the jurists of the 'Abbāsid period, they distinquished two basic taxes, one on the land always called Kharāj, and one on 'the head', that is, a poll-tax, always called Jizya. Something like this distinction had nearly always been present, but the words had not had a precise sense, so that one could speak of a Kharāj on the head and a Jizya on the land. The confusion is increased by the fact that the Arabs normally in each province took over the existing tax-system, and in many cases we have no exact information about this. Many things seem to have happened which were not in accordance with the later system of the jurists.

The financial crisis about the beginning of the eighth century came about through the conversion of non-Arabs to Islam. This affected the state in two ways. In Iraq, when a villager became a Muslim, he usually went to the town and left the other villagers to farm his land and pay the tax on it. So long as the converts were a small minority, this created no problems. Towards the end of the seventh century, however, there was a great spate of conversions; and the remaining villagers were too few to farm all the land properly and produce all the taxes expected of them. Because of this al-Ḥajjāj, the governor of Iraq, decreed that converts in the towns were to go back to their villages and be responsible for the same taxes as before conversion. This was taken to include a poll-tax, so that in effect they were prevented from becoming Muslims. In some parts of Khurasan, on the other hand, the poll-tax had been levied as a lump sum on the district. The consequence was that, when some persons became Muslims, those who were not converted had to pay more; if the converts were numerous, this could be a crippling burden. We therefore find the local nobles, who were responsible for collecting the tax, trying to prevent conversions to Islam.

The steps taken by ʿUmar II to solve this crisis in accordance with Islamic principles and without discouraging conversion seem to have been chiefly two. Firstly, it was insisted that the Kharāj was a tax on the land and not on the owner or occupier of the land, and that therefore it had to be paid whatever the status of the person involved. This applied to all land paying Kharāj at the time of the decree, but at the time of the conquests or later some Muslims had been given tax-free grants of land and these remained exempt. Secondly, the Jizya was made strictly into a poll-tax of so much per head, though with the possibility of different rates according to a man's wealth. This meant that the conversion of some men did not place a heavier burden on the unconverted remainder, while it would appear that the state lost little since it collected *zakāt* or legal alms from the new converts. Because of the differences between provinces there were some problems in the application of these principles to the various provinces.

The conversion of non-Arabs to Islam did not at first bring about any change in the structure of the Islamic polity. It remained a federation of Arab tribes, to which were attached a large number of other groups – the various communities of *dhimmīs*. Arab ideas of protection required that it should always be a group which was responsible for the safety of the individual. It was for this reason that, when a convert ceased to be a member of a group of *dhimmīs*, he had to be attached to an Arab tribe; and this was done by the relation of clientship. The clients or *mawālī* felt that their status was something less than the full brotherhood implicit in the central conceptions of the Qur'ān, and their dissatisfaction was an important factor in the success of the ʿAbbāsids. In return the ʿAbbāsids seem to have quietly suppressed the conception of the Islamic state as a federation of Arab tribes.

The head of state

The distinctive names applied to the head of the Islamic state were *khalīfa*, 'caliph', and *amīr al-mu'minīn*, 'prince of the believers' or 'commander of the faithful'. Though these names are new, the office may be regarded as developing out of that of the *sayyid* or chief of a nomadic tribe (or sub-tribe). The *sayyid* presided in the assembly of the adult males of the tribe, but did so as *primus inter pares*. All the members of a tribal assembly felt themselves equal in principle, but a young man would hesitate to oppose a wise and respected *sayyid*. The *sayyid* could not impose his views on the assembly, but, if he wanted a particular decision, had to obtain it by his personality and oratorical skill. On certain points he might be better informed, because he was responsible for the external affairs of the tribe; and this might carry some weight. He was not usually the leader of the tribe in war.

The caliph differed from the *sayyid* in that, following the example of Muḥammad, he was leader in war, and this carried with it responsibility for the main provincial appointments. Apart from this, however, the power of the Umayyad caliphs was limited by the need to consult an assembly of Arab nobles in Damascus in respect of many details. When towards the end of the Umayyad period tribal feuds assumed serious proportions, the need to consult an assembly created difficulties for the caliphs.

The caliph was also responsible for the organization of the judicial processes by which disputes between Muslims were settled. Some cases he might decide himself; others he would entrust to subordinates such as provincial governors. If there were many cases, one official might devote all his time for a period to hearing them, and would have the title of *qāḍī* or 'judge'; but he was not a specialist in law and might move on to some other administrative post. The conception of the *qāḍī* may have owed something to the pre-Islamic office of the *ḥakam* or 'arbiter'. The *ḥakam* was a man respected for his wisdom and knowledge of tribal custom to whom cases might be submitted, though he had no executive power and could only get the parties to promise to accept his decision. In the Islamic state under the Umayyads, however, the basis of decisions had become more complex, even though there was as yet no law in the strict sense. There were Qur'ānic rules on a wide variety of matters, such as marriage and divorce, inheritance, permitted and forbidden foods, the prohibition of wine-drinking and usury, the punishment of adultery and theft, and the freeing of slaves. In cases where these rules applied in an obvious way they were usually followed. In other cases, however, the judge might have to consider ancient Arab practice or the local provincial custom; and he had to use his own initiative to decide which set of considerations was to be given most weight. This was far from being an ideal legal system, but it is nevertheless to the credit of the Umayyads that they produced a judicial procedure which actually functioned and which was not grossly unfair.

When the title of *khalīfa* was first selected, it was probably taken as meaning 'successor', since Abū-Bakr succeeded Muḥammad in respect of temporal matters, though not of spiritual. The Umayyads, however, tried to magnify the office of caliph by linking it with a passage in the Qur'ān (2.30/28ff.) in which God says to the angels, 'I am making a *khalīfa* in the earth', and then, when the angels protest, teaches Adam the names of things so that he is later able to instruct the angels. In this passage *khalīfa* may have meant no more to the first hearers than a settler in the earth, with perhaps some suggestion of exercising authority. The Umayyads, however, insisted that it meant 'deputy' – a possible meaning of *khalīfa* – and made their title *khalīfat Allāh*, 'the deputy of God'. From this they drew the inference that their decisions were made by the authority of God and that whoever disobeyed them was an unbeliever. To discredit this claim of the Umayyads a story was put into circulation by opponents (followers of Ibn-az-Zubayr). According to this story, when the office was offered to Abū-Bakr, the title *khalīfa* of God was suggested, but he declined it saying, 'I am not the *khalīfa* of God, but only the *khalīfa* of the Messenger of God'. This story cannot be true, since in 632 no one could have thought of Abū-Bakr either as succeeding God or as deputizing for him.

The character of the Umayyad régime

The Umayyads in general, or Mu'āwiya in particular, are often charged with transforming the true or prophetic caliphate (*khilāfat an-nubuwwa*) into a *mulk*. The word *mulk* can mean 'kingship', 'sovereignty' or simply 'possession', but especially in later times the critics of the Umayyads took it to mean 'kingship' with the connotation of tyranny and secularity. In the time of the Umayyads, however, their court poets used *mulk* in an honourable sense of their 'sovereignty'. Thus al-Farazdaq could say, 'I saw that the sovereignty of the sons of Marwān was firmly established by a true council . . .', presumably referring to the council or *shūrā* which appointed ʿUthmān, from whom the Umayyads claimed to have inherited the caliphate. The first person to use *mulk* in a pejorative sense was apparently a pious scholar of Medina, Saʿīd ibn-al-Musayyab (d. 712) who exclaimed, 'God deal with Muʿāwiya! he was the first to make this office (*amr*) a *mulk*'. It is also recorded, however, that this man refused to take an oath of allegiance to two sons of ʿAbd-al-Malik during the latter's lifetime; so the presumption is that he objected to keeping the caliphate in one family and meant by *mulk* a 'possession' which can be inherited. The pious circles would doubtless have liked a *shūrā* on the occasion of each vacancy; but this would have led to intolerable confusion and would have destroyed the empire. The Umayyads therefore introduced the dynastic principle, and, since primogeniture was not practised among the Arabs, tried to smooth over the change of ruler by having allegiance sworn to the heir (or heirs) apparent during the preceding reign. This was an innovation, but it was a desirable and necessary one.

After the fall of the Umayyads all sorts of slanders were attached to them with little justification. One of the more serious charges was that brought by members of the pious circles or the general religious movement to the effect that they were irreligious. The seriousness of this charge was not in its criticism of the private lives of the Umayyad caliphs and their retinue, for, though they were by no means perfect, they were probably no worse than the ʿAbbāsids, and several were to some extent devout. The point of the criticism was that the Umayyads did not adopt the policy of making Islamic principle the basis of all their administrative decisions. Under the Umayyads the Islamic state was largely based on Arab ideas, so that Julius Wellhausen spoke of it as 'the Arab kingdom'. The dynasty claimed to have inherited the caliphate from ʿUthmān, and this claim was linked with the thoroughly Arab conception that the heir was the man who accepted responsibility for avenging the death. In judicial decisions, too, Arab custom still played an important part. Thus in various ways the empire of the Umayyads was not an Islamic state.

Since modern students are often led astray by statements about the *mulk* of the Umayyads into thinking that their outlook was mainly secular, it is worth quoting some of the verses of their court-poets, Jarīr and al-Farazdaq. While it is clear from these poets that the main justification of their caliphate given by the Umayyads was that they had inherited it from ʿUthmān, there are also two religious or theological lines of argument. Firstly it is asserted that the Umayyad dynasty had many noble deeds to its credit, such as fighting on behalf of Islam.

When the sons of Marwān meet [enemies], they unsheath
for God's religion angry swords
[And] sharp, by which they defend Islam;
the sword-blows fall only on the doubt-raisers.

Secondly it is maintained that the caliphate has been bestowed by God on the Umayyads.

The earth is God's; he has entrusted it to his *khalīfa*;
he who is head in it will not be overcome.

God has garlanded you with the caliphate and with guidance;
for what God decrees there is no change.

In addition to this the caliphs are regarded as having certain religious functions.

Were it not for the caliph and the Qur'ān he recites,
the people had no judgements established for them and no communal worship.
We have found the sons of Marwān pillars of our religion
as the earth has mountains for its pillars;
And for this religion you are like the direction mark
by which people are guided when they go astray.

Even if some of this is ascribed to adulation, the fact that it is expressed in religious terms indicates that a religious outlook was widely spread through society.

These religious claims of the Umayyads had theological repercussions which will be considered in the next section.

4

RELIGIOUS ASPECTS OF UMAYYAD RULE

As long ago as 1943 Jean Sauvaget (in his bibliographical *Introduction à l'histoire de l'orient musulman*) remarked that, though the Umayyad period was of exceptional interest, it was extremely badly known; and in the interval since that date this state of affairs has not been greatly altered, although there have been some important books on specific aspects of the period. The difficulty is that, while we know much about the political events, possess many of the poems and other literary works, and know a little about the scholars, we are unable to grasp Islamic life as a whole during this period and to see the significance of all the facts and patterns. The difficulty is particularly great in the case of an attempt to understand the place of religion during the period. For one thing it is difficult to distinguish what really happened in the religious sphere from what in later periods was alleged to have happened under the Umayyads. For another thing the religious aspect was often assumed or implied and not directly described. Most important of all, however, the Arabs had a tendency to deal with different aspects of life in relative isolation whereas it seems not impossible that it was precisely religion that unified and gave a wholeness to the life of the Islamic empire. This is at least a hypothesis worth examining, and to it the present section will be devoted.

The absence of non-Islamic thinking

The fundamental point in this discussion seems to be that something so tremendous happened to the Arabs during Muḥammad's lifetime that even those who opposed the Islamic state were *unable to think except in Qur'ānic terms*. One piece of evidence is the wars of the Ridda or 'apostasy'. It may be allowed that the reasons for these wars were mainly, perhaps exclusively, political and economic. Yet it was apparently impossible for the leaders to express their opposition to the caliph in Medina except in religious terms. More specifically, they had to claim to be prophets like Muḥammad and to try to produce revelations like the Qur'ān. Another important piece of evidence is that virtually all the leaders of revolts against the Umayyads and early 'Abbāsids professed an Islamic basis for their activity. This implies that there was for these men no serious possibility of turning right away from Islam to paganism or Christianity or Judaism. Just after the Hijra some of the Meccans tried to base opposition to Muḥammad on an appeal to paganism; but this seems to have been ineffective and was soon forgotten. A little reflection shows that there were numerous reasons why Christian and Jewish groups did not become centres of revolt. The nearest to a non-Islamic basis for opposition was the so-called Manichaeanism of the early 'Abbāsid period which will be mentioned later.

This wide, and in a sense universal, acceptance of the Islamic state and the Qur'ānic world-view is thus a historical fact which has to be noted, given due weight, and if possible explained. One inference which seems inevitable when the events are looked at in this way is that nearly all the men involved must have passed through a deep and profound experience. It is just as certain that this was not an experience of conversion as that is cultivated in various forms in evangelical Christianity. Indeed, in the case of most of the Arab Muslims there was probably nothing that could be called 'religious experience' as that is commonly understood in the West. If we want to find what moved these men so profoundly, we must cast our net more widely. The view to be maintained here is that what transformed the outlook of these Arabs was the total experience of belonging to the community led by Muḥammad. Within this total experience we may distinguish a number of factors or aspects, and doubtless some men were more moved by one and some by another.

At the centre must have been the personality of Muḥammad himself. The attempts of the Ridda leaders to imitate him make this point clear. Muḥammad attracted men by his confidence in his mission, by his air of authority and by his vitality. Because he believed whole-heartedly in the Qur'ānic world-view those who admired him tended to do the same. Included in this world-view was the belief that Muḥammad came at the end of a long line of prophets. This line of prophets included those whose teachings were followed by the great empires of the day. Thus Muḥammad had an important place in history, in God's purpose for the world. It followed that the community of Muḥammad's followers also had an important place in history and in God's purposes.

Thus the Arab who became a Muslim received a new sense of identity. He now belonged to a body greater and more glorious than the Arab tribe in which he had grown up. Something of this sort was probably felt in Muḥammad's lifetime after the conquest of Mecca and the victory of Ḥunayn when many of the Arab tribes came to seek alliance with him. After the defeat of the Byzantine and Persian empires there must have been an enhancement of this sense of belonging to a glorious community with an important place in world history. In joining in the wars of expansion the ordinary nomadic Arab was doubtless motivated chiefly by the excitement of the razzia and the prospect of plunder; but he got caught up into the tremendous experience of being a member of this vital, confident, victorious Islamic community. There was no moment of 'conversion' presumably, but rather a gradual assimilation of the experience, until it had so taken hold of him that there was no going back on it. A very few disliked life in the new provinces and went back to the freedom and hardship of the desert and presumably, in the main, to the old pre-Islamic outlook. For those who remained in the provinces, however, or even in Medina and Mecca, there was no alternative to the Qur'ānic world-view. To try to think otherwise was to choose loss of identity, emptiness and death.

By the reign of Muʿāwiya, then, practically all Arabs, whatever their 'religious' experience or lack of it, and whether they were opposed to the caliphal government or not, had a firm allegiance to the community of believers, that is, to the social and political body which had arisen out of the activity of Muḥammad. The usual way of defining this body was to say that it was based 'on the Book of

God and the Sunna or practice of Muḥammad'. The latter seems originally to have had a vague sense, but it was precisely delimited in the early 'Abbāsid period. Even the anti-caliph Ibn-az-Zubayr had homage rendered to him on the basis of the Book and the Sunna.

Though most of the Muslims may not have been 'religious' in the modern sense, the fact that, however vaguely, they accepted the Book and the Sunna meant that certain Qur'ānic ideas determined aspects of the life of the community. It has already been noted that the practice of the razzia was transformed into the Jihād by the ideas that conversion to Islam was open to everyone and that all Muslims were brothers; for it followed that there could be no razzia against Muslims. Again from the idea that Muḥammad was the last in a long series of prophets came the practice of accepting the followers of other prophets as 'protected persons' attached to the Islamic federation. Most important of all in the Umayyad period was another implication of the idea that conversion was open to all, namely, the accession to Islam of thousands of persons from the protected groups. These converts are in fact those who have already been encountered as *mawālī*. It might perhaps be claimed that the ultimate cause of this phenomenon was Judaeo-Christian universalism, but the immediate cause was certainly the Qur'ānic idea. Though social, political and economic factors were also present, the moulding of the Islamic world in certain ways came about only because of ideas present in the Qur'ān, and because of the inevitability of Muslims thinking in terms of these ideas.

The basic architecture of the Islamic state had no doubt been determined by 'Umar, building on the foundations laid down by Muḥammad, but much of the structure had still to be created or elaborated, and this took place under the Umayyads. Judicial and administrative practice, as has been seen, was an amalgam of Qur'ānic, traditional Arab and various local or regional elements; but, as fresh problems demanded a solution, the question had constantly to be asked, 'On what principles is the decision to be made?' One of the two main possibilities was to decide each case in the way that seemed appropriate for it; and this seems to have been what the Umayyads usually did. The danger inherent in this course was that what would seem appropriate would often turn out to be what was in accordance with traditional Arab practice. The treatment of the *mawālī* could be given as an example of this. In the early days when there were non-Arab Muslims for whom protection had to be arranged, the natural thing to do was to make them clients of Arab tribes belonging to the Islamic federation; and presumably this practice was simply continued when the numbers became large and protection was not so urgent. Yet this was something distinctly Arab; and since it placed Arabs in a position of privilege as compared with non-Arab Muslims, it was contrary to the equality of all believers implied by the Qur'ān.

The other main possibility was to try to bring administrative and judicial practice more into line with Qur'ānic principles. This was the course favoured by an amorphous body of men, which is sometimes called 'the pious opposition' or 'the neutral party' but is here designated 'the general religious movement'. By this phrase is intended the whole body of men who were loyal to the Islamic community as they had experienced it and who wanted to maintain it in a satisfactory condition. They did not all hold the same views on political questions, though there was some measure of agreement among them. Unfortunately there are serious difficulties to be overcome in studying the subdivisions and internal variety of the general religious movement, especially during the first two centuries of Islam. Later Sunnite Islam rejected any idea of development and presented the material about the early scholars in such a way as to give the image of a monolithic community with its religious doctrines fully formed in essentials from the beginning and accepted by almost everyone except a few heretics. If the modern student digs a little below the surface, however, he can find many small scraps of information which, when pieced together, give an idea of the political and religious views of a number of men and roughly indicate the various groups into which they were divided. A beginning has been made with studies of this kind, but much remains to be done.

The point most in need of emphasis in the present context is that at this time there was no body of central 'Sunnite' opinion, since Sunnism was still in process of formation. Consequently the views of every scholar must have had some affinities to one or other of the heresies to be described. The more eminent and reputable scholars did not hold heretical views in an extreme form; but they could hardly avoid having definite views on the political questions of the day and these political views had doctrinal implications.

The Khārijites

The first group of sects to be looked at is that later known as the Khārijites (or Khawārij). They were originally many separate groups, though with some similar ideas, and it was only later systematizers who found it convenient to have a common label for them. The murderers of ʿUthmān were claimed by later Khārijites as their forerunners, but the first clear manifestation of Khārijism was in ʿAlī's army, both at the battle of Ṣiffīn and in the months afterwards. Groups 'went out' or 'seceded' (*kharajū*) from the army to Ḥarūrā' and then to Nahrawān. ʿAlī was reconciled to some, but at Nahrawān an intransigent minority was massacred. Two principles were implicit in this political activity, and may also have been made explicit. The first was that there should be 'no decision but God's' (*lā ḥukm illā li-llāh*), meaning that such questions as the selection of the caliph should be decided by principles taken from the Qur'ān. This slogan is known as the *taḥkīm*, and those who used it became 'the first Muḥakkima'. Strictly speaking this is not a heresy but a form of the contention that the Islamic state must be based on Qur'ānic principles. In the course of time some modification was necessary, since it was found that the Qur'ān did not give guidance on all matters of practice, but that supplementary principles had to be brought in from Tradition (the practice of Muḥammad), and that both sets had to be further extended by certain forms of reasoning. This first principle of the Khārijites, then, was a first approximation to a formula for one of the bases of the community of Muslims, namely, that its political and administrative decisions should be in accordance with Islamic principles. In this respect the Khārijites contributed to the formation of Sunnism.

The second principle was that 'the grave sinner (*ṣāḥib kabīra*) is excluded from the community'. This expresses a deep moral concern. The Islamic community is to be a community of saints. This is, of course, much too severe a standard for ordinary human weakness, since it means that for every misdemeanour the punishment is either death or banishment. Nevertheless it is important to notice that this second Khārijite principle has also its positive value. It expresses a concern for the moral quality of the life of the community as a whole; and this moral concern was retained in later Sunnism, even though it was denied that the grave sinner was excluded from the community. Indeed, until matters had been adequately thrashed out, there was a tendency to bring a charge of moral laxity against some unguarded expositions of the non-exclusion of the grave sinner.

The second principle could easily be abused, especially since exclusion from the community meant the loss of all rights whatsoever. The principle gave a justification for the murder of 'Uthmān. Since he had, it was alleged, committed a grave sin, he was excluded from the community, and that meant that to kill him was no sin and might even be regarded as a duty. The most extreme application of the principle was made by a group known as the Azraqites (or Azāriqa), the followers of Nāfi' ibn-al-Azraq. This man was at first (in 683 or 684) inclined to support Ibn-az-Zubayr as caliph, but later apparently realized that Ibn-az-Zubayr was not in sympathy with his ideals. When a Zubayrid governor came to Basra, Ibn-al-Azraq opposed him and was forced to flee eastwards. In 685 he was killed by a Zubayrid army, but the Azraqites under other leaders continued till about 698 as a body of rebels, brigands and terrorists. Wherever they were strong enough and the opponents weak – and this happened several times, both near Basra and further east – whole districts were exposed to pillage, arson and massacre. This was justified by the second Khārijite principle, extended by the insistence that God had commanded the Muslims to fight the unbelievers, and that therefore everyone who had not joined the Azraqite force had broken this command and was an unbeliever. In other words the Azraqites were the only Muslims.

Much more important for the development of Islamic doctrine were the moderate interpretations of the Khārijite principles. These were not the work of the small groups of insurrectionaries, who justified the identification of 'Khārijite' with 'rebel', but of men who were concerned for Islamic principles and who kept the peace. Many such were found in Basra after the end of the Second Civil War. Mention may also be made of the Najdites, followers of a man called Najda who from 686 to 692 was effective ruler of much of central Arabia. The nature of his administrative responsibility meant that he could not punish every case of theft or adultery by death or exile, and he therefore adopted the modified view that exclusion from the community came about only through ignorance or rejection of certain fundamentals, namely, knowledge of God and of his prophets, acceptance of the Qur'ān, and acknowledgement that the life and property of every Muslim was sacrosanct.

Those who settled down in Basra under a non-Khārijite governor had to find some theoretical justification for living peaceably under someone who in their eyes, strictly speaking, was not a Muslim. One line they followed was to introduce refinements into the distinction between 'the sphere of Islam' and 'the sphere of war' (*dār al-islām*, *dār al-ḥarb*), the first being the lands under Islamic rule and the second everywhere else (as possible objectives for razzias). It was suggested that in a place like Basra one was in 'the sphere of prudent fear' (*taqiyya*), where one did not express one's true beliefs publicly. Then it was argued that one must distinguish between 'unbeliever' (*kāfir*) and 'idolater' (*mushrik*), and that one could apply the latter term only to one who rejected or was ignorant of the doctrine of God; on this ground it could be said that non-Khārijite Muslims though not 'believers' were at least 'monotheists' (*muwaḥḥidūn*). Correspondingly the 'sphere' could be described as that 'of monotheism' (*tawḥīd*).

This partial acceptance of other Muslims led in time to further problems, such as whether it was lawful to sell 'believing' (that is, Khārijite) slave-girls to 'unbelievers' (other Muslims). This matter is said to have been raised when a man called Ibrāhīm was kept waiting by a slave-girl and swore he would sell her to the bedouin (non-Khārijites). He was challenged on the legality of this transaction by Maymūn, a member of his sub-sect, on the ground that the Qur'ān forbids the marriage of a Muslim woman to any but a Muslim man (and a slave-girl would normally be a concubine and have marital relations with her owner). In Basra, however, most Khārijites seem to have acted like Ibrāhīm and regarded themselves, despite theological differences, as belonging to the wider community of Muslims.

Yet another subtlety was introduced by the group known as the Wāqifa or Wāqifiyya, 'those suspending judgement'. They held that in this case the correct attitude was not to follow either Ibrāhīm or Maymūn but to suspend judgement. They seem to have justified this position by asserting that they were living in 'the sphere of mixing' (*dār al-khalṭ*), where not all rules can be precisely stated and where it is necessary to have a measure of imprecision and even compromise. Such an assertion brings one near to an abandonment of the doctrine of the exclusion from the community of the grave sinner.

Apart from the first formulation of Khārijite principles by the first Muḥakkima, the Ḥarūriyya (men of Ḥarūrā), the Azraqites and perhaps the Najdites, the chief Khārijite contributions to theology were made at Basra during the half-century after about 690. Round about the year 800 one or two Khārijite 'theologians' (*mutakallimūn*) are mentioned as having taken part in discussions, probably both in Basra and Baghdad. The most important seems to have been al-Yamān ibn-Ribāb, who wrote a book on the subdivisions of the Khārijites. Khārijite doctrine also spread to several regions in Persia, Arabia and North Africa; but the Khārijite groups there were cut off from the main stream of Islamic thought. Indeed Khārijism changed and became a method of constituting a small closely-knit community and maintaining it in relative isolation from the rest of the surrounding Islamic world. One Khārijite sub-sect, the Ibāḍites, has remained in existence until the present day. It is the dominant form of Islam in the sultanate of Muscat and Oman (whence it spread to Zanzibar), and there are several small pockets of Ibāḍites in North Africa. They probably number less than half a million in all.

A true assessment of the Khārijites must see them not merely as fanatical heretics or rigid puritans but as men who in their zeal for a truly Islamic polity made an important contribution to the development of the Islamic community. Had it not been for men like them who insisted on a Qur'ānic basis for administrative and judicial decisions, the Umayyad state would probably have slipped back into a more Arab way of doing things, and Islam would never have become a world religion. By insisting on a Qur'ānic basis they were also insisting that the Islamic state should be a state pursuing a moral ideal. This was indeed implicit in their contention about the grave sinner; but to exclude him from the community was not a feasible method of getting the community as a whole to accept the moral ideal.

The Shīʿites

The study of Shīʿism during the Umayyad period is particularly difficult. Apart from the obstacles met with in any study of sectarian views in the Umayyad period, there is an additional element of confusion in that Imāmite-Shīʿite propagandists from the later ninth century onwards presented a version of events from 632 to 874 which supported their doctrinal and political views, but which is now held by occidental scholars to be at variance with what actually happened. Sunnite scholars always denied some points in this version of events, but were inclined to accept others since these were directed not against Sunnism but against deviant forms of Shīʿism. In the present context a detailed critique of the sources would be out of place, and the correctness of the conclusions of recent occidental research will therefore be assumed. Many matters remain obscure, but there is agreement about the presence of ideas and currents of thought which can be labelled Shīʿite.

In the first place, as noted above, there was widespread respect for 'the family', and this was one of the roots of Shīʿism, even though not all who held 'the family' in high esteem were Shīʿites in any sectarian sense. This was in accordance with the traditional Arab idea that, if a man performed noble deeds, it was because he came of noble stock; that is to say, they believed that the capacity for achievements of outstanding quality was transmitted in the tribal and family stock. It was therefore natural for Arabs to suppose that some of the exceptional qualities present in Muḥammad would be found in his family or clan. It appears, however, that different people took 'the family' in different senses. The narrowest sense – that of the later Imāmites – restricted the persons among whom exceptional qualities might be expected to the descendants of ʿAlī and Fāṭima. Others were prepared to allow that 'the family' included all the descendants of ʿAlī or all the descendants of Hāshim (that is, the clan of Hāshim). Certain assertions in support of Umayyad claims seem to have tried to extend 'the family' to include all the descendants of ʿAbd-Manāf (the father of Hāshim and grandfather of Umayya), so that they themselves would be in 'the family'; but this idea does not seem to have found much favour. ʿAbbāsid propaganda emphasized the special character of the whole clan of Hāshim.

Another current idea, and one more characteristic of Shīʿism, was that of the imam or charismatic leader. By most Shīʿites the imam was thought of as divinely inspired and divinely preserved from sin and error. He was thus a person who could be relied on to bring the community safely through a crisis; and this may be why many people looked to an imam when things were difficult. It was often held that there was only one imam at a time and that he designated his successor (just as Muḥammad was alleged to have designated ʿAlī to succeed him). The Imāmites eventually (after 874) recognized a series of twelve imams, beginning with ʿAlī, al-Ḥasan, al-Ḥusayn, and then going from father to son. Other imams, however, were recognized by various people during the Umayyad period. Some held that al-Ḥusayn had been succeeded by his half-brother Muḥammad ibn-al-Ḥanafiyya; and it was also alleged that he had been succeeded by his son Abū-Hāshim, who in turn had designated a member of the ʿAbbāsid branch of the clan of Hāshim. Yet others held that any member of the clan of Hāshim who claimed the imamate (understood as also comprising the caliphate) and substantiated his claim by military success, was entitled to receive allegiance. This view is sometimes called 'Zaydite' after Zayd ibn-ʿAlī (a grandson of al-Ḥusayn) who revolted against the Umayyads at Kufa in 740 but speedily met his death. A similar claim was made, again unsuccessfully, by a descendant of ʿAlī's brother Jaʿfar called ʿAbd-Allāh ibn-Muʿāwiya in the years 744 to 746; and of course the ʿAbbāsids themselves were in a position to make a claim of this type, since they were descendants of Hāshim and had made good their right to rule by force of arms.

While some believers in 'the family' were looking for a successful military leader, others apparently abandoned all hope of immediate success and adopted a form of messianism. This has its focus in the conception of the 'hidden imam'. The general idea was that an imam had gone into 'concealment', usually in mysterious circumstances, and that in the fullness of time, when the world was ready for him, he would return and set everything right. One of the names given to this expected deliverer was the Mahdī, 'the guided one'. In so far as the Mahdī was 'the hidden imam' this was a purely Shīʿite conception; but there is also a Sunnite conception of the Mahdī, and the best-known examples, like the Mahdī of the Sudan in the nineteenth century, were Sunnites. There was, of course, many a man of whom at some point is was claimed that he was the hidden imam; but during the Umayyad period the chief candidate for the honour was Muḥammad ibn-al-Ḥanafiyya. The conception of the hidden imam was in general associated with political quietism. It implied that for the moment the conditions of life were just tolerable, or at least that nothing could be done in the immediate future to improve them; but at the same time it gave hope for a more distant future.

Besides these ideas and currents of thought which were taken up into the more developed forms of Shīʿism, there was widespread admiration and respect for 'the family' and especially for ʿAlī. An example of this attitude is Ibrāhīm an-Nakhaʿī (d. *c.*714), the leading scholar and jurist of Kufa in his time. He is reported to have said that ʿAlī was dearer to him than ʿUthmān, but he balanced this by adding that he would rather forfeit Heaven than speak ill of ʿUthmān. He also reproached a man who said ʿAlī was dearer to him than Abū-Bakr and ʿUmar, and remarked that this view would have been objectionable to ʿAlī himself; and he apparently dissociated himself from any form of belief in the hidden imam.

The complexity of attitudes on these matters is illustrated by the uses of the term 'Shīʿa'. The word merely means 'party', and during ʿAlī's lifetime there was a body of close friends and followers who were known as *shīʿat ʿAlī*, 'the party of ʿAlī'; but there is nothing to show that these men thought of ʿAlī as having any special charisma. There is indeed a story of some men who came to ʿAlī and said they would be friends of those he was friends with and enemies of those to whom he was an enemy; but this willingness to accept ʿAlī's judgement, and perhaps to recognize a measure of charisma, does not appear to have been widespread at that date, and the story might even be a later invention. Most sect names are nicknames and connote something bad, but Shīʿa and Shīʿite have a good connotation and are names people want to apply to themselves. As late as the middle of the ninth century we find Aḥmad ibn-Ḥanbal (d. 855) claiming that he and his Sunnite associates (whom he calls Ahl as-Sunna wa-l-Ḥadīth) were the true *shīʿa* of ʿAlī, since they had due affection for the family of Muḥammad and, in particular, recognized the rights of ʿAlī. Nearly a century later a follower of Aḥmad's still distinguished the true Shīʿite from the heretical Rāfiḍite; the former acknowledges Abū-Bakr as well as ʿAlī and does not decide between ʿAlī and ʿUthmān, whereas the latter puts ʿAlī above ʿUthmān. Towards the end of the ninth century the Sunnite writer Ibn-Qutayba (d. 889) produced a list of Shīʿa which excluded those he called Rāfiḍites and included Ibrāhīm an-Nakhaʿī and other noted Sunnite scholars. It was presumably not till after the definition and consolidation of Imāmite Shīʿism about the year 900 and the establishment of an Ismāʿīlite (Fāṭimid) state in 909 that the word Shīʿite came to have its modern sense.

The early, ill-defined form of Shīʿism may be said to be behind the risings of al-Ḥasan in 661, of al-Ḥusayn in 680 and of al-Mukhtār from 685 to 687. There was also military action from 683 to 685 by a body known as 'the Penitents' who wanted to make reparation for having failed to support al-Ḥusayn. After the utter failure of all these attempts there was no rising of Shīʿite inspiration until 737 when the Umayyad caliphate was on the point of dissolution. Apart from the revolt, already mentioned, of Zayd ibn-ʿAlī and his brother Yaḥyā in 740 and that of another Hāshimite, ʿAbd-Allāh ibn-Muʿāwiya, from 744 to 746, there were revolts or potential revolts associated with the sects of the Bayāniyya, the Mughīriyya and the Manṣūriyya, none of which had more than local significance. In a sense the rising which brought the ʿAbbāsids to the throne was another such Shīʿite rising.

The Murji'ites

Of the main Islamic sects the Murji'ites are the most difficult to describe clearly. The collective noun Murji'a is a nickname, but it was used differently by different people. There is virtually no Sunnite scholar of the eighth and ninth centuries who was not dubbed Murji'ite by some opponent or other. The important Sunnite jurist Abū-Ḥanīfa was regarded as a Murji'ite by other Sunnites, including al-Ashʿarī. This caused serious difficulties to later writers about sects, since they regarded Murji'ites as heretics, and it was unthinkable that the founder of one of the legal rites could be a heretic. The doyen of the writers on sects, ash-Shahrastānī (d. 1153), found it impossible to provide any tidy scheme of the subdivisions of the Murji'a; they seemed to overlap with other sects. So he spoke of Murji'a of the Khārijites, Murji'a of the Qadarites, Murji'a of the Jabrites (extreme determinists), and pure Murji'a. When he came to Abū-Ḥanīfa and could not avoid noticing the assertion that he was a Murji'ite, he tried to escape from the impasse by saying that he and his disciples had been called the Murji'a of the Sunna. The following account is based on a critique of the sources.

It is generally agreed by Muslim scholars that the name is derived from a Qur'ānic phrase (9.106/107), 'others are deferred for the command of God to see whether he will punish them or whether he will relent towards them'. This is said to refer to the three Muslims who without any reasonable excuse stayed behind from Muḥammad's great expedition to Tabuk in 631. The word translated 'deferred' is *arja'a* (verbal noun *irjā'*), whose basic meaning is 'to postpone, to place later or after'; but *irjā'* can also be the verbal noun of another word *arjā*, 'to cause to hope'. This made it possible to interpret the nickname of Murji'a in several ways.

The first application of the idea seems to have been to the 'postponing' of a decision about ʿAlī and ʿUthmān, that is, not saying whether each was a believer or unbeliever, and so assigning him to heaven or hell. This 'postponing' implies a rejection of the Khārijite view that ʿUthmān was an unbeliever and so excluded from the community, and probably also of the Shīʿite attitude of unreserved approbation for ʿAlī. A poet of the Umayyad period expressed the Murji'ite position by saying that ' ʿAlī and ʿUthmān are two servants of God who did not associate any deity with him, and they will be rewarded according to their striving, which is known to God'. Thus the Murji'ites accepted both ʿUthmān and ʿAlī as rightful rulers of the community, and thereby showed their concern for the unity of all Muslims. During the Umayyad period this acceptance of ʿUthmān would also have the connotation that the Umayyads were the legitimate caliphs.

Another application of the idea was the 'postponement' of ʿAlī to fourth place. A question that was frequently asked during the first two or three centuries of Islam was: 'Which was the most excellent of the community after Muḥammad?' The Shīʿites firmly insisted that it was ʿAlī. Most others held that it was Abū-Bakr, followed by ʿUmar, but some were then inclined to place ʿAlī third. The Murji'ites, however, placed ʿUthmān third and ʿAlī fourth. A large proportion of the early Murji'ites whose names are recorded lived in Kufa, and this view is a mark of opposition to the strong sympathy for ʿAlī and his descendants found in that city.

In the third place there may be a 'postponement' of the decision about the grave sinner. This means that in practice he remains a member of the community and is regarded as a believer. A man ceases to be a believer, on this view, only if he falls into the sin of idolatry or polytheism (*shirk*), expressed in Arabic as 'associating other beings (or deities) with God'. This leads on to the doctrine that 'belief' or 'faith' by itself is what makes a man a believer, and that works are not considered – a doctrine which laid the Murji'ites open to the charge that they 'postponed' works to belief, though it could be said in their defence that their name meant those who 'gave hope' to the grave sinner. Indeed the Murji'ites were accused of belittling sins and of lacking moral earnestness.

All this increases the problem of how the Murji'ites came to be regarded as heretics, for the points in respect of which they received the name Murji'ites were eventually accepted as Sunnite doctrine. Later Sunnite creeds have an article to the effect that the chronological order of the first four caliphs is also the order of excellence, thus placing ʿAlī fourth. It is also agreed that grave sin (other than 'associating other deities with God') does not lead to exclusion from the community; and it is also generally held, though with some slight variations in detail, that everyone who remains a Muslim will eventually go to heaven. (The 'postponement' of the decision about ʿAlī and ʿUthmān comes to be taken up into the other points.) Thus for the most part Murji'ism is an early form of Sunnism, though particular Murji'ites might differ from later Sunnite doctrine in respect of points which in their day had not been explicitly formulated. The heretical deviations labelled 'Murji'ite' by writers on sects were relatively unimportant variants which helped to make up the number of seventy-two sects at which they were aiming.

The Qadarites

It is tolerably certain that the doctrine of Qadarism arose in reaction to some of the theological assertions made on behalf of the Umayyads, such as the verse already quoted:

> God has garlanded you with the caliphate and with guidance;
> for what God decrees [*qaḍā*] there is no change.

In a story about al-Ḥasan al-Baṣrī a friend is reported to have said to him, 'These princes shed the blood of Muslims and seize their goods, and act in various ways and say, "Our acts occur according to God's determination [*qadar*]".' When such a claim is made, those who want to oppose the people who make it have to oppose their theological doctrine. It is therefore not surprising to find that most of the Qadarites are political opponents of the Umayyads. The fact that not all opponents of the Umayyads are Qadarites is probably to be explained by the low level of theological interest in such persons, and one may still maintain that there is a significant connection between Qadarism and opposition and that this is found in religious-minded persons. Thus Maʿbad al-Juhanī, allegedly the first Qadarite, supported Ibn-al-Ashʿath when the latter was in revolt from about 701 to 704 and was subsequently executed.

One of the most prominent of the early Qadarites was Ghaylān ad-Dimashqī, who had a position as secretary in the Umayyad administration at Damascus. During the reign of ʿUmar II (717–20) he is said to have written to the caliph complaining of the deterioration of the state from a religious point of view and urging the caliph to give a lead in the restoring of religious principles. Part of his complaint was about the luxury of the court at a time when many were going hungry; and ʿUmar apparently gave him power to take certain measures to improve things. At the same time ʿUmar was critical of Qadarism and warned Ghaylān that his sympathy for it was dangerous. At some point in the reign of the caliph Hishām (724–43), who was less friendly than ʿUmar to the religious point of view, Ghaylān and a friend judged it prudent to flee to Armenia, but they were eventually apprehended and, after imprisonment, cruelly put to death, probably near the end of the reign of Hishām. The works on sects do not speak of the revolutionary implications of Ghaylān's teaching; but in dealing with this period the historians give the name of Qadarites to a group of opponents of the régime who took up arms and who eventually brought Yazīd III to the throne in April 744. There are various indications that these men followed the doctrines of Ghaylān. Qadarism was only part of Ghaylān's position; thus he did not regard grave sinners as excluded from the community, and in this respect is reckoned a Murji'ite.

The Qadarites are often regarded simply as upholders of the freedom of the human will, but from what has been said about the political implications of the doctrine it will be seen that the central point was rather the denial that the acts of the Umayyads were divinely determined. This point could be elaborated in various ways. Something of the subtlety with which it was developed can be seen from a *Risāla* or epistle on the subject written to the caliph ʿAbd-al-Malik by al-Ḥasan al-Baṣrī (624–728), the leading religious thinker of the

Umayyad period. A short account of his life and thought is therefore appropriate at this point.

Al-Ḥasan was the son of a Persian or persianized inhabitant of Iraq who had been made prisoner in 635 and brought to Medina, where after a time he had gained his freedom. Al-Ḥasan was probably born in Medina and brought up in the neighbourhood, but went to Basra about 657 and spent most of the rest of his life there. He took part in a campaign on the eastern frontier and later was secretary to the governor of Khurasan. Before 680 he was back in Basra, for he protested at the oath of allegiance given to Yazīd I as heir apparent while his father was still alive. Nevertheless after 694 he was for a time on good terms with the stern governor al-Ḥajjāj. In the rising of Ibn-al-Ash'ath (701–4) he remained loyal to the governor and caliph and urged his friends to do likewise. About 705, however, he fell into disfavour with al-Ḥajjāj, perhaps because of his outspoken criticisms where he thought some religious principle was at stake. He remained in hiding until the death of al-Ḥajjāj in 714; but in 717 he became *qāḍī* (judge) of Basra for a short time. When Basra was in the hands of the rebel Yazīd ibn-al-Muhallab in 720, al-Ḥasan spoke against him and called on men to remain loyal to the Umayyads. Perhaps because he was now a respected elder statesman he did not suffer for this, but on the restoration of Umayyad rule he was publicly honoured.

Al-Ḥasan could perhaps be best described as a saintly puritan. In addition to the *Epistle* many of his ascetic and ethical sayings have been preserved. He constantly insisted on uprightness of life, both for himself and for others; and he was very conscious that failure to carry out God's commands put a man in danger of being consigned to Hell. He saw it as a scholar's duty to warn his fellow-Muslims about this. On the other hand he had some sympathy with the Murji'ite view that the man who avoids the great sin of 'associating gods with God' might hope for pardon of all other sins; and he advocated the pronouncing on one's deathbed of the words 'there is no god but God'. His view of the grave sinner came between those of the Khārijites and Murji'ites, for Al-Ḥasan called him a 'hypocrite' (the term applied in the Qur'ān to nominal Muslims of Medina). In the field of politics he accepted the first four caliphs and the Umayyads as legitimate rulers. Like many later pious Muslims he was opposed to rebellion (as noted above), and thought that *de facto* rulers should be obeyed provided they did not command something contrary to the divine law. To those who complained of the misdeeds of rulers he said, 'If these matters are a punishment from God, you cannot with your swords deflect God's punishment; but if they are a trial sent by him, you should patiently wait God's judgement; in neither case should you fight.' At the same time he could preach outspoken sermons before governors and others in authority, warning them of the danger of Hell if they themselves did not obey God's commands.

Since shortly after the death of al-Ḥasan it has been vehemently argued whether he was a Qadarite or not, and the arguments have continued until the present century. It is now possible from the *Epistle* to ʿAbd-al-Malik to form some idea of what al-Ḥasan really believed. Where opponents had argued for predestinarianism from such a Qur'ānic verse as 'God sends astray whom he will' (13.27), he insisted that God did this only after men had themselves chosen evil, and supported this view with another verse, 'God sends astray only the evildoers' (14.27/32). In his presentation of his own view he emphasizes that, since God has commanded men to worship him and to do various things and has forbidden certain other things, men must have been given the power or ability to act as God wants; if they have not this ability, God is wronging them by commanding something and then preventing them doing it. Thus in his view men are able to fulfil or not to fulfil God's commands, and to this extent al-Ḥasan is a Qadarite. Unlike the contemporary Qadarites, however, al-Ḥasan refused to use violent means against rulers of whom he disapproved. On the other hand he seems, like the pre-Islamic Arabs and the Qur'ān, to have believed that man's provision or sustenance (*rizq*, that is, food and drink) is predetermined and also the date of his death. Al-Ḥasan well illustrates the connection between Qadarism and deep religious concerns.

A transformation came over Qadarism in the generation after al-Ḥasan. One sign of this was the clear demarcation between Qadarites and non-Qadarites. In the circle of scholars round al-Ḥasan during his lifetime the upholders of different attitudes to Qadarism seem to have fraternized easily with one another. Later, however, even in Basra among men influenced by al-Ḥasan there was a cleavage between those who emphasized the Qadarite side of his teaching, like ʿAmr ibn-ʿUbayd, and those who emphasized the opposite aspects. Perhaps the violence associated with the Qadarism of Ghaylān helped to produce this cleavage. It must be remembered, however, that the change of dynasty in 750 affected the attitude to Qadarism. The ʿAbbāsids justified their rule on quite other grounds than the Umayyads. Hence it was no longer necessary to be a Qadarite to oppose the government, and to hold predestinarian views no longer had the connotation that one approved of wicked rulers. In short, Qadarism gradually ceased to have political implications, and this made it possible for Sunnite Islam to reject Qadarism. The basic reason was doubtless that it was felt to be at variance with the central Qur'ānic vision of human life.

5

THE BEGINNINGS OF ISLAMIC CULTURE

Sir Hamilton Gibb (in *Mohammedanism*, chapter 1) seems to have been the first to maintain that 'the fundamental and decisive contribution of the Arabs' to the culture of their empire was an intellectual one; and this assertion is so important, and at the same time so surprising, that it is worth considering it more fully. Sir Hamilton, of course, did not intend to deny that it was the military effectiveness of the Arabs which created the empire and their administrative genius which first made it a viable political entity; and it is clear that the material splendour of ʿAbbāsid Baghdad and Fāṭimid Cairo came not from the Arabs but from the centuries-old material culture of Iraq and Egypt. The strength of Sir Hamilton's assertion emerges when one compares the Arabs with the Romans. The Romans also had the military power and the administrative ability to create an empire, but the intellectual life of their empire came to be dominated by Greece and in many fields aspirants to scholarship had to have a knowledge of Greek. By way of contrast, when the Arabs conquered lands where there was a strong intellectual tradition based on the use of Syriac and, to a lesser extent, Greek, these languages gradually faded out, and Arabic became the linguistic vehicle of the intellectual life of the vast empire. Even when the Persians came to have a large share in the empire, so that Persian became a kind of second language, it was chiefly used for poetry and mysticism. Arabic remained the language of the main intellectual disciplines.

Arabic literature before Islam

This achievement of the Arabs is all the more amazing when it is remembered how slight their literature was at the time of the Prophet's death in 632. Up to this date the Arabs' literary tradition had been virtually restricted to poetry and oratory. Oratory is of its nature evanescent where writing is little practised; but there are grounds for thinking that pre-Islamic oratory was in general character not unlike the special type of formal prose known as *saj'*, consisting mainly of short phrases, balancing one another, and often showing parallelism of structure together with rhyme or assonance. The aim of the orator was to sway the audience in favour of his policies, and, in conditions where weighty decisions were taken at meetings of the tribe or clan, oratorical power was an asset for any political leader. The tradition of poetry, which was cultivated especially by gifted individuals among the nomadic tribes, is commonly held to have reached its greatest height of achievement in the age immediately before Islam, with the seven outstanding odes known as the *Mu'allaqāt*. The ode (*qaṣīda*) is no rough or ingenuous folk ballad, but a highly sophisticated type of poem, complex metrically and conceptually. It represents the culmination of at least a century of poetic effort – and perhaps of a longer period, for its origins are unknown – and during this time not merely had the poets increased their skills, but their audiences had shown a parallel development in aesthetic feeling.

Apart from oratory the only Arabic prose which existed in 632 was the Qur'ān and a small number of documents containing treaties, statements of land rights and other business matters. It has sometimes been thought that parts of the Bible had been translated into Arabic by 632, but on the whole this seems unlikely. The language of the documents is somewhat crude, terse and inelegant, and often difficult to understand – hardly a model for later prose. The earlier parts of the Qur'ān are in a form of *saj'*, the later parts in more ordinary prose, though with a special flavour. The documents, of course, were written, and by 650 the Qur'ān had all been written down, though in an imperfect script which could be read in various ways. To begin with, the Qur'ān had probably not been written but only remembered; and the same holds of the poetry. Naturally an oral literature is still literature, and may indeed be great literature.

Yet nothing can conceal the fact that the *total* literary heritage of the Arabs in 632 was no more than poetry, oratory, the Qur'ān and some business documents. Four hundred years later Arabic literature counted many thousands of books; besides poetry and belles-lettres there were works of history, geography, theology, philosophy, jurisprudence, political theory, literary criticism and other subjects. The language had been expanded to deal elegantly with all these. It is a staggering achievement. Perhaps the feeling for words and skill in their use which produced the *Mu'allaqāt* indicate the presence of literary gifts which contributed to this process.

We know that this literature developed, for many of the later works still exist; but we do not know in detail how the development came about, especially in its early stages. As has already been noted, Arabic scholars had no concept of development, and regarded Islamic institutions and doctrines as having existed from the first in what was later accepted as their standard form. Since the works of the pioneers of the first two Islamic centuries did not always accord with the standard form, they were forgotten and lost; it was impossible to appreciate what they contributed to a process of development. The names have been preserved, however, and occasionally some anecdotes or isolated sayings. From such materials and from our general knowledge of the period it is possible to give some idea of how this new culture – or should we say 'cultural vehicle'? – was created.

The first legal discussions

The central discipline of Islamic higher education, once that came into being, has always been jurisprudence; and in dealing with the Umayyad period it is thus helpful to consider first those who may be termed jurists, even though their discipline was still in an embryonic stage. Whatever name we give to it, there was a strong body of opinion that was concerned that the practice of the Umayyad state should come to be more in accordance with Qur'ānic principles. This body of opinion was constituted by many ordinary Muslims – mostly Arabs at first, but later also non-Arabs from Iraq and elsewhere. In each of the main cities there were one or more groups of such men, who would meet for discussion in mosques or courtyards or private houses. The aim of their discussions would be to discover, in respect of the new problems which were constantly arising, which course of action was in accordance with Qur'ānic principles. In each centre the local group usually formed a common mind on most points and so constituted what have been called 'the ancient schools of law'. Frequently there was also a minority group which disagreed with the majority.

During the Umayyad period the specifically Islamic element in the legal discussions was supplied almost exclusively by the Qur'ān, since little attention was paid to that other 'Islamic' source, the Traditions (*ḥadīth*), until after 750. This use of the Qur'ān, however, implied agreement about the actual text. About 650 the caliph 'Uthmān had appointed a committee which had produced a standard or 'canonical' text, and this put an end to most textual disputes, although, owing to the imperfection of the script, minor variants were still possible (and even – in the tenth century – were in part recognized as canonical). As an example of the differences which could occur previously 5.89/91 may be cited, where it is stated that for a poor person the expiation for the breaking of a contract made on oath is to fast three days. The 'Uthmānic text has simply 'the fasting of three days', but Ibn-Mas'ūd, an early scholar associated with Kufa, had with others read 'the fasting of three successive days'. The standard text may be interpreted to mean either separate days or successive days, whereas Ibn-Mas'ūd's reading excludes the former interpretation. The later legal schools mostly said that separate days were intended, but it is noteworthy that the school of Abū-Ḥanīfa, also associated with Kufa, while following the standard text, held that the days must be successive.

The example just given leads to the further point that, after agreement is reached about the text, differences of interpretation are still possible. At first the questions of interpretation were doubtless included in the discussion of practical problems. Gradually, however, it came to be seen that *tafsīr*, the interpretation or exegesis of the Qur'ān, was a discipline on its own in which a man could specialize by devoting most of his time to it. *Tafsīr* had many different aspects. One could remember what Muḥammad or someone close to him had said about the interpretation of a particular verse. One could compare phrases in different verses. One could quote verses of pre-Islamic poetry to justify an interpretation of an obscure word. One could consider from a grammatical standpoint different ways of understanding the construction of a verse. The stories told allusively in the Qur'ān could be filled out from Jewish or Christian or traditional Arab sources, or sometimes, it would seem, from sheer imagination. One could try to discover on what particular occasion a passage had been revealed and to what specific person or group it referred. Many of the activities mentioned developed into separate disciplines such as grammar, lexicography and the collection and study of pre-Islamic poetry. These branches of philology were only beginning to emerge at the end of the Umayyad period, and will be described in the next chapter; but before 750 many men had become noted in the field of *tafsīr*, and some will be mentioned presently.

History

Another group of disciplines come under the heading of history. As time went on, men were probably led to take up the study of history by motives of a general kind, such as the desire to understand the place of the Arabs in world history or to know more fully the background of events referred to in the Qur'ān, or even sheer curiosity. To begin with, however, there were considerations of a more immediate and practical nature, for political arguments often involved references to alleged historical events. One such matter was the question: Must the head of the Islamic state be a member of the Meccan tribe of Quraysh, or were the men of Medina also eligible? Those who held the latter view argued that when Sa'd ibn-Mu'ādh (the leading Medinan Muslim at the time) had come to the assembly to pass judgement on the Jewish clan of Qurayẓa, Muḥammad had said 'Rise for your chief', addressing the whole company and so implying that a Medinan could be in the position of *sayyid* or chief to Meccans. The upholders of the other view parried this argument in various ways; they could hold that Muḥammad's words were addressed only to the man's own clan or tribe, or they could expand the story to include an objection by the Meccans present to the term 'chief', so that either they did not rise or they did so only when it was clear that they were not acknowledging Sa'd as their chief.

Even weightier political issues – issues which continued for centuries to have a contemporary relevance – were implicit in the events of 632 (what arrangements, if any, Muḥammad had made for the succession) and 656 (what happened after the assassination of 'Uthmān). At first biased versions of these events were circulated to support one or other political standpoint. Then followed more sophisticated, and apparently more objective, versions, though still with a political aim. It is only towards 900 with aṭ-Ṭabarī that we find something like critical history. Apart from political concerns, some interest in history probably grew out of the desire to glorify one's ancestors. There were family anecdotes about what grandfathers had done in the Prophet's expeditions. Yet another preliminary of historical writing was the continuation of the Arab poetic tradition. There were persons who memorized the ancient poems, and these persons were often also experts in genealogy and knew stories about the more notable men. In the early Umayyad period this traditional lore was doubtless still preserved orally, and interest in it was probably declining; but before it was completely lost the study of Qur'ānic lexicography led to a revival of interest in the old poetry, and many of the poems and anecdotes were written down. Some use of genealogy was made by Umayyad administrators, because the payment of stipends was based on tribal lists.

In this way from a combination of various motives historical writing emerged as a branch of scholarly activity. The earliest works dealt with Muḥammad's *Maghāzī* or 'Expeditions', and with some of the controversial events of the period between 632 and 661. Gradually the desire for completeness led to fuller and more systematic accounts of Muḥammad's career and the subsequent periods – accounts which were not limited to the disputed matters, though they still tended to have a particular standpoint. Material from the Old Testament and other Jewish sources was also contributed by scholarly Jews who had become Muslims; and in the middle of the eighth century historical study was extended to pre-Islamic Arabia and the non-Arab world.

The Traditions

A word must also be said here about that important section of Arabic literature known as *Ḥadīth*, usually rendered as Tradition or Traditions (sometimes with a capital to indicate the technical sense). A Tradition here means an anecdote about something Muḥammad said or did. A simple example (al-Bukhārī, *Īmān*, 4) is: 'The Prophet said, "The Muslim is he from whose tongue and hand the Muslims are safe".' At a certain period the use of Traditions became important as a basis for legal and other arguments, and it was soon realized that it was easy to invent sayings of Muḥammad. The habit then developed of giving one's authority for the authenticity of a Tradition; and this came to be in the form 'I heard from (on the authority of) N that the Prophet said . . .'. In time it came to be seen that the only satisfactory proof of authenticity was a chain of transmitters stretching back without a break to the Prophet himself. Such a chain was known as an *isnād* (support). The full form then becomes: al-Bukhārī writes, 'There related to me Adam AI, who said, "There related to me Shuʿba from ʿAbd-Allāh AS and Ismāʿīl from ash-Shaʿbī from ʿAbd-Allāh ʿA. from the Prophet, who said . . ." .' It must further be known that each of the persons named had sound views, a good memory and the opportunity of hearing Traditions from his predecessor (the person after him in the list). If these conditions were fulfilled, the Tradition was accepted as 'sound'; and, as will be seen later, collections were made of 'sound' Traditions and regarded as canonical.

The Muslim scholars' view of sound Traditions thus implies that from the lifetime of the Prophet onwards pious Muslims were handing on his sayings to the younger generation. In particular this means that there must have been much study of Traditions throughout the Umayyad period. Much of this view has been rejected by modern occidental scholars. On the one hand, they have made the point that it is easy to invent an *isnād*. Joseph Schacht spoke of producing the *isnād* 'backwards'; this meant that he found legal texts where a saying had a restricted *isnād* of one or two names, and then another legal text thirty or forty years later with a complete *isnād* right to the Prophet. (The additions are, of course, the earlier names chronologically.) The implication is that the later scholars, because of a greater interest in the *isnād*, added the earlier names *without having heard them from the man who transmitted the saying*. The added names were not necessarily a sheer invention, but may have been based on a general knowledge of the scholars active in a given locality.

A second point made by occidental writers is that in Arabic works of the seventh and eighth centuries there is often no mention of Traditions at places where some reference might have been expected.

Thus there are numerous Traditions expressing predestinarian views, but in his *Epistle* al-Ḥasan al-Baṣrī does not argue against any of them, from which we may at the least infer that they were not in general circulation at this period. Again, Ibn-Is'ḥāq (d. 768), in his *Sīra* or 'Life of the Prophet', gives numerous *isnāds*, but there is also some material without any *isnād* and much with only an incomplete *isnād*. So even by the middle of the eighth century the *isnād* was far from being a *sine qua non*. The person mainly responsible for the change of attitude to the *isnād* was the jurist ash-Shāfi'ī (d. 820) who, in writing of the Sunna (or standard practice) of the Prophet as one of the 'roots of law', insisted that the Sunna should be defined by 'sound' Traditions.

The implication of the usual Muslim view is that throughout the Umayyad period countless scholars spent much time transmitting Traditions in a formal way. The occidental view, by way of contrast, maintains that there was no formal study of Traditions until after 750, and that such study did not become a recognized discipline until the 'Abbāsid period. Some stories about Muḥammad may indeed have been passed on, but, if so, it was done incidentally and informally. The conclusion, then, is that the Traditions are not to be regarded as an aspect of Arabic literature under the Umayyads.

Some leading scholars

Let us now turn to look briefly at one or two of the chief figures among the scholars, arranging them geographically rather than according to subjects. During the Umayyad period there was no real specialization, so that, even if a man achieved something of note in one discipline, he must be presumed to have ranged through most of the field of contemporary studies.

In Mecca the leading figure is Ibn-'Abbās, more fully 'Abd-Allāh ibn-al-'Abbās, the cousin of Muḥammad and ancestor of the 'Abbāsid dynasty – the first two 'Abbāsid caliphs were actually his great-grandsons. Whether all that is ascribed to Ibn-'Abbās is really his is a doubtful matter. Some scholars living under the 'Abbāsids may have tried to gain the favour of the ruling family by exaggerating the achievements of their ancestor; and once he was the recognized authority on the exegesis of the Qur'ān it would be natural to ascribe to him all sorts of views in order to gain their general acceptance. He was nearly fifty years younger than Muḥammad, having been born in 619. Though his father was still a pagan, his mother is said to have brought him up from the first as a Muslim. As a young man he took part in campaigns both to the east and to the west, but he took no active part in politics until ʿAlī, also his cousin, came to the throne in 656. For a time he was governor of Basra but he lost ʿAlī's confidence when he disapproved of his rejection of the Arbitration and his treatment of the Khārijites. He reappears, however, as a general under al-Ḥasan, and seems to have helped to negotiate the latter's agreement with Muʿāwiya. Following that he lived in Mecca for over twenty years and occasionally went to the court at Damascus as a spokesman for the Hāshimite family. Hāshimite loyalty and in particular friendship with Muḥammad ibn-al-Ḥanafiyya made him refuse to acknowledge ʿAbd-Allāh ibn-az-Zubayr. He was eventually exiled to aṭ-Ṭā'if, where he died about 687.

Stories are told of how he gave lectures in the mosque each day of the week on a different subject, but this is probably something of an exaggeration. The centre of his scholarly concern was the interpretation of the Qur'ān, and in working at this he doubtless made use of all his knowledge of Muḥammad and his background and of the early history of Islam. He is also said to have made use of information he received from Jewish converts to Islam. Because he was both a great authority on the interpretation of the Qur'ān and the ancestor of the ʿAbbāsid dynasty, many points were ascribed to him which were not really his. From such works as the great thirty-volume Qur'ān-commentary of aṭ-Ṭabarī it should be possible to reconstruct in detail much of the teaching of Ibn-ʿAbbās, but this has not been done so far. Aṭ-Ṭabarī quotes many interpretations specifically attributed to Ibn-ʿAbbās or to his chief pupils ʿIkrima and Mujāhid. ʿIkrima (d. 723) was a freedman of Ibn-ʿAbbās, perhaps of Berber origin, who travelled widely and belonged to Medina as much as to Mecca. Mujāhid (d. 721) was also a freedman, though possibly of Arab origin. He is said to have favoured rationalistic interpretations, whereas ʿIkrima was held to have Khārijite sympathies. Another pupil of Ibn-ʿAbbās was ʿAṭā' ibn-Abī-Rabāḥ (d. 732), a freedman of African descent. Though he did not neglect Qur'ānic studies, his chief importance is as the first man in Mecca to have gone deeply into questions of jurisprudence.

Medina, as the centre of government during the life of Muḥammad and until 661, seems to have had a more varied intellectual life than Mecca. The leading scholar in Medina from among the Companions of Muḥammad was Zayd ibn-Thābit (611–66). He was a native of Medina of the tribe of al-Khazraj, who wrote down Qur'ānic passages for Muḥammad as they were revealed, and in other respects acted as his secretary. Muḥammad realized that he had a gift for languages and made him learn Syriac in order to deal with correspondence in that language – less probable is the version according to which he learnt Hebrew and read the Jewish scriptures. ʿUmar placed him in charge of the distribution of the booty after the battle of the Yarmuk, and ʿUthmān made him head of the commission to stabilize the text of the Qur'ān.

Another Companion in Medina was ʿAbd-Allāh ibn-ʿUmar, son of the second caliph, who died in 693, aged over eighty. He was respected for his piety and uprightness, though he was also held to be unduly serious and to lack a sense of humour. He maintained an attitude of neutrality between ʿAlī and his opponents in 656, but later recognized the Umayyads. While Ibn-ʿUmar kept somewhat aloof from the practical work of administration, there were a number of pious men in Medina who were deeply concerned that government should be in accordance with Islamic principles. A group of such men, with death-dates between 710 and 725, came to be known as 'the seven lawyers of Medina', though we cannot now be certain about their precise contributions to the discussion or even, since there are variant lists, about who constituted the seven. The best-known in the usual list are Saʿīd ibn-al-Musayyab (d. after 710) and ʿUrwa ibn-az-Zubayr (d. 712).

Among the pupils of these two and others was a man who became the most learned scholar of the Umayyad period. This was Muḥammad ibn-Shihāb, usually known simply as az-Zuhrī (*c.*670–742). He belonged to the clan of Zuhra of the Meccan tribe of Quraysh. His father had been a supporter of the Zubayrid party in the Second Civil War, but he himself, though very friendly with ʿUrwa ibn-az-Zubayr (brother of the anti-caliph) and his son Hishām (d. 763), was on good terms with the Umayyad caliphs ʿAbd-al-Malik (probably), Yazīd II and Hishām. Later Muslim scholars assigned to him a high reputation in jurisprudence and also regarded him as one of the first persons to write down the information he received. This last matter gives point to a story about his marital relations. He had only one wife, but when he was at home he spent all his time poring over books, so neglecting the poor woman that she exclaimed in exasperation, 'Those books! they are worse for me than three other wives would have been.' Books must have been a rarity in the early eighth century in Medina, but, if they were his own notebooks, this would explain the situation. Modern scholars have, on the other hand, tended to think of az-Zuhrī primarily as one of the founders of Islamic historiography. He wrote on the biography of the Prophet, the genealogies of the Meccans, and other subjects. Though none of his own works is extant, he is frequently quoted, presumably verbatim, by Ibn-Is'ḥāq and aṭ-Ṭabarī.

Not much need be said about Damascus, since, although it was the capital, it was less lively in intellectual matters than several cities In it resided a Companion who was outstanding for his knowledge of the text of the Qur'ān, Abū-d-Dardā' (d. 652), a member of the Khazraj tribe from Medina, and also noted as an ascetic. After him another scholar of Damascus, Ibn-ʿĀmir (d. 736), produced a set of readings which came to be recognized as one of the seven 'canonical' sets. There was naturally some study of law in Damascus, and the chief name in this field is that of Mak'ḥūl (d. *c.*731), who was apparently of Afghan or Persian stock and had for a time at least sympathized with the Qadarites. Because of his Qadarite leanings Mak'ḥūl may have been somewhat suspect to the Umayyad administration, but one of his pupils, al-Awzāʿī (d. 774), apparently from Sind, is said to have headed a school with official recognition. Since al-Awzāʿī's birth is placed in 706, he cannot have reached his full stature as a scholar much before the fall of the Umayyads. After 750 he lived a retired life in Beirut, his career ruined by the change of dynasty. In general it seems that the Syrian school – if we can speak of one at all – was checked at an embryonic stage by the course of events.

In Kufa in contrast to Damascus there seems to have been much intellectual activity. Kufa had been the chief centre of support for ʿAlī in Iraq, and continued to have many persons who were at least in a vague sense of Shīʿite outlook. Since many of the earliest Murji-'ites are from Kufa, it is probable that the name was first given to the minority (?) in Kufa who were not whole-heartedly in favour of ʿAlī and his descendants. There must have been much study of the

Qur'ānic text in Kufa, for three of the seven 'canonical' sets of readings come from Kufa. One of these, that of 'Āṣim (d. 744) in the version of Ḥafṣ (d. 805), is the most widely accepted of all the sets. The Companion specially associated with Kufa was ('Abd-Allāh) Ibn-Mas'ūd (d. 653), who had a peculiar set of readings rejected by the commission under 'Uthmān. The first scholar of whom we can form a clear idea was Ibrāhīm an-Nakha'ī (*c.*665–714), who was of Yemenite Arab stock. Various reports about his political attitudes indicate a moderate position: though he had a high regard for 'Alī, he did not attribute any special charisma to him and would not place him above Abū-Bakr and 'Umar; and though he preferred him to 'Uthmān, he would not speak ill of 'Uthmān. As has already been indicated, these were not academic historical matters (as they sound to us), but had to do both with actual political issues and with the use of the example of these men to justify actual legal and ritual practices. Longer-lived than Ibrāhīm but probably less influential was ash-Sha'bī (*c.*640–722), also of Yemenite stock, who on one occasion went to the Byzantine emperor as envoy for 'Abd-al-Malik. Much was done for the development of jurisprudence by a pupil of Ibrāhīm's, Ḥammād ibn-Abī-Sulaymān (d. 738), who was in turn the teacher of the celebrated Abū-Ḥanīfa (pp. 121f.). His general attitude was Murji'ite.

While Kufa had supported 'Alī, Basra had supported the 'rebels' Ṭalḥa and az-Zubayr. While Kufa had many Shī'ites (or at least admirers of 'Alī) and Murji'ites, the most distinctive sects in Basra were Khārijites and Qadarites. In both cities there were scholars moving towards a moderate or Sunnite position, but the starting-point of each group was the set of ideas most discussed in their own city. Another curious difference is that whereas in the early 'Abbāsid period Basra was the scene of important intellectual advances (notably the acceptance of aspects of Greek thought), in the Umayyad period it was much less active than Kufa. Al-Ḥasan al-Baṣrī, who has already been described, was really the only scholar in the first rank, and his chief interests were the interpretation of the Qur'ān and the discussion of doctrinal questions. There were some competent scholars of the text of the Qur'ān, but there was no jurisprudence to speak of. Many men and women in Basra were deeply concerned about holiness of life – a concern that is seen in al-Ḥasan and his younger associate Qatāda (679–736). The group of four sometimes regarded as forerunners of the developed form of Sunnism had as their oldest Ayyūb as-Sakhtiyānī (d. 748); the others lived on into the ʿAbbāsid period. Qatāda was an Arab, Ayyūb a non-Arab.

Egypt played a very small part in the intellectual life of the Umayyad caliphate, and was not prominent under the ʿAbbāsids, though there was some study of jurisprudence and of the history of North Africa. This may have something to do with the fact that the Copts seem to have little talent for abstract rational thinking, for this would affect the form of any inter-religious discussion which took place, while some of the Arab invaders may have married Coptic wives. The great school of Alexandria (which in any case was moved to Syria about 718) was mainly a Greek affair and had little influence on the Copts who constituted the vast majority of the pre-Islamic population.

Arab attitudes

After this review of scholarly activity in the main Islamic centres during the Umayyad period, we may look again at the assertion of Sir Hamilton Gibb about the importance of the *intellectual* contribution of the Arabs. Other modern writers have tended to take the contrasting view that the intellectual developments in the Islamic world were due mainly to the non-Arab clients. As far as possible it has been indicated in the above review whether the scholars were Arabs or not; and it is clear that at least under the Umayyads the Arabs themselves achieved much. It is even more important, however, to notice that the clients who took part in the early intellectual movement had, as far as we can tell, become arabized in that they had accepted and become bearers of the Arab ethos. One mark of this is their enthusiasm for the Arabic language. Even if not all the writers were Arabs, it was mainly Arab influences which were moulding the new intellectual culture.

The underlying reason for this appears to be the unbounded self-confidence of the Arabs. Nearly every Arab was convinced of the nobility of his own tribe and the baseness or inferiority of other tribes. The main point of pre-Islamic poetry was the expression of these convictions. Somehow or other this developed into an unshakeable conviction of the superiority of the Arabs to all other peoples. It would be anachronistic to speak of anything like a national consciousness in the seventh century, but there was some awareness of a distinction between Arabs and foreigners or *'ajam*. This distinction is based on language; the Arabs are the 'clear-speakers', the *'ajam* the 'unclear-speakers', presumably meaning those who are and who are not mutually intelligible. The Arabs of the seventh century were also conscious of common descent (in two groups). This common consciousness would be further fostered by the references in the Qur'ān to its being 'an Arabic Qur'ān' and 'in clear Arabic speech'. After the conquests the relatively small number of Arabs in the new provinces would be drawn together by their common language and also, at first, by their religion. The Qur'ān encouraged a sense of superiority in so far as it spoke of the corruption and so inferiority of the Jewish and Christian forms of monotheism.

This self-confidence of the Arabs was probably the chief reason for the dominant position assumed by the Arabic language in Islamic culture. Because the Arabs believed themselves superior to other peoples and their religion superior to other religions they could not be expected to take over from others things they regarded as inferior. One aspect of this attitude is well illustrated by the following, presumably apocryphal, story. After the conquest of Alexandria the caliph 'Umar was asked what was to be done with the books in the great library there. He replied: 'if they are in accordance with the Qur'ān, they are unnecessary and may be burnt; if they are contrary to the Qur'ān, they are dangerous and ought to be burnt'. To persons with this attitude it was unthinkable that their Arabic Qur'ān should be replaced even by a translation, say into Syriac or Persian. What was basically a deep innate or traditional attitude was reinforced by the theological doctrine that the Qur'ān was the actual speech of God. With the Qur'ān thus irreplaceable, scholarly works growing out of it could hardly have been in a language other than Arabic, even if in the early days the proportion of non-Arab scholars had been greater. Arab self-confidence, coupled with their political dominance under the Umayyads, also explains the readiness of non-Arabs to become arabized.

In certain circumstances the Arabs were prepared to accept what foreign sources provided. They accepted much Biblical and extra-canonical Jewish material from Jewish converts like 'Abd-Allāh ibn-Salām (d. 663) and Ka'b al-Aḥbār (d. 654) and from the Yemenite of Persian descent, Wahb ibn-Munabbih (d. 728/32); but they presumably felt that this material was not entirely foreign, since it was an elaboration of passages of the Qur'ān. In other cases foreign material was accepted and its foreign origin disguised by making it into a saying of Muḥammad or some other Arab Muslim.

Poetry

In this section the chief emphasis has been on the new disciplines in Arab speech, since their development amounted to the creation out of almost nothing of Arabic prose literature. Nevertheless it must not be forgotten that the Arabic poetical tradition continued. There was no lack of would-be poets, but their productions were mostly not of a high quality. In their great period the pre-Islamic odes had been closely linked with the outlook of the nomadic Arabs. When so many Arabs had left the desert in the conquering armies, even those who remained and continued to follow the traditional mode of life must have experienced a great change in their circumstances, and it is thus not surprising that the odes of the old type produced in this period should have been second-rate. The best poems of the Umayyad period were those that reflected some aspect of the new life in which the Arabs were now immersed.

At the end of the seventh century and beginning of the eighth there emerged a group of three men who are generally reckoned the greatest poets of the time. In some ways they are close to the spirit of the desert, but the fact that their audience consisted of urbanized tribesmen and wealthy patrons subtly affected the general tone of their poetry. The oldest of the three was al-Akhṭal (d. *c*.710) who, though a Christian from the Christian tribe of the Taghlib, became acquainted with the Umayyad family during the reign of Muʿāwiya I and was official court poet for ʿAbd-al-Malik. Despite some gentle pressure from his patrons he refused to become a Muslim, saying he could not give up the use of wine, and he ostentatiously went about the Umayyad court with a cross round his neck. Besides singing the praises of the Umayyads, he engaged in the usual boasting of the glories of his own tribe and the satirizing of the shameful and dishonourable features in the lives of other tribes, either enemies of his own tribe or the tribes of rival poets.

The other two of the trio, Jarīr and al-Farazdaq, are usually named together, doubtless because over a period of forty years they were engaged in a series of diatribes against one another, which have been described as 'slanging-matches on parallel themes' and which gave scope for the display of their ingenuity and command of the language. Both belonged to the tribe of Tamīm but to different subdivisions, and both died in 728. Jarīr found favour with the governor al-Ḥajjāj and was received at the court of ʿAbd-al-Malik, though with little enthusiasm, probably because of his hostility to the court-poet al-Akhṭal. On the other hand he became a favourite with the pious ʿUmar II. Al-Farazdaq lived mostly in Basra, and was usually on bad terms with the individuals and groups with whom Jarīr was on good terms and vice versa. He was the official poet of al-Walīd I and Sulaymān, but moved somewhat into the shade under ʿUmar II. This illustrates how in this time of 'rapid social change' the poets not merely reflect the general unsettlement but are caught up into the political currents. Other stories about these poets indicate how considerable was their influence.

One of the great changes the conquests had brought was that many Arabs could now live in luxury and ease. This was particularly so in Mecca and Medina, and affected the poetry produced there. Instead of the pre-Islamic ode (*qaṣīda*) with its glorification or vilification of an individual or group, there appears the love-lyric (*ghazal*). In Medina the poet Jamīl (d. 701) perfected the *ghazal* of 'hopeless love', based on his experiences with a woman of his tribe, who was married off by her parents to another man. The lover, in the purity of his love, continues to worship the beloved, though it brings him suffering and death. Because Jamīl belonged to the tribe of ʿUdhra, this kind of poetry came to be known as ʿUdhrite, and has continued to have a great attraction for many Arabs.

The outstanding composer of *ghazals* under the Umayyads was ʿUmar ibn-Abī-Rabīʿa (d. *c.*712), who belonged to the Meccan clan of Makhzūm and spent most of his life in Mecca. He is said by a biographer to have been 'celebrated for his *ghazals*, his witticisms, his adventures and his wanton and disorderly life'. His poems are all about love, and no doubt derive from his own experience, for his ideal of love is fresh, tender and chivalrous. The moralists disapproved of him; al-Ḥasan al-Baṣrī is reported to have said, referring to the belief that this ʿUmar was born on the night on which the caliph ʿUmar was murdered, 'what worth was taken away and what worthlessness brought'. The Meccan *ghazal* was taken up at the court in Damascus and associated with a local tradition of wine-songs. Among the exponents of this last genre was the caliph al-Walīd II (d. 744).

There is thus a cleavage between the prose and the poetry of the Umayyad period. The prose is developing in the service of religion, while the poetry rests on traditional Arab values. It is true that Jarīr and al-Farazdaq used religious achievements as material for the praise of their patrons (see p. 56 above); but one wonders how far this was lip-service to Islam. It is also true that some of the old virtues are hardly mentioned. The basic fact, however, is that the outlook of the Umayyad poets is essentially this-worldly. Perhaps even the attraction of 'hopeless' ʿUdhrite love is due, not to 'eternal longings' but to unconscious desires for the desert life which urban Arabs had decided to abandon.

II

The First ʿAbbāsid Century

750–850

ʿABBĀSID CALIPHS

750 (749)	as-Saffāḥ
754	al-Manṣūr
775	al-Mahdī
785	al-Hādī
786	Hārūn ar-Rashīd
809	al-Amīn
813	al-Ma'mūn
(817–19	Ibrāhīm, in Baghdad)
833	al-Muʿtaṣim
842	al-Wāthiq
847–61	al-Mutawakkil

THE 'ABBĀSID DYNASTY (1)

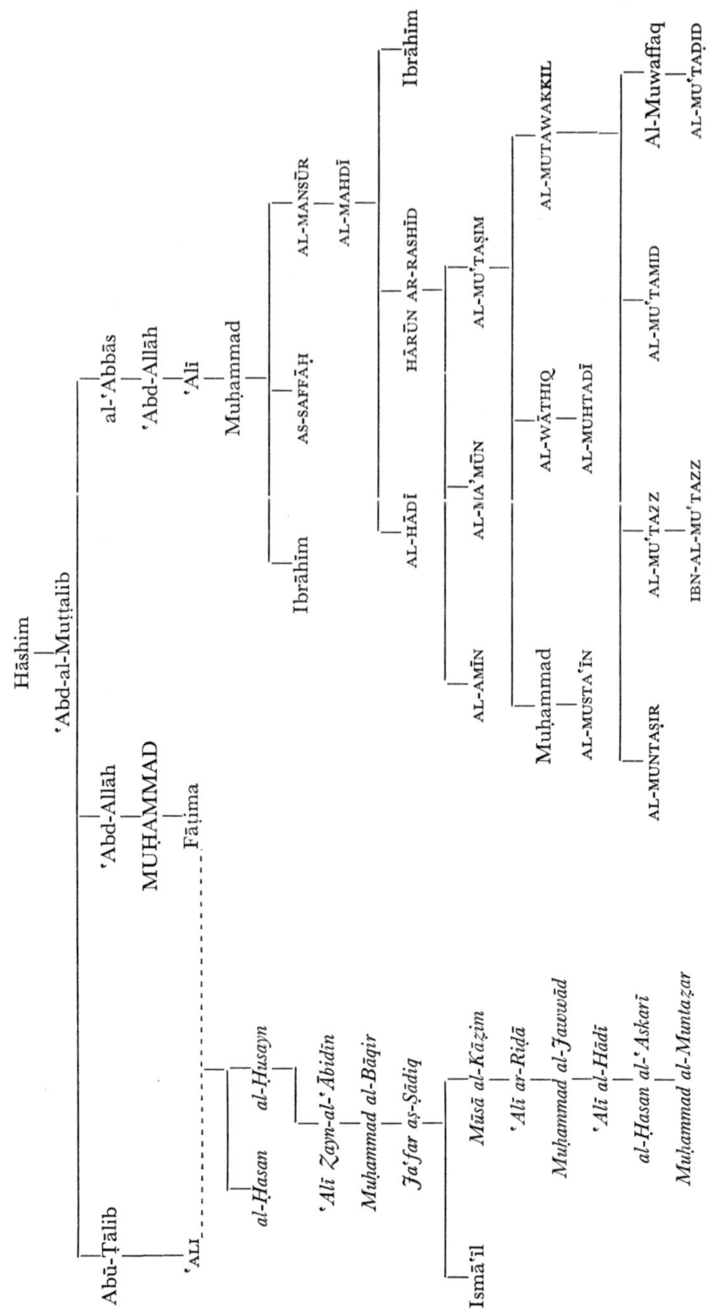

Note: Names of caliphs are in small capitals; of Imāmite imams in italics.

1

THE ESTABLISHMENT OF 'ABBĀSID RULE

The basis of 'Abbāsid power

The events of the 'Abbāsid rising, which brought Abū-l-'Abbās as-Saffāḥ to the caliphate and led to the death of the last Umayyad caliph Marwān II in 750, have already been described (pp. 30f.). The fall of the Umayyads was traced to the growing strength and dissatisfaction of the *mawālī* or non-Arab Muslims, the disunity of the Arab tribes, the disaffection of most members of the general religious movement, and the widespread desire for a political saviour, a charismatic leader. These four factors are indicative of the various forces operative in the empire, and the victory of these forces in combination was bound to bring about great changes in the social and political structure. At the same time, the support for the 'Abbāsids included so many heterogeneous elements that some of the extremists among them were bound to be dissatisfied. This last matter will be considered under the heading of 'the maintenance of internal order'. First, however, it is convenient to look at the influence of the four factors after the caliphate had passed to the 'Abbāsids.

The discontent of the non-Arab Muslims had much to do with the fall of the Umayyads because their numbers were constantly growing. The 'Abbāsids were thus compelled to try to remove the causes of this discontent, not merely out of gratitude for the contribution to their victory, but also because of the importance of the non-Arabs in the caliphate. Ancient Muslim and modern western writers have sometimes spoken as if the *mawālī* who had political power in the caliphate about the middle of the eighth century were almost exclusively Persians; but this is not so. There were also men from Syria, Egypt and Iraq; and even if most of the last group could be described as 'persianized Aramaeans', the *mawālī* as a whole were not consciously acting as Persians. It would be anachronistic at this period to suppose the existence of any common Persian or Iranian consciousness. It is mainly in respect of traditions of government that the label 'Persian' is appropriate, as will be seen presently.

The non-Arab Muslims wanted above all to be accepted in every respect as the equals of the Arabs. They were no longer to be second-class citizens, suffering under various disadvantages, but were to share in all the privileges of the Arabs, not least in the economic field. At the same time, the politically influential *mawālī* were mostly town-dwellers, earning a livelihood as small merchants or artisans; they were thus opposed to an expansionist policy, and instead wanted one aiming at stability, good order and prosperity through the growth of trade. Quietly and unobtrusively the ʿAbbāsids did in fact adopt these aims. On the negative side they simply refrained from mounting any large-scale military operations beyond their frontiers. Such expeditions as they sent against the Byzantines may be described as defensive; they were certainly not expansionist. When we read about the many revolts the ʿAbbāsids had to quell, it might seem that they had no energy left for expansion; but this can hardly have been so, since the empire in general was very prosperous, and so the absence of expansion must be assigned to deliberate policy, at least in the sense of giving priority to other aims.

The disunity of the Arabs seems to have been linked with the general problems of the empire, even though it was expressed in terms of tribal antagonisms. Concern for maintaining Arab privileges and avoiding concessions to the *mawālī* was prominent among the Qaysites, whereas the Yemenites were rather aware of the need to make use of the energies of the non-Arabs and in return to give them a fair share of the benefits of empire. The Qaysites were therefore expansionist and tended to follow Arab political traditions, whereas the Yemenites were 'assimilationist' and more inclined to insist on Islamic principles. The coming to power of the ʿAbbāsids and their lack of inclination or opportunity for expansion made this quarrel of the Arab groups irrelevant. Those Arab privileges linked with expansion faded away, and the leaders of the movement for retaining them became redundant. Those Arabs whose sympathies were with the granting of equality to non-Arab Muslims and basing the state on Qur'ānic principles became merged in the general religious movement.

It is convenient to speak of the general religious movement, but the term can be misleading if it leads one to suppose that it refers to a group of men completely separate from such other groups as the *mawālī* and the Yemenites. From what has just been said it should be clear that there was a considerable degree of overlap. Because the 'Abbāsids were aware of the strength of the general religious movement and of the widespread concern that government practice should be based on Islamic principles, they themselves tried to show by various public actions that they accepted such a basis for their rule. In particular most of the appointments to judicial posts were given to men from the embryonic schools of law, while at the same time pressure was brought to bear on the schools in the different cities to try to reach agreement on the content of the law. It is to be noted, however, that there were certain limitations on the 'Abbāsid acceptance of an Islamic basis for their rule, and these limitations probably corresponded to limitations of the concerns of the men in the general religious movement. The latter were mostly ordinary town-dwellers who had little or no experience of the work of administering an empire. What they got the caliphs to accept was an Islamic basis for a social structure leading to good order and justice among ordinary Muslims. Numerous incidents, however, such as the execution of Ja'far the Barmakid, suggest that for men in the higher echelons of the administration there was little protection in Islamic principles.

Those of the 'Abbāsid supporters who had been looking for a political saviour were probably the most difficult to satisfy, since they had very divergent ideas about the nature of such a person. While the name of Shī'ites is often given to such persons, it must not be supposed that there was any organized sect or group of sects or any widely held credal affirmations. In the eighth century there was an amorphous body of opinion, united solely in feeling that they could be delivered from their troubles and that life would be better, if only they could find a political leader with some more-than-human qualities. Beyond that they were disagreed. Some looked for an actual leader in the present or immediate future, while others were content with the prospect of a messianic figure at some unspecified and perhaps distant date. Again, some thought that almost any member of the clan of Hāshim might have a sufficient charisma, while others wanted to restrict the field from which the leader might come. Despite these disagreements the presence of this desire for a political saviour made it possible, when a likely candidate actually appeared or was alleged to be just off-stage, to organize round him a close-knit movement capable of military action on a local scale. Several of the movements with which the early ʿAbbāsids had to deal were of this type, as indeed was the movement which brought them to the throne. The particular constellations of ideas which gave such movements temporary cohesion tended to dissolve after military defeat, but the separate ideas were still available for inclusion in subsequent constellations.

The ʿAbbāsids had instructed their agents to say that their movement was on behalf of 'him of the family of Muḥammad who shall be approved', and thereby they doubtless got the support of some who did not approve of the ʿAbbāsids. They justified their assumption of the caliphate, however, on the ground that the son of Muḥammad ibn-al-Ḥanafiyya had bequeathed the office of imam or head of the community to the grandfather of the first two ʿAbbāsid caliphs, and that he had then handed it on to his son and grandsons. In the reign of al-Mahdī (775–85), however, they abandoned this form of legitimation of their rule and claimed instead that the office of imam had been conferred directly by the Prophet on their ancestor al-ʿAbbās. In both cases they were trying to meet the demand among their followers for a charismatic leader. It would seem, moreover, that during the first half of the ninth century there was more apologetic along these lines but that this had mostly been passed over by the historians since it could be described as Zaydite, and Zaydism had come to be regarded as a heresy. This is a complex matter, however, and is best reserved until the next section. In the same context attention will be given to the way in which the factors just considered entered into the political struggles under the ʿAbbāsids once they were established.

The distinctive features of the ʿAbbāsid state

Because of the nature of the problems which had developed under the Umayyads and the nature of the forces which combined to bring about their overthrow, what happened in 750 was a revolution rather than a mere change of dynasty. Some of the changes which affected the central administration may now be looked at briefly.

One of the most important changes was that the capital of the empire was moved eastwards from Syria to Iraq. When an ʿAbbāsid army entered Kufa in 749, it was natural for them to make this their provisional centre of administration, since most of their support came from the eastern provinces and they had not yet penetrated to Syria. Even after the defeat of the Umayyads and the occupation of Syria and Egypt, as-Saffāḥ and al-Manṣūr continued to reside in Kufa. This area continued to be the centre of their real power, since they had no secure control of the provinces west of Egypt and probably felt that the Arabs of Syria had been so closely associated with the Umayyads that they were unlikely to give wholehearted support to their successors. Shortly after his accession al-Manṣūr moved to a new castle somewhere near Kufa called al-Hāshimiyya. Then in 758 al-Manṣūr, having apparently decided that this general region was most suitable for a capital and centre of government, selected a more advantageous site within it, that of Baghdad. The Tigris was navigable to this point and there was also a navigable canal to the Euphrates, which was here relatively close. Goods could also be brought down the Tigris and Euphrates on light vessels. Convenient routes from almost all directions converged on Baghdad. In short, for the purposes of the ʿAbbāsid empire it was a magnificent site. In 762 al-Manṣūr took up his residence in the Round City, of some two miles in diameter, designed as a secure administrative centre for the caliph, his chief officers, his guards and the like. Outside the Round City a commercial area soon appeared, and eventually the whole became a vast metropolis. The official name was *Madīnat as-Salām*, the City of Peace.

The caliph himself ceased to be merely *primus inter pares* like an Arab shaykh and was clearly raised above other men. His seat was higher than those of others, and access to him was difficult for ordinary mortals, since a series of chamberlains had first to be passed. His absolute power of life and death was symbolized by the constant presence of the court executioner. The title 'God's caliph' was possibly used more frequently, and that of 'Shadow of God of the earth' also came into use and was given a more honorific sense than it originally had – it seems to have meant 'the one appointed by God to give protection'. Some of these changes may have been made chiefly for reasons of efficiency, for there are some hints that the Umayyads were already trying to move in this direction. There may also have been some deliberate imitation of Persian (Sasanian) imperial practice, which may be said to have embodied the quintessence of what men had learned from running empires in this very area for over two millennia. Moreover, full use came to be made of officials taken from among the people of Iraq, some of whose ancestors may have held similar posts under the Sasanians.

It has often been suggested that another Persian feature taken over by the ʿAbbāsids was the office of vizier (*wazīr*). Recent investigations, however, show that this hypothesis of Persian origin is so far unproved. The word *wazīr* appears to be Arabic, originally meaning 'helper' or 'support', and is so used twice in the Qur'ān of Aaron in relation to Moses. While it is thus preferable for the time being to admit that the problem of the origin of the vizierate has not been solved, there is no doubt of the growth of the office from the time of al-Manṣūr onwards. Abū-Salama, the representative of the ʿAbbāsids in Kufa in 749, is called 'vizier of the family of Muḥammad'. but this title does not seem to have implied the later vizierate. The outstanding early examples are the Barmakids, though they are not altogether typical, since they consist of a group of a father (Yaḥyā ibn-Khālid) and his two sons (al-Faḍl, Jaʿfar), who worked closely with one another. In principle the vizier combined some of the functions of a prime minister with some of those of a head of the civil service. He had to carry out the orders of the caliph, but at the same time he had an important share in the formation of policy and a wide area of responsibility. Unlike his modern counterparts he had usually, if he wanted to be really efficient, to form and train his own corps of under-secretaries and clerks. It was the competence of Yaḥyā the Barmakid at this point which enabled him to dominate the policy of the caliphate for seventeen years from the accession of Hārūn ar-Rashīd in 786. Apart from the office of vizier the ʿAbbāsid system of administration was a continuation and extension of the Umayyad *dīwāns*.

One small point in which the ʿAbbāsids differed from the Umayyads was in the use of what may be called 'throne-names'. The ʿAbbāsid caliphs had all the usual names of the Arabs of the period; thus al-Manṣūr was Abū-Jaʿfar ʿAbd-Allāh ibn-Muḥammad, and could have been called al-Hāshimī. At what date he adopted or was granted the name of al-Manṣūr is apparently not known. It means 'the one helped to victory [by God]', and was doubtless chosen not so much to enhance the caliph's dignity as to make those who looked for a divinely endowed saviour feel that the head of state was indeed supported by God. All the later throne-names of the ʿAbbāsids have this implicit reference to God in respect of his guidance, succour and the like. In a formal mention of a caliph the reference to God could be explicit, though it was always omitted in common usage. Thus al-Mutawakkil, 'the trusting', is properly al-Mutawakkil ʿalā llāh, 'the trusting in God'. Some ʿAbbāsid princes who did not become caliphs had a name of this type; and in Umayyad Spain in 981 after a victory the chamberlain Ibn-Abī-ʿĀmir, who was *de facto* ruler of the country, took the title of al-Manṣūr (bi-llāh). In English it has become customary to refer to the fifth ʿAbbāsid caliph by his own name Hārūn (Aaron) as well as his throne-name ar-Rashīd, 'the rightly-guided'.

With the coming to power of the ʿAbbāsids the composition of the army inevitably changed. Their military victory was mainly due to an army recruited in Khurasan, and for over half a century they continued to rely largely on Khurasanite troops. With the establishment of the general Ṭāhir as semi-independent governor of Khurasan in 820, the supply of men from Khurasan dried up, and the caliphs began to recruit men of various Turkish tribes, first from within the empire and later also from beyond it. The Turks were excellent fighters, and mostly horsemen, so that by the end of the ninth century they were the main part of the ʿAbbāsid army and a power to be reckoned with in politics. Other changes were linked with these. It had long ceased to be the practice for ordinary able-bodied Muslims to go on campaign, and the army really consisted of professional soldiers who were paid for their service. The early Umayyad system of stipends therefore disappeared completely, though the state still paid stipends to members of the clan of Hāshim. When temporary recruits joined an expedition, they might be rewarded by a share of the booty. In dangerous frontier areas there were also volunteer bands of soldiers of fortune with the honourable title of *ghāzī*, 'campaigner' (*sc.* against the infidel), who lived partly from booty and partly from non-military activities.

Along with these changes in the forms of government and administration there may be mentioned the growth of industry and commerce. In part this was simply the result of the formation of an empire, since the empire constituted a vast 'common market' which facilitated trade and thereby stimulated local industries. There was a great expansion, for example, in the production of the textiles in which certain regions specialized. The caliphs, too, with their Meccan mercantile background, encouraged many kinds of economic development. The draining of swamps and the extension of irrigation increased the agricultural yield of Iraq. Advantage was taken of the capture of some Chinese papermakers at a battle in Central Asia in 751 to learn the technique and establish this new industry, which gradually spread westwards and into Europe (though the Europeans do not appear to have established their own paper-mills until the fourteenth century). Paper soon replaced papyrus, and by making books much cheaper fostered the growth of literature. An interesting feature was the growth of a complex banking system. The eastern part of the empire, following the Persians, used a silver dirham, whereas the western part, following the Byzantines, used a gold dīnār. Since the relative value of the two metals fluctuated, every commercial centre had to have its money-changers. Some of these worked out a system which was so efficient that a cheque drawn in Baghdad could be cashed in Morocco. Because Islam prohibits usury, most of the bankers were Jews or Christians.

The maintenance of internal order

The reigns of as-Saffāḥ and al-Manṣūr were largely taken up with quelling insurrections. The disorders of the last decade of Umayyad rule had encouraged various groups of discontented persons to take to arms to have their grievances redressed. Most of the revolts were local affairs, though some became the focus of the discontent over a wide region.

In particular a whole series of revolts can be traced to deep-rooted feelings of dissatisfaction, especially among the Persian peasantry.

These had led to the communistic rebellion of Mazdak against the Sasanians in the fourth century. Although that had come near to success and had then been savagely put down, the discontent continued and had led many to support the ʿAbbāsid movement, only to be disillusioned when its actual achievements fell far short of their hopes. Mazdakite ideas seem to underly the revolt of Bihāfarīd in Nishapur about 749, that of Sunpādh in western Persia in 755, that of Is'ḥāq at-Turkī in Transoxiana in 757, and that of Ustadhsīs in Khurasan in 767. These were minor affairs. More serious was the rising of a man called al-Muqannaʿ, 'the veiled one', from his habit of wearing a veil over his face, who claimed to be the final prophet. He was killed after three years' fighting in 781, but his movement continued for several years longer. Still more serious was the revolt of Bābak with its centre in Azerbaijan some fifty miles north of Tabriz, for it began in 816 and lasted until Bābak himself was captured in 837, while some of his followers were not subdued for another year or two.

These revolts connected with Mazdakism were by no means the only ones with which the early ʿAbbāsids had to deal. As-Saffāḥ had to quell a revolt in Syria in 750 and another in Oman in 752. In 758 al-Manṣūr was attacked in his castle of al-Hāshimiyya by a group of fanatics called Rāwandites who wanted to see in him an incarnation of deity; they were nearly all killed by the caliphal guards. Then there were half a dozen revolts spread over most of the century and led by descendants of ʿAlī. The best known are those of Muḥammad 'the Pure Soul' (*an-nafs az-zakiyya*) at Medina in 762; of al-Ḥusayn ibn-ʿAlī 'the man of Fakhkh', the place near Medina where he was killed in 786; of Abū-s-Sarāyā in Kufa in 815 as agent of certain ʿAlids; and of Muḥammad ibn-Qāsim in aṭ-Ṭaliqān in Khurasan in 834. These revolts are usually described as 'Zaydite', but in this context this seems to mean no more than that they were led in person by a descendant of ʿAlī. The name is derived from the first descendant of the Prophet to lead a revolt, Zayd ibn-ʿAlī, a grandson of the martyr of Kerbela, who met his death in an insurrection in Kufa in 740. Zaydism as a political theory will be discussed later. It is almost certain that none of the men named held this theory. They seem to have been motivated partly by personal ambition and partly by a concern to redress local grievances. There were also other non-ʿAlid revolts including one of Khārijite inspiration which continued in different districts of Khurasan from 795 until 820 under a man called Ḥamza ibn-Adrak.

This list of revolts gives an idea of the difficulties in keeping order with which the caliphal government had to cope, but it does not invalidate the assertion that the first ʿAbbāsid century was one of peace and prosperity. Those revolts which lasted for any length of time were in remote districts. The main centres of population were relatively little disturbed.

The beginnings of provincial autonomy

While the ʿAbbāsids were thus establishing control over most of the territory conquered by the Arabs, certain provinces on the periphery were beginning to slip from their grasp. This might happen in one of two ways: either a local leader might lead a successful rising and assert complete independence, or a man appointed as governor by the caliph might become so strong that he could not be replaced and had eventually to be succeeded by his sons. The examples of the first way of gaining independence are from North Africa and indicate how the removal of the capital to Iraq lessened the ability of the central government to control that region.

The first province to be lost was Spain. For some years before 750 there had been fighting between different groups of Arabs and Berbers, and the situation was confused. In 755 it became known that a young Umayyad prince, a grandson of the caliph Hishām, later called ʿAbd-ar-Raḥmān the Incomer or ʿAbd-ar-Raḥmān I, was on the North African side of the straits after having escaped from the ʿAbbāsids. Some of those involved in the fighting in Spain thought that the presence of an Umayyad prince would help their cause, and they brought ʿAbd-ar-Raḥmān to Spain. In 756 he and his supporters defeated their opponents, and he was able to bring most of Spain under his control. During the thirty-two years of his rule the new emirate acquired a degree of stability and was ruled by the descendants of ʿAbd-ar-Raḥmān – the Umayyads of Spain – until 1031. The Spanish Umayyads were content to rule in Spain and to have at times some influence in the nearer parts of North Africa; they did not aspire to recover the empire of the caliphs of Damascus. For them the ʿAbbāsids were enemies, the murderers of their family, but they needed no theological justification for their independence. Intellectually Spain remained part of the greater Islamic world.

Soon after the loss of Spain there began in Tripolitania an insurrection with a theological basis which led in the end to the 'Abbāsids losing most of North Africa. In 757 certain Berber tribes of the Jebel Nefusa, which had adopted the Ibāḍite form of Khārijism probably as an expression of anti-Arab feeling, occupied Tripoli and in the following year also Cairouan. The 'Abbāsid governor of Egypt had to send several expeditions westwards before he recovered Cairouan, and did not succeed in asserting his power farther to the west. Indeed Cairouan was lost again to the 'Abbāsids for a time about 772. Meanwhile Ibn-Rustam, an Ibāḍite leader of Persian origin, established himself in Tahert (the modern Tiaret) and created a kingdom in what is now western Algeria which flourished under his descendants, the Rustamids, until the arrival of the Fāṭimids in 909. To the south-west round Sijilmasa in Morocco there was a small autonomous region ruled by the Miḍrārid dynasty and acknowledging the Ṣufrite form of Khārijism. These territories were completely lost to the 'Abbāsids. The Khārijism practised in them was moderate, since it was the religion of the mass of the people and not merely of robber bands.

In somewhat accidental fashion much of Morocco came under a diluted form of Shī'ism. Idrīs ibn-'Abd-Allāh, a great-grandson of 'Alī's son al-Ḥasan and brother of Muḥammad 'the Pure Soul', after taking part in the abortive revolt of Fakhkh, managed to escape to North Africa, where he was accepted as leader by a group of Berbers and set about building Fez as his capital near the site of the Roman town of Volubilis. Fez was occupied by the Fāṭimids in 921, but this was not quite the end of the Idrīsid dynasty, since it had become fragmented under pressure from the Berber nomads and some of the local units were able to maintain themselves for at least another half century. Their Shī'ism seems to have amounted to little more than a belief in the charisma of the Shorfā', the descendants of al-Ḥasan and al-Ḥusayn, the two sons of 'Alī by Fāṭima.

It was doubtless the loss of provinces to the Rustamids and Idrīsids and the difficulty of controlling the Berbers further east which led the 'Abbāsids to enter into the special arrangements which resulted in the founding of the Aghlabid dynasty. In 800 Ibn-al-Aghlab, the son of a Khurasanian army officer, was appointed governor of Ifrīqiya (modern Tunisia) by the caliph with a large degree of autonomy; in return he was to be responsible for an annual tribute of 40,000 dīnārs. He was able to bequeath his position to his son, and it remained in the family until the coming of the Fāṭimids in 909. Not merely did the Aghlabid dynasty hold Tunisia on behalf of the 'Abbāsids, but they brought Sicily under Muslim domination in a series of campaigns beginning in 827 and lasting about half a century. This arrangement between the central government and the Aghlabids was particularly advantageous to the former. They shed their responsibility for maintaining order in the province and defending it from its neighbours on the west, but at the same time had an assured annual tribute.

A similar arrangement was made in Khurasan with the Ṭāhirids, but lasted little more than half a century. The founder of the dynasty, Ṭāhir, was of Persian descent and was one of the two generals responsible for al-Ma'mūn's victory over his brother al-Amīn. In 820 he was sent as governor to Khurasan, but this appointment was mixed up with a struggle for power between several of the leading men of the caliphate, and it is not clear exactly what happened next. In 822, however, when Ṭāhir died, perhaps poisoned, he was succeeded by his son Ṭalḥa, and he in turn in 828 by his brother 'Abd-Allāh ibn-Ṭāhir and then by other members of the family, until in 873 they were expelled from their capital by the founder of a rival dynasty, the Ṣaffārids.

Despite the immediate advantages of this arrangement with the Aghlabids and the Ṭāhirids and at least one minor group, it was in the long run a source of weakness to the caliphate, since the caliph had really lost control over these autonomous governors and had reduced his own effective military strength. It is not surprising, then, that in the middle of the tenth century the caliph lost all his secular authority. The arrangement with Ibn-al-Aghlab was thus the beginning of the break-up of 'Abbāsid power.

2

THE CONTINUING POLITICAL STRUGGLE

In the previous section there was given an analysis of the forces which brought the ʿAbbāsids to power; and this was followed by an account of the various insurrections and revolts which gave vent to local discontents and of the steps by which the outlying provinces were removed from central control. At the same time, however, a struggle was taking place at the heart of the caliphate, which was essentially a struggle between two different conceptions of the nature of the caliphate as a political structure and of the general policies it ought to pursue. To this struggle we now turn, looking first at the various economic and social groups involved in it, and then at what may be called the intellectual form of the struggle.

The opposing interest-groups

The factors leading to the ʿAbbāsid victory were brought under four heads: positively there was the support they received from discontented clients, discontented members of the general religious movement, and discontented believers in a leader with charisma; and negatively there was the dissension among the Arabs over matters which were less and less relevant to contemporary events. The interests thus supporting the ʿAbbāsids were so heterogeneous that it was inevitable that after victory some should be disappointed. The events mentioned in the previous section are mostly due to minor disappointed groups, especially Persian clients with Mazdakite leanings and descendants of ʿAlī who thought they themselves possessed more charisma than the ʿAbbāsids. When the events of the next century are examined, however, it appears that some of the major groups supporting the ʿAbbāsid revolution remained only partly satisfied. These groups are best understood if they are regarded as coalescing to form two great blocs, which will here be labelled 'constitutionalist' and 'autocratic'.

Foremost in the constitutionalist bloc would come the general religious movement of the Umayyad period, that is, the men who believed that the activities of the government and the judiciary should be based on Qur'ānic principles. Even under the Umayyads these men had not seen eye to eye on particular legal and political questions, and under the ʿAbbāsids still further diversification took place. The Qur'ān did not supply sufficient principles for all the needs of the complex urban and agricultural empire, and it therefore came to be supplemented by the Traditions, that is, anecdotes regarded as normative about what Muḥammad had said or done on specific occasions. For a time – as will be described more fully in the next section – there was tension between those who emphasized the importance of Traditions and those who preferred to follow what in their city had come to be recognized as the Sunna or 'standard practice' of the Prophet; but by the early ninth century the view was coming to be generally accepted that the Sunna had to be defined by the Traditions. The Sunna, however, as so defined, was held to have the same divine authority as the Qur'ān itself. The essential belief of the group could therefore be expressed by saying that the state must be based on the Sharīʿa or 'revealed law', that is, on the principles found in the Qur'ān and the Traditions. (In modern times Sharīʿa has come to be identified with 'law', but in the earlier centuries of Islam the meaning was closer to 'revelation'.)

The acceptance, at least in part, by the ʿAbbāsids of the principle that the state should be based on the Sharīʿa led gradually to the emergence of a 'religious institution'. If judges were to be taken from men 'trained' in the various 'schools' of law, the 'training' had to become more formal. Just how this happened is not altogether clear, but some men came to be recognized as authorities in one or other of the specialized religious disciplines which were developing. Those who had been adequately 'trained' under recognized masters may be said to have entered the corps of ulema (*'ulamā'*) or 'scholars' from whom judges and similar officials were selected. This corps of ulema was the religious institution, and it claimed that it alone (acting through those of its senior members who were recognized as authorities) could formulate the application of the Sharī'a to particular cases. In other words, the ulema and they alone had the right to formulate the rules and regulations stating how the divinely-given law implicit in the Qur'ān and Traditions was to be applied in actual governmental and judicial practice. Ideally the caliph and his subordinates could operate only within the framework of these rules and regulations formulated by the ulema. The term 'constitutionalist' is intended to indicate the parallel between the Sharī'a and a constitution by which rulers and subjects are alike bound.

The constitutionalist bloc, however, included many others beside the ulema. Presumably most Arabs of the Yemenite party would be found here in so far as they favoured a state based on Islam rather than Arabism where the difference of privilege between Arab and non-Arab would cease to exist. Most of the clients who had supported the 'Abbāsids would become constitutionalists, since it was through the supremacy of the Sharī'a that their grievances were best redressed. In respect of social class it would seem that most of the ordinary people, especially the city-dwellers, were on the constitutionalist side. The greatest successes of the ulema were in creating and maintaining a social structure in which ordinary men were treated with a considerable measure of justice and fairness. In the accounts of the persecution of Aḥmad ibn-Ḥanbal by the government it is clear that he had a large proportion of the populace of Baghdad on his side.

The autocratic bloc consisted first and foremost of those who believed in the desirability or necessity of a leader with charisma or, to use the Arabic term, an imam. To understand the situation in the middle of the eighth century it is best to express the view thus in general terms. Some men believed they knew who the imam was or ought to be, but others believed more in the principle of having an imam than in the suitability of any particular individual as imam. This belief in the need for an imam has to be understood as contrasting with the belief of the ulema and other constitutionalists in the supremacy of the Sharīʿa. The question at issue was: is the voyage of the ship of state likely to be more prosperous if it is steered by a divinely-inspired leader or if it is steered by the instructions contained in a divinely-given law?

Among the groups included in the autocratic bloc were the 'secretaries', who had some of the functions of modern cabinet ministers, and some of modern civil servants, and were the people at the centre chiefly responsible for the running of the empire. They were the persons who carried out the orders of the caliph (or imam), and also who had some share in the framing of policy. The greater the authority of the caliph, the greater the authority they themselves wielded. They were in some respects the rivals of the ulema, and must have felt that the latter put many obstacles in the way of the smooth functioning of government. Moreover, many of them were Persians or persianized Aramaeans, the descendants of men who had exercised similar functions under the Sasanians. Other Persians may also have been included in the bloc, especially the local squires or *dihqans*, many of whom had latterly acted as agents of the Umayyad government; but it would be wrong at this period to imagine that all Persians were believers in a charismatic leader.

Though genuine evidence is scanty, it would appear that the ʿAlids (descendants of ʿAlī) as a group supported the autocratic bloc. They must all have been aware that a large body of popular opinion ascribed a charisma to the family. In 750 there was no generally recognized imam among them – witness the various leaders of risings – and so an ambitious individual might hope that he himself would be recognized as imam, or would become the chief minister of someone who could be pushed into this position. Other Hāshimites also – among whom were at least some of the ʿAbbāsid family – might wonder if they had not an endowment of charisma so that they might be recognized as imam. Among the ʿAlids and Hāshimites probably only certain individuals were fully convinced of the presence of the charisma in the family, but most would be ready to make use of the popular belief in the charisma.

Can anything be said about the social and economic position of the groups which supported the autocratic bloc? Who would have benefited from more autocratic rule, untrammelled by the ulema? Whose interests were in contrast to those of the urban masses? Again the evidence is slight; but it might be suggested as a hypothesis that they included the wealthier merchants and the great landlords and those dependent on such men and ready to follow them in all respects.

The intellectual form of the struggle

This characterization of the two blocs in external social terms is a necessary preliminary to an attempt to understand the political significance of the religious ideas held by men of influence at the centre of the caliphate during the first 'Abbāsid century. It has been seen in the previous chapter that even by the time of Muḥammad's death the minds of the Muslims and of other Arabs in contact with them were so dominated by the Qur'ānic picture of the world that political opposition to the Islamic state had to be based on Qur'ānic categories. This was still more the case under the 'Abbāsids, except that to religious or theological ideas had been added certain historical matters.

In the first place there may be mentioned a relatively unimportant movement or trend of thought, against which the 'Abbāsids felt compelled to take strong measures round about 772 and again from 782 to 786 or later. This movement or trend was called *zandaqa* and the individual adherent a *zindīq* (plural *zanādiqa*). At this period *zandaqa* (which might perhaps be rendered 'irreligion') was not so much a specific set of beliefs as any mode of thought which was felt to threaten the security of the state. It usually implied denial of the Sharī'a in some form, and was sometimes connected with Manichaean doctrines, though the traditional Manichaean communities in Iraq were not directly involved in the charge of *zandaqa*. Most of the persons against whom the charge was preferred at the dates mentioned belonged to the class of secretaries, and were doubtless expressing in this way their dislike of the Islamic state. One such was Ibn-al-Muqaffa', the first great Arabic prose-writer, who was probably put to death for *zandaqa* in 756 or soon afterwards despite important services to al-Manṣūr. Among the books ascribed to him was one attacking the Qur'ān (of which a refutation is extant). These men must have professed Islam, at least nominally. The persecutions presumably showed them that such open forms of opposition were too dangerous. More subtle were the literary productions of the Shu'ūbite movement, which emphasized the demerits of the Arabs and the merits of the Persians and other non-Arabs; and others turned to some form of the belief in a charismatic imam and are therefore labelled Shīʿites.

When we turn to consider Shīʿism in the first ʿAbbāsid century, we are faced with a very difficult problem. From about the year 900 the Imāmite Shīʿites began to spread an account of earlier events which was really political propaganda and is at variance with other historical accounts for which there is good evidence. Certain parts of the Imāmite account were taken over by writers about sects, and have been taken over somewhat uncritically by occidental scholars.

This commonly accepted view is somewhat as follows. Before Muḥammad died he indicated in some way that his cousin and son-in-law ʿAlī was to be his successor; moreover ʿAlī was the most excellent (*al-afḍal*) of the community after Muḥammad. ʿAlī was thus rightfully imam of the community of Muslims from 632 onwards, though he was not recognized as such by most of the Companions of Muḥammad. He handed on the position of imam to his sons by Fāṭima, al-Ḥasan and al-Ḥusayn, and then it was handed on from father to son until it came to the twelfth imam. The eleventh imam, al-Ḥasan al-ʿAskarī, died on or about 1 January 874. The Imāmites assert that he had a son, whom they call Muḥammad al-Qā'im, who was born during his lifetime, who was alive at the time of his death, and who 'went into concealment' a few years after his death. It is usually said that this boy was four or five when his father died, and that he went into concealment when he was between six and nine, that is, between 875 and 878. From his concealment al-Qā'im 'the Upholder' (*sc.* of the law or command of God), will return at the time appointed by God and will fill the earth with justice and equity.

The Imāmites are also called the Ithnāʿashariyya or 'Twelvers' because they have twelve imams. They are the most important group of Shīʿites, though rather less than ten per cent of all Muslims. Imāmism is the official religion of Persia, and there are also important bodies of Imāmites in Iraq and India. The next most important group are the Ismāʿīlites, also called Sabʿiyya or 'Seveners' because they recognize seven imams in the first place (though the line does not end with the seventh). The first six are the same as those of the Imāmites, but they reject the seventh, Mūsā al-Kāẓim son of Jaʿfar aṣ-Ṣādiq, and instead have his brother Ismāʿīl. They are nowadays far less numerous than the Imāmites. Another group, very small at the present day, are the Zaydites, who are rather different from both the Imāmites and the Ismā'īlites. More will be said about them presently, since they were important in the eighth and ninth centuries.

A close examination of this account of the imams and their followers shows that it must be extensively modified at several points. While it is true that there was a large body of opinion looking for an imam or charismatic leader, it is clear from the sources that there was no wide agreement about the identity of the leader. Several 'Alids led risings, and were to that extent accepted as imam, though their names are not among the twelve; some of these were mentioned in the last section. Again, there are indications that in 749 Abū-Salama, called the 'vizier of the family of Muḥammad', would have liked to make an 'Alid the caliph by identifying him with 'the approved one of the house of the Prophet' but could find none recognized by the others and himself willing to stand forward. It is, of course, obvious that before 874 there could be no theory of *twelve* imams, since no one could know that the line was going to end by the twelfth going into concealment. There is much evidence of disagreement, too, in a book called *The Sects of the Shī'a* by an-Nawbakhtī, himself an early tenth-century Imāmite writer, but this evidence has to be handled carefully since at times the author may be following the usual Imāmite practice of rewriting past history.

It is further clear, that, even if the imams had been in some way recognized as such during their lifetime, this recognition could not have implied that they were leaders of a movement aiming at placing them on the caliphal throne instead of the 'Abbāsids. The 'Abbāsids had a good information service and would quickly have got rid of all the 'Alids, had they thought them guilty of treasonable activities; on the contrary the early Imāmite sources allege no more than spells of imprisonment. Perhaps the most telling point, however, is that there are reports about Imāmites – usually called Rāfiḍites at this period – arguing for their point of view in political discussions held in the presence of the Barmakid viziers or the caliph al-Ma'mūn. It is unthinkable that these men were arguing that the imam of the time was the rightful ruler of the caliphate. The conclusion seems inescapable that during their lifetime the twelve imams were not recognized as imams in the sense which was later given to that word. If they had any post, it can only have been as family spokesman and representative, since the family seems to have had some organization linked with its special privileges.

If then the advocates of Imāmism were not in their political discussions arguing for the rights of a particular imam, what were they arguing for? A clue is given by what an-Nawbakhtī reports of the views of the Imāmite ʿAlī ibn-Mītham, who took part in discussions in the salon of Yaḥyā the Barmakid. He held that ʿAlī as best of men after the Prophet was deserving of the imamate, and that the community of Muslims was in error, though not sinfully, in recognizing Abū-Bakr and ʿUmar as caliphs instead of ʿAlī. It is to be noted that there is no mention here of any imams other than ʿAlī himself. These Imāmites could hardly have remained friendly with the Barmakid vizier if they had been supporters of the supposed imam of the time, Mūsā al-Kāẓim, for the latter was regarded with grave suspicion by Hārūn ar-Rashīd and imprisoned on two or three occasions. Implicit in the report is the view – known from other sources to have been held by the Imāmites of the time – that Muḥammad had clearly 'designated' ʿAlī as his successor. This was one assertion which had contemporary relevance. A second was that most of the Companions had disobeyed the Prophet.

The contemporary relevance of these assertions is to be understood as follows. The idea of 'designation' in the case of ʿAlī is to be applied also to the actual ʿAbbāsid caliph. The reigning caliph comes at the end of a line of men, each of whom has been designated by a predecessor. This at least is the theory, though there may have been difficulty with some details. Such designation means that the ruler gets his authority from above, as it were, and does not owe it to the acclamation by the people or election by their representatives. In other words, the Imāmism of the late eighth and early ninth centuries was the advocacy of a more autocratic policy for the ʿAbbāsid caliphs, not an attempt to replace them by ʿAlids. The second assertion is in line with this. The disobedience of most Companions to the Prophet's designation of ʿAlī means that they are not upright persons; and the practical consequence is that the Traditions on which contemporary ulema base many of their arguments are not worthy of credence. Imāmite doctrine is thus a defence of more autocratic policies and an attack on the constitutionalist position.

Next an attempt must be made to understand the relevance of Zaydism to the politics of the early ninth century. The nature of

Zaydism at this period is obscured rather than clarified by the treatment in the books of sects. These tend to restrict their account to a few persons who can be clearly labelled Zaydite and who were in some sense forerunners of the later Zaydite state in the Yemen. In the early ninth century, however, there was a widely held set of ideas (with immediate political relevance) which were essentially those of the groups called Zaydite, even though at certain points the ideas were vaguer and the persons holding them may never have been called Zaydites (which after all is a nickname). Zaydism in this extended sense differs from Imāmism in various ways. It does not make use of the idea of designation. Though it agrees with Imāmism in holding that 'Alī was the best of the community after Muḥammad, it does not reject the caliphate of Abū-Bakr and 'Umar. Since these two were *ex hypothesi* inferior to 'Alī, the recognition of their rule is sometimes described as a recognition of 'the imamate of the inferior'. Beyond this the Zaydites rejected the idea of an imam who remained hidden or even inactive, and insisted that the imam must assert his rule by force of arms if necessary.

Zaydism is mainly a political doctrine, but there are close connections between this and the theological group known as the Mu'tazilites of Baghdad, though some obscurities in the relationship have not yet been elucidated. An early writer on sects speaks of these Mu'tazilites as a subdivision of the Zaydites, and a slightly later Mu'tazilite writer describes many of them as holding the doctrine of the imamate of the inferior. The contemporary relevance of these facts is that certain of these Mu'tazilites of Baghdad were in high favour at court from the reign of al-Ma'mūn until the early years of al-Mutawakkil. Al-Ma'mūn's policy of the Inquisition (see below) was based on their theological views. If they were in the extended sense Zaydites, then so was al-Ma'mūn. This is not so strange a conclusion as it sounds when first formulated. Al-Ma'mūn was a member of the house of the Prophet (taken as including his uncle al-'Abbās) who had asserted his right to rule by the sword; so also were the first two 'Abbāsid caliphs. He apparently also claimed to be the best of the community and, first of the 'Abbāsids, adopted the title of imam. He did not reject the rule of Abū-Bakr, 'Umar and the Umayyads, though he may have had some hankerings after a more autocratic, Imāmite conception of his position. A man with the responsibility of rule cannot, of course, follow exactly a doctrinaire theory, but the signs are that al-Ma'mūn and possibly also his successors had strong sympathies with the general Zaydite attitude.

Something must now be said about the political position of the Muʿtazilites, though the main account of their contribution to Islamic theology will be reserved to the last section of this chapter, While all Muslims agreed that the Qur'ān was the speech of God. the Muʿtazilites asserted that it was created speech in contrast to most members of the general religious movement who held that it was uncreated speech. This appears to be a hair-splitting argument. Yet towards the end of his reign al-Ma'mūn instructed certain governors to summon into their presence the judges and other ulema and to require them to profess publicly their belief that the Qur'ān was created, not uncreated. This is known as the Miḥna or 'Inquisition', and it lasted intermittently until about 848. The difference between created and uncreated speech appears to be in respect of the relation of the speech to the eternal nature of God. If the Qur'ān is God's uncreated speech, then it expresses his eternal nature and must be unchangeable, whereas if it is created, he might presumably have created it otherwise than it now is. The implication in the latter case is that there would be no objection to it being overridden by the decision of a divinely inspired imam. The Inquisition as a political policy is thus seen to rise out of the tension between the autocratic and constitutionalist blocs. It is best regarded as an attempt at compromise. By denying the uncreatedness of the Qur'ān it weakens the position of the ulema, but it does not go all the way to accepting the Imāmite doctrine of 'designation'. The Inquisition was finally abandoned not because one or two important men refused to make the public profession required but because, as a compromise, it failed to satisfy either bloc.

Finally a word must be said about the main body of the general religious movement. They are the forerunners of Sunnism, though they cannot yet be properly called Sunnites since there was still no clear idea of what constituted Sunnism. The men in question merely thought of themselves as truly following the Islam taught and practised by Muḥammad; but a similar claim was made by most of the heretics. The external observer, however, can see that these forerunners of Sunnism were characterized by certain distinctive beliefs. They fully accepted Abū-Bakr and ʿUmar as caliphs, further coming to assert that Abū-Bakr was the most excellent of the community after Muḥammad, and 'Umar after Abū-Bakr. They accepted the Sharī'a as the basis of the state, claiming that they followed the Sunna of the Prophet (though this concept was itself in process of being more strictly defined in the course of the first 'Abbāsid century). They accepted all the Companions as trustworthy – a point that was linked with the later acceptance of Traditions as defining the Sunna. Most of the general religious movement also had certain other doctrines in common, but a few disagreed. Needless to say they belonged essentially to the constitutionalist bloc.

The course of the struggle

After looking at the main tension at the centre of the Islamic empire during the first 'Abbāsid century and at the ideas in which this tension was expressed, the course of events may be looked at briefly to try to discover how the tension worked itself out in detail. The reader must be warned, however, that the matter is a complex one and the motives of the chief actors were never simple. A few points have recently been studied in detail, and these studies have shown that black and white generalizations tend to be inaccurate in various degrees. Yet in the space available here such generalizations cannot be avoided.

In their early years the 'Abbāsids got rid of two of their chief supporters, Abū-Salama in 750 and Abū-Muslim in 755, presumably because the former was sympathetic to the 'Alids and because the latter had connections with the Persian Mazdakites. While these events are not unrelated to it, the main tension which has been described begins to become apparent only in the reign of Hārūn ar-Rashīd. Indeed to discern it even there one has to work backwards from the civil war between his sons, al-Amīn and al-Ma'mūn. Hārūn decided that al-Amīn should be his heir and al-Ma'mūn next in succession after him. He also made al-Amīn governor of Syria and al-Ma'mūn of the eastern provinces. On Hārūn's death in 809 al-Amīn established himself as caliph in Baghdad, while al-Ma'mūn remained in the east. When al-Amīn began to encroach on al-Ma'mūn's privileges, matters drifted into a war which ended in 813 with the defeat and death of al-Amīn and the acknowledgement of al-Ma'mūn as caliph. In this war there emerged something like the two blocs described. On the one side al-Amīn had the populace of

Iraq, most of the general religious movement and many Arabs, while on the other side were the inhabitants of the eastern provinces and sympathizers with the ʿAlids and with Imāmism.

This conflict has sometimes been presented by occidental scholars as a struggle between Arabs and Persians, but it is now realized that the respective 'national' aspirations were not a primary issue. Yet it is true that al-Ma'mūn was 'the son of the Persian woman', and that his vizier up to 818, al-Faḍl ibn-Sahl, was of Zoroastrian Persian stock, whereas al-Amīn's mother was Arab and his vizier, al-Faḍl ibn-ar-Rabīʿ, though of obscure origin, was a client of an Arab tribe and had pro-Arab sympathies. This latter had also had much to do with the fall of the Barmakids in 803 and had replaced them in Hārūn's favour. In turn his successful rival, al-Faḍl ibn-Sahl, was a protégé of the Barmakids. The Barmakids, however, were not Persian as was once thought, since it is now known that their ancestor was the Barmak or 'superior' of a Buddhist convent near Balkh (close to the Oxus river). They were closely associated, however, with the class of secretaries and apparently sympathetic to the 'autocratic' attitude. The end of Barmakid domination, however, was not primarily due to any question of policy, but to the fact that Hārūn felt threatened by their great power and wealth. Thus before 803 there are some indications, but no more than indications, of the tension between the blocs; and it may well be that accidental features of the struggle between Hārūn's sons had much to do with the final alignment of interests and polarization of programmes.

Despite the victory of al-Ma'mūn the tension continued. In 817 al-Ma'mūn took the unusual step of naming as heir not one of his sons but one of the ʿAlids, ʿAlī ar-Riḍā, later recognized as eighth imam of the Imāmites. This was presumably intended to be some sort of political compromise, but exactly what is not clear. Al-Ma'mūn already had the support of most of the autocratic bloc, doubtless including many Imāmites, and what he needed most was the goodwill of the constitutionalists, especially since a few months after his proclamation of ʿAlī ar-Riḍā as heir, while al-Ma'mūn still remained in the east, his uncle Ibrāhīm was proclaimed caliph in Iraq with much constitutionalist backing. Against this the favour of the ʿAlids, if he succeeded in gaining it, was of slight importance. Perhaps he had miscalculated. The sources suggest that the vizier al-Faḍl ibn-Sahl had kept him misinformed about the situation in

Iraq and that it was his new heir who opened his eyes; but these suggestions may be no more than court gossip. What is certain is that al-Faḍl ibn-Sahl was murdered in a public bath early in 818 and that ʿAlī ar-Riḍā died some six months later; the latter's death, according to later Imāmite historians, was due to poison administered by al-Ma'mūn. It is impossible now to determine if the vizier was murdered by order of the caliph or by irate opponents from Iraq. In any case the essential change of policy – the decision that the caliph should return to Baghdad – had been made before the murder. On the other hand, there is no obvious reason why the caliph should want to get rid of his heir, and the Imāmite accusation should probably be rejected.

The return to Baghdad was certainly important, especially when it is remembered that in 820 the general Ṭāhir was sent to the east and proceeded to make himself autonomous; but to make Iraq the primary basis of the caliph's power did not necessarily indicate any radical change in political belief. The document appointing ʿAlī ar-Riḍā as heir has been preserved and has nothing to suggest a rapprochement with Imāmism. There is no mention of 'designation' and ʿUmar is quoted with respect, while the good caliph is described as 'upholding the Book and the Sunna of the Prophet' – a 'constitutionalist' phrase. The mention of the excellent personal qualities of ʿAlī ar-Riḍā is, if anything, Zaydite in the extended sense noted above. Thus the death of ʿAlī ar-Riḍā, though giving al-Ma'mūn the opportunity of 'thinking again' and indeed forcing him to do so, did not lead to any fundamental change of view. Some of the Muʿtazilite–Zaydite group who came to be closely associated with the caliph in Baghdad had already been prominent at his court in the east.

The final attempt of al-Ma'mūn to reduce the central tension was the so-called policy of the Inquisition, of whose theological basis an account has already been given. What might be called a pilot scheme was produced in 827, but it was not until 833, a few months before al-Ma'mūn's death, that the main policy was implemented. As indicated above it was a compromise intended to weaken the ulema and thereby strengthen the caliph and his officials. The policy was by no means a personal one based on the whim of a single man, for it was continued during the next two reigns and indeed as long as the Muʿtazilite–Zaydite ascendancy lasted.

Further attempts to deal with the tension are probably also to be seen in the two cognate matters of the increasing reliance on Turkish troops and the transference of the capital to Samarra. Al-Ma'mūn is credited with inaugurating the practice of employing slave soldiers from the periphery of the empire, mostly either Berbers from the Sahara or Turks from beyond the Oxus. Such men were not engaged to one side or the other in the party strife and – what is probably the primary consideration – they were better soldiers. Under al-Muʿtaṣim (833–42) the number of Turkish troops increased greatly – to as many as 70,000, it is said. Moreover, some of those trusted by the caliph were appointed to the higher ranks. The power of this foreign soldiery incurred the anger of the older inhabitants of Iraq, whether Arab or Persian. The populace of Baghdad became more and more hostile to the Turks and incidents multiplied. This is given as the reason for the removal of the caliph's residence and the seat of government to Samarra; but it may be that both the introduction of the Turks and the move away from Baghdad were intended further to weaken the power of the ulema by reducing the influence of the mobs which followed them.

Samarra lies about sixty miles north of Baghdad on the Tigris, and was occupied for less than sixty years – from 836 to 892. Yet the ruins of the mud-brick walls of the ordinary houses stretch for nearly twenty miles along the Tigris and in places have a width of nearly five miles. These ruins are an astounding record of the vast wealth and energy the Islamic empire was able to devote to a single project. Whether the departure from Baghdad was wise is doubtful. It may have relieved the immediate pressure from the mobs, but it almost certainly contributed to the decline of the ʿAbbāsid dynasty. Where there was nothing to balance the power of the Turks, these were more and more able to dictate policy.

3

ARAB SELF-ASSERTION IN RELIGION

The process of creating a new Islamic culture, which had begun under the Umayyads, continued during the first ʿAbbāsid century. There was much scholarly work in all the various branches of Islamic learning, such as the textual criticism of the Qur'ān and its interpretation. Much of this work was of a plodding, pedestrian kind, and the account in this chapter will therefore concentrate on the fronts on which an important advance was made. The present section deals with the founding of the main schools of jurisprudence, together with the cognate matter of the development of the study of Tradition as a further discipline, while the beginnings of systematic theology will be left to the next section.

The early Ḥanafite and Mālikite schools

The chief contributions to the growth of jurisprudence were first of all made in Kufa and Medina. The intense intellectual activity which had characterized Kufa during the Umayyad period continued during the first few decades of the ʿAbbāsid period, but it subsequently declined, doubtless owing to the rise of Baghdad.

The leading intellectual figure in Kufa in the early years of the new dynasty was Abū-Ḥanīfa. He was a client of an Arab tribe, born about the turn of the century, but it is not clear whether his grandfather came from Afghanistan or was of local Aramaean stock. Abū-Ḥanīfa spent nearly all his life in Kufa, and earned a living as a manufacturer and seller of silk – a reminder that scholarship had not yet become a profession. He was able, however, to attend the lectures and discussions held in Kufa, and eventually himself gave instruction to a large number of disciples. He died in prison in Baghdad in 767, perhaps because he had been compromised in the rising of Muḥammad 'the Pure Soul' in 762, though a common version is that it was because he had refused to serve as *qāḍī*.

Because he was not involved in the actual making of judicial decisions, he was freer than his chief rival in Kufa, the judge Ibn-Abī-Laylā (d. 765), to work out his legal theory in a logical fashion. Though this led him to conclusions which were unacceptable in practice, it was important at this stage in the growth of legal theory that someone should attempt to systematize the field. Later he came to be regarded as the great proponent of the principle of *ra'y* or 'personal judgement', but modern research suggests that in his use of *ra'y* he differed little from his contemporaries. He himself wrote no legal works, but his teaching was perpetuated by his disciples, especially Abū-Yūsuf and ash-Shaybānī; but though these two and other later scholars elaborated and developed the teaching of Abū-Ḥanīfa to a considerable extent, they always regarded him as the founder of their school, which thus came to be known as Ḥanafite.

Abū-Yūsuf was a pure Arab born about 731 and brought up in Kufa, where he studied under Abū-Ḥanīfa and others, but he also visited Medina and heard lectures from Mālik ibn-Anas. Because of his intellectual ability and sound common sense he was brought to the notice of the caliphal court, and probably in 785 was appointed *qāḍī* of Baghdad, a post which he held until his death in 798. He was the first person to be called grand *qāḍī* (*qāḍī l-quḍāt*), a title conferred by Hārūn ar-Rashīd. At the latter's request he wrote a book which has survived on taxation and similar subjects; it has been translated into French under the title of *Le livre de l'impôt foncier*. The names of other books have been preserved, but hardly any of the actual texts. His practical experience as a judge seems to have led him to modify some of the harsher opinions of the master, and even to change his own views from time to time. His polemical writings helped to give a distinct identity to the nascent school.

The man whose writings became the real basis of the Ḥanafite school was ash-Shaybānī (Muḥammad ibn-al-Ḥasan), of Syrian stock but born in Wasit in 749 and brought up in Kufa, where he was chiefly under the influence of Abū-Yūsuf. He also studied in Medina under Mālik for a time. In 796 he became *qāḍī* of av-Raqqa, but did not retain the post for long. Hārūn ar-Rashīd took him with him on his last journey to the east, and ash-Shaybānī died near Rayy in Persia in or about 804. His importance in the Ḥanafite school is shown by the large number of manuscripts of his works which exist and by the large number of commentaries written on them. Both he and Abū-Yūsuf placed more reliance on Traditions than did Abū-Ḥanīfa – a point whose significance will become evident presently.

While the Ḥanafite school was burgeoning in Kufa and then Baghdad, an outstanding jurist was active in Medina. This was Mālik ibn-Anas, from whom the Mālikite school took its name. Born about 710 or a little later, he was of Ḥimyarite descent and spent most of his life in Medina. He absorbed all the religious learning of Medina, and at a relatively early age became an authority on legal matters in accordance with the views approved by the majority of religious scholars in Medina. During the rising of Muḥammad 'the Pure Soul' at Medina in 762 he apparently gave it as his considered opinion that the oath of loyalty taken to the 'Abbāsids was not binding since it had been taken under duress, and this opinion must have helped to swell the support for the rebel. Though Mālik himself remained in his house and took no active part in the rising, he was in disfavour with the 'Abbāsid governor and was stripped and flogged. He seems to have regained favour, however, and was treated with respect by the caliphs al-Mahdī and Hārūn ar-Rashīd. He died in 795. Of his chief work *Al-Muwaṭṭa'*, 'The Beaten Path', more will be said presently. It is essentially a comprehensive statement of the normal or standard practice observed in Medina. The Mālikite school developed through the work of disciples of Mālik, such as Ibn-al-Qāsim al-'Utaqī (d. 806) and 'Abd-Allāh ibn-Wahb (d. 812) in Egypt, and Saḥnūn (d. 854) in Cairouan.

In the case of both the Ḥanafite and Mālikite schools there must have been several steps between the teaching of the master to an amorphous body of disciples and the formation of a school in the full sense of the word; but these steps are obscure. The men described, however, represent an important stage in the development of jurisprudence, though its character can best be understood in connection with the growth of interest in Traditions.

The Traditionist movement

It was shown in the previous chapter that an important question during the Umayyad period was whether the empire was to be based on Islamic principles. Such was the success of the general religious movement in asserting the necessity of an Islamic basis that by 750 most of the inhabitants of the empire were ready to pay at least lip-service to this ideal. Even a rebel like al-Ḥārith ibn-Surayj (d. 746), who was prepared to support non-Muslims against Muslims, claimed that he was summoning men to 'the Book of God and the Sunna of the Prophet'. This formula was widely accepted, and there was no difficulty about the primacy of the Qur'ān; but the Sunna of the Prophet, that is, his 'standard practice', could be understood in different ways. Indeed the earliest form of the phrase may simply have been 'the Book and the Sunna', and the Sunna could have been thought of as the practice of the Islamic state in so far as it was continuing the practice of Muḥammad and his Companions. With the territorial expansion of the state countless problems emerged for which there was no specific instruction in the Qur'ān. Muḥammad himself had to deal with some such problems. A man like the caliph 'Umar, when faced with a novel situation, presumably decided as he thought Muḥammad would have done or in accordance with principles followed by Muḥammad. So presumably also did later caliphs and judges, at least in so far as they tried to act according to 'the Book and the Sunna'. Thus the Sunna came to be the actual practice of the community in so far as it was claimed to be Islamic.

During the Umayyad period also the legal discussions by members of the general religious movement in various cities led to a measure of agreement in each city about the truly Islamic practice in all sorts of matters; and each city would identify this with 'the Sunna', perhaps even 'the Sunna of the Prophet'. The 'Abbāsids recognized the general religious movement, but at the same time exerted pressure on the jurists in different cities to come to some agreement with one another; and it was doubtless these and similar factors which forced the jurists to offer some justification for their assertion that such and such was the Sunna.

An advanced stage, though not the final one, in this process of justification is illustrated by the *Muwaṭṭa'* of Mālik. His book is arranged according to topics, and these include not merely questions of law (in the European sense) but also questions of ritual. Frequently his main evidence consists of Traditions from the Prophet, but in other cases the emphasis is rather on a Companion or later doctor of the school of Medina; among those most cited are 'Umar ibn-al-Khaṭṭāb, 'Abd-Allāh ibn-'Umar and 'Urwa ibn-az-Zubayr, while 'Umar (II) ibn-'Abd-al-'Azīz is occasionally mentioned. Sometimes he makes a statement such as: 'The rule agreed upon among us, and which I heard from the scholars in our city, in respect of obligatory shares of inheritances is that ...'; in this way he clearly indicates that he is following the consensus of the scholars of Medina. He hardly ever speaks of the Sunna, but he is said to have remarked: 'It has come to my knowledge that the Messenger of God said, "I have left two things among you, and as long as you cleave to them you will not go astray; they are the Book of God and the Sunna of his Prophet." ' It is noteworthy that he mentions no source for this saying, and that the concluding phrase could be from Mālik himself or one of the unnamed transmitters.

Similar methods of justifying his views are found in Abū-Yūsuf's book. There are many Traditions from the Prophet, though sometimes with an incomplete list of authorities. Thus he can say: 'I had it from 'Abd-Allāh ibn-al-Muḥarrir, following az-Zuhrī, who gave his authorities, that the Prophet said, "Honey owes the tithe ..." .' In a smaller number of cases he is content with the authority of later Muslims. In connection with the question of amber and other precious objects from the sea, he bases his view (which is contrary to that of Abū-Ḥanīfa and Ibn-Abī-Laylā) on a report from 'Abd-Allāh ibn-al-'Abbās by three named intermediaries to the effect that 'Umar ibn-al-Khaṭṭāb in reply to a question about such objects said 'The fifth is due on these objects', together with the remark of Ibn-al-'Abbās, 'That is also my opinion'.

These examples show the different ways in which legal rules could be justified. The earliest way was probably to refer to an action or saying of someone like 'Umar ibn-al-Khaṭṭāb who was commonly regarded as a good Muslim who followed the Sunna of the Prophet. For a long time this probably satisfied the majority of the jurists. Eventually, however, certain rules were objected to on the basis of some saying of Muḥammad's which appeared to imply the opposite. This presented a certain difficulty for those who claimed they were following the Sunna of the Prophet, but there were ways of parrying the objection, such as producing an apparently contrary saying of the Prophet, or interpreting the original saying so as to avoid the implication.

The significant event here is the emergence during the eighth century of the Ahl al-Hadīth or 'Traditionist movement'. (The Traditions were described in the previous chapter.) In later times nearly every scholar of this century was regarded as a transmitter of Traditions and so a 'traditionist' (*muḥaddith*); this was the case even with Abū-Ḥanīfa himself. By no means all transmitters of Traditions, however, were members of the 'Traditionist movement', but only those who disapproved of the majority of jurists when they claimed that 'the rule agreed upon among us' represents the Sunna of the Prophet. The Traditionist movement insisted that the Sunna could be known only from the report of a saying or action of Muḥammad. They also objected to the methods of reasoning and 'personal opinion' employed by the jurists; and on religious and moral grounds they objected to some of the specific rules of the jurists. While the jurists of the general religious movement were critical of Umayyad legal practice, the Traditionist movement thought these jurists had accepted elements of compromise and were not sufficiently Islamic. Thus a cleavage grew between the Traditionist movement and the main body of jurists who, though not in full agreement with Abū-Ḥanīfa, were in a broad sense Ahl ar-Ra'y, followers of 'personal opinion'.

The arguments between the Traditionist movement and other jurists led to refinements in the study of Traditions. It was soon realized that an anecdote about Muḥammad could easily be invented, and that therefore it was not enough to say 'It has come to my knowledge that the Messenger of God said . . .' A source had to be given for the story; and it was further seen that the only satisfactory source was a whole chain of transmitters, an *isnād*, going back to a Companion or actual associate of Muḥammad. These transmitters must be known to be trustworthy persons, not holders of heretical views. It had also to be known that there was no impossibility in each man hearing the Tradition from the previous link in the chain; for example, a man could not have heard an anecdote from someone who died before he was born.

In this way the study of Traditions led to a whole series of disciplines. Not merely had the Traditions themselves to be memorized, but also for each the chain of transmitters or *isnād*. Then attention had to be paid to the methods of criticism; and there had to be some basic biographical information about every transmitter.

The growth of the Traditionist movement forced the jurists, even while they resisted Traditionist arguments, to make more and more use of Traditions. This is seen in the works of Mālik and Abū-Yūsuf. It was the work of ash-Shāfiʿī to overcome to a great extent the cleavage between the Traditionist movement and those who made some use of *ra'y*.

The achievement of ash-Shāfiʿī

Muḥammad ibn-Idrīs ash-Shāfiʿī was born in 767 in Gaza or Ashkelon, but spent his early life in Mecca in poor circumstances. After preliminary studies there he went to Medina at the age of about twenty to continue his training under Mālik. His exceptional intellectual gifts were recognized and he was given an administrative post in the Yemen, but somehow became involved in an ʿAlid intrigue and in 803 was tried in Baghdad before Hārūn ar-Rashīd. Though some others were executed, he was set free, perhaps through the advocacy of ash-Shaybānī. He certainly made contact with the Ḥanafites in Baghdad, and this proved to be a significant factor in the development of his juridical thought. On a visit to Mecca the divergence of his views from those of Mālik and his followers was becoming apparent. This may have influenced his decision to go to Egypt about 814 and to spend the remainder of his life there. Until his death in January 820 he was busy in teaching disciples and writing voluminously in exposition of the mature form of his legal theories. After his death these disciples created the Shāfiʿite legal school, probably the first 'school' in the later sense.

Ash-Shāfiʿī's greatest achievement in the field of law lies in the founding of a new discipline, the study of *uṣūl al-fiqh*, 'the roots of law', or, as we might say, the principles of jurisprudence. For ash-

Shāfiʿī these roots' are four; the Book, the Sunna, the consensus (*ijmāʿ*) of the community, and analogical reasoning (*qiyās*). The Book is given the primary place, and is frequently quoted in the short summary of his teaching on the 'roots', known as the *Risāla*. It should be noted, however, that, whereas the Qur'ān as God's speech must be accepted without qualification, there is not the same certainty about the specific interpretation and practical application of Qur'ānic rules. In particular there may be a Sunna of the Prophet which shows that a certain rule is to be taken in a restricted sense and not as of general validity. In making this point, however, he insists that no Sunna can be at variance with the Book.

His greatest innovations are in his treatment of the Sunna of the Prophet. He himself normally uses the word Sunna of a single command or exemplary action. A Sunna is something which has been laid down by Muḥammad by giving an order or by acting in a certain way. A Sunna can in general be known only by a Tradition from a Companion of the Prophet which has been handed on by an uninterrupted chain of named transmitters. Whereas previously, however, the words and acts of Muḥammad were regarded as evidence for the practice of the community on much the same level as the words and acts of a man like the caliph ʿUmar, ash-Shāfiʿī gave them a much higher status. He took verses of the Qur'ān which spoke of Muḥammad as being sent to 'teach the Book and the Wisdom', and asserted that the Wisdom (*ḥikma*) here was to be identified with the Sunna of the Prophet. He further asserted that in laying down any Sunna Muḥammad had been divinely inspired, and that God had commanded the Muslims to obey Muḥammad. In this way the Sunna was elevated to become an aspect of the Sharīʿa or revealed law. Although these general principles were thus made clear, the matter remained one of great complexity, since all sorts of apparent contradictions had to be ironed out in a systematic fashion.

The consensus allowed as a 'root' by ash-Shāfiʿī was different from the agreement or consensus of the jurists of Medina of which Mālik had spoken. The latter consensus had been reached after argument, but ash-Shāfiʿī was concerned rather with the fact that there were certain practices universally accepted by Muslims for which there was no Qur'ānic prescription and no Tradition with named transmitters. In such cases he argued that the general public could not have been ignorant of a Sunna of the Prophet, and could not have agreed on what was contrary to a Sunna or in error, and that therefore the practice in question was obligatory.

In his admission of analogical reasoning he was to some extent accepting the views of the Ḥanafites. They had been noted for their belief in *ra'y* or *ijtihād ar-ra'y*, meaning literally 'opinion' or 'personal effort in forming an opinion' and amounting in practice to almost any kind of reasoning. Ash-Shāfiʿī agreed that some reasoning was necessary, but insisted that this must be confined to strict analogy

Thus ash-Shāfiʿī was deeply influenced by the intellectual and rationalizing approach to legal questions of the school of Abū-Ḥanīfa, and developed this into a systematic study of the 'roots of law'. At the same time he accepted much of the position of the Traditionist movement, and indeed raised the status of Traditions, though also subjecting the use of Traditions by jurists to rational scrutiny. In its totality his legal theory was so coherent and so much in line with the deepest feelings of religious men that it carried all before it. While the use of Traditions had previously been spreading, it was now recognized that the Sunna could be determined only by Traditions, and that the Sunna was part of the Sharīʿa. Both the Ḥanafites and the Mālikites came to accept a modified version of ash-Shāfiʿī's theory of the 'roots of law'.

The Ḥanbalite school

The persons who were least satisfied with the theory of ash-Shāfiʿī were the extreme opponents of reasoning among the members of the Traditionist movement. Within this group one man came to a position of eminence through his brave resistance to the policy of the Inquisition inaugurated by al-Ma'mūn (pp. 116, 119). This man was Aḥmad ibn-Ḥanbal.

Aḥmad ibn-Ḥanbal belonged to the Arab tribe of Shaybān and was born in Baghdad in 780. He was primarily a student of Traditions, and in quest of Traditions travelled to the main centres in Iraq, Syria and the Arabian peninsula. He had attended lectures by Abū-Yūsuf and knew something of the teaching of ash-Shāfiʿī, though he may not have met him more than once; but he belonged first and foremost to the Traditionist movement. He appears to have become a teacher of Traditions in Baghdad, and by 833 he had attained sufficient of a reputation to be summoned in the Inquisition and asked to profess publicly the createdness of the Qur'ān, which he vehemently refused to do. The death of al-Ma'mūn prevented him from appearing before that caliph, but he was kept in various prisons until September 834 when, on refusing before al-Muʿtaṣim to make the required profession, he was severely beaten and then allowed to go home. From this date until the end of the Inquisition he seems to have done no teaching, sometimes because he was forbidden, and sometimes because he judged it imprudent. As far as Aḥmad ibn-Ḥanbal was concerned, things were not much better after al-Mutawakkil came to the throne in 847, for the gradual change of policy was very complex and mixed up with court intrigues. It was not until 851 or 852 that al-Mutawakkil actively tried to gain Aḥmad ibn-Ḥanbal's support, but by this time the latter was over seventy and in poor health, besides being out of sympathy with many of the caliph's ministers and officials; so when he asked permission to leave Samarra, this was granted, and he ended his life quietly in Baghdad in 855.

After his death the rump of the Traditionist movement was transformed by his disciples into the Ḥanbalite legal school. At a later date this school produced treatises expounding its doctrine of the 'roots of law', but Aḥmad ibn-Ḥanbal himself seems to have given only the outline of such a doctrine, and that only verbally. His essential position was that the only 'roots of law' are the Book and the Sunna, and that the divine law is not in any respect dependent on human reasoning. He allowed a certain weight, however, to formal legal decisions of the Companions, since the Prophet had commended the following of such persons. Despite its appearance of being anti-intellectual, the Ḥanbalite school in later centuries attracted many men of first-rate intellectual ability.

* * *

It was thus the first ʿAbbāsid century which created the schools of law and the corpus of Traditions which to a great extent moulded Islamic civilization and dominated its intellectual life.

4

THEOLOGY AND THE STIMULUS OF HELLENISM

Arguments between the sects

It was seen in the previous chapter that the beginnings of theology in Islam came from disputes between bodies of opinion within the community of Muslims in which religion and politics were inextricably intertwined. The Khārijites went to extremes in insisting that the community should be based on Islamic principles, for they excluded the 'grave sinner'; and this led to complex discussions about what makes a man a member of the community of Muslims and believers. The Shīʿites (if the term may be used in a loose sense) emphasized religious aspects of sovereignty in the Islamic state. Then, when the Umayyads claimed to have been appointed by God it was necessary for their opponents to justify opposition by the Qadarite doctrine of human freedom and responsibility.

In a sense the central politico-religious issue of the early ʿAbbāsid period was a continuation of the dispute between the Khārijites and the Shīʿites, though in a more moderate form. It was a question of what balance was to be maintained between the authority of Qur'ānic principles and the authority of the inspired imam. The policy of the Inquisition was an attempt at compromise, though weighted slightly in favour of the imam or caliph. The question of the createdness or uncreatedness of the Qur'ān led to all manner of theological refinements.

At the same time another division of opinion emerged which cut across the divisions based on politico-religious issues. This was the question of how far reason and rational conceptions might be used in matters of theological doctrine. In a sense this was an extension of the question which had appeared in the field of jurisprudence, though some of those who approved of the use of reason in legal matters were hesitant about its use in theology. The difference of attitude was in part due to the fact that after the Muslims became familiar with Greek thought, many foreign ideas were introduced into theological discussions. This matter will presently be looked at further.

Arguments with other religions

Not a great deal is said in theological or other books about the relationship between Islam and other religions, though it must have been a constant problem in practice. After the conquests the majority of the inhabitants of the heartlands like Iraq, Syria and Egypt, were protected minorities, and these were mostly Christians, with some Jews, Zoroastrians and others. Although there must have been many daily contacts, these would be largely restricted to a formal level. As time went on, there were converts to Islam from these religions, who must have brought right into the heart of Islam something of their previous experience and attitudes. Thus the Muslim, educated or uneducated, had to know how he stood with regard to other religions. The problem went back to the lifetime of Muḥammad himself. Implicit in his belief in what it was to be a prophet was the idea that there had been many previous prophets, each of whom had brought to his fellow-countrymen a message from God, which was in essentials identical with all the others. This meant that the Muslims had to regard the sacred books of the Jews and Christians – the Torah brought by Moses and the Evangel brought by Jesus – as in essentials identical with the Qur'ān. There were hardly any educated Jews or Christians in Mecca, but after Muḥammad went to Medina he was in contact with educated Jews, who proved somewhat of a trial to him. The Qur'ān instructs the Muslims how to reply to various Jewish arguments, and accuses the Jews of 'corrupting' or 'altering' the scriptures, though by this it seems to mean no more than that they played various verbal tricks on the Muslims. It also definitely asserts (7.157/156) that the coming of Muḥammad as Messenger and Prophet was foretold in the Torah and Evangel, and charges the Jews with concealing this. There is a rather smaller amount of polemic against the Christians.

In the course of the next two centuries these slight references in the Qur'ān were greatly elaborated and extended. Stories were invented – doubtless intended as a defence against Christians for illiterate people – of how the description had been physically concealed by such methods as pasting two pages together. Then the Qur'ānic verses about 'corrupting' or 'altering' the scriptures, which had probably referred originally to single passages, were interpreted as applying to the whole text or to all the interpretations of the text. This gave a weapon of defence to more educated Muslims, since any Jewish or Christian argument based on the Bible could be countered by saying 'Yes, but your scriptures are corrupt'. The very vagueness of the theory was an advantage, since, if one form did not convince the opponent, another might. The next stage was that a few scholars actually read parts of the Bible to find verses foretelling Muḥammad. In the life of the Prophet by Ibn-Is'ḥāq (d. 768) it is claimed that the *paraklētos* of John 15.26 is Muḥammad (a claim thought to rest on a confusion with *periklytos*, 'famous', which is roughly equal to *muḥammad*, 'praised'). About the year 782 the caliph al-Mahdī, in an argument with the Nestorian Catholicos Timothy (recorded by the latter) repeated this verse and added two others. Ibn-Qutayba (d. 889) had a sizeable list, but an ex-Christian ʿAlī aṭ-Ṭabarī, writing in 855, had no less than 130. Very few Muslim scholars ever read the Bible; and soon there were Traditions in circulation which discouraged or forbade the questioning of Jews and Christians or the use of their books; it was insisted that they were in error or had corrupted their scriptures, so that one never knew where one was with them. Before this prohibition came into effect, of course, most of the Biblical material necessary for an understanding of the Qur'ān had been accepted by Muslims (cf. p. 89).

While arguments with Christians and Jews were relatively frequent, these were not the only religions with which the Muslims were in contact. The Persian empire had been officially Zoroastrian, but

Zoroastrianism had not been in a very healthy state, and there seem to have been more arguments against the modified form of dualistic religion already described as *zandaqa* or Manichaeanism. Despite the fact that the Barmakids came from a Buddhist milieu, the Muslims had very little knowledge of Buddhism in the ninth century. There are reports of arguments with an obscure group called Sumaniyya, who have been described as 'hinduizing sceptics'. Thus Islam had some contact with other religions, but was not very interested in learning about them. Perhaps it was hoped that, if they were neglected and not spoken about, they would gradually die out.

It has often been suggested that Islamic theology owes something to Christian influences. There is some plausibility in supposing that Muslim discussions of whether the Qur'ān is the created or uncreated Word (or Speech) of God were influenced by Christian discussions of whether Christ, the Word of God, was created or uncreated. The older discussions of such influences, however, are unsatisfactory since they paid little attention to the precise nature of influence. It is ridiculous to suggest that Muslims adopted the view that the Qur'ān was the uncreated Word of God because they had heard Christians saying something similar. The idea of an uncreated word may well have been taken over from Christians, but it was not taken over because it was in itself intellectually attractive. The adoption of the idea must have come about when a group of Muslims, already involved in fierce arguments with other Muslims, noticed that this conception, applied to the Qur'ān, would make their case against their fellow-Muslims more effective. What drives men to make this theological formulation is their involvement in an intra-Islamic debate – an entirely Islamic motive. The only 'influence' is that a Christian idea has suggested a useful weapon.

The translation of Greek books

When the Muslims conquered Iraq, they found themselves in contact with a living tradition of Hellenistic learning. Several colleges had been established, mostly by Christians, the most prominent being one at Gondeshapur near the head of the Persian Gulf. This latter was run by Nestorian Christians, and was famous for both medical and religious studies. The language of instruction was

Syriac, and the necessary books had been translated from Greek into Syriac. The medicine was chiefly of Hippocrates and Galen, and closely associated with it were studies of the philosophy of Aristotle, Plato and their successors, together with mathematics and other sciences. Some of the clients from Iraq who became Muslims during the Umayyad period presumably knew a little about the scope of these intellectual disciplines and may even have attended a college. The Muslim administrators seem to have been interested first of all in having Christian physicians to attend them. The ʿAbbāsid caliphs had a Nestorian as court physician from 765 to 870. The translation of medical works from Syriac into Arabic is said to have begun under the Umayyads, but the real impact of Greek thought began after al-Ma'mūn had established a library and a team of translators in 'the House of Wisdom'.

At first the translations were made from Syriac by Iraqian Christians, but the greatest of the translators, Ḥunayn ibn-Is'ḥāq (809–73), had learnt Greek, and would collate manuscripts before embarking on a translation. As the Arabic language developed and knowledge of the subject-matter increased, the translations were revised. This process went on at least until the eleventh century, by which time the Arabs had taken all they wanted from the Greeks. The extent of the work of translation is impressive. In a list of translations of which either the titles are known or manuscripts exist, there are found over eighty Greek authors; and men like Aristotle, Plato, Galen and Euclid are each represented by several works. It is to be noted, however, that the works translated were entirely philosophical and scientific – there were no poems, plays or histories. Even in philosophy, it seems, only those works were translated which were valued in the late Hellenistic schools.

The translation of the Greek books was one factor in the intellectual ferment which stirred up the Islamic world of the ninth century, and which continued in some measure until the twelfth. There were indeed other translations, especially Indian books which had previously been translated into Pahlevi, the language of the Sasanian empire; but the main stimulus came from the Greeks. It is important, however, to see Greek influence in a proper perspective. The Muslim mind was not a *tabula rasa* whose empty spaces could be filled up with Greek ideas. There probably were some relatively small blanks in restricted areas, such as the particular sciences. Over a wide field, however, there had been intense intellectual activity among the Muslims before the translations appeared, notably about legal questions and in the doctrinal arguments between the sects. Had it not been for this prior intellectual activity, the Muslims would not have been in a position to assimilate as much as they did of Greek thought. In other words, Greek thought was able to have some influence in the Islamic world because there was an on-going intellectual process into which certain Greek ideas could be taken up.

The acceptance of Greek ideas

Greek ideas may be said to have entered the intellectual world of the Muslims in two waves. The first wave is linked with the first translations, and extends roughly over the first ʿAbbāsid century and perhaps a little way into the second. The second wave is associated with the work of al-Ghazālī round about 1100. It was particularly at these two periods that Greek ideas came into the main stream of Islamic thinking; but besides this main stream there was also a side-stream in which there was a more intense study of Greek philosophy and science. From the Greek word *philosophos* there was formed an Arabic word *faylasūf* (with the plural *falāsifa*) which was used in a wide sense. There was less specialization in the medieval period than at the present time, and there were several Muslims who were outstanding both as philosophers and as physicians. Among the Falāsifa (as we shall call them) there were many whose works were later translated into Latin and made an important contribution to the development of European philosophy and science. Because these men were known in some measure to modern occidental scholars, there has been a tendency to assume that they played a prominent part in the intellectual life of the Islamic world; but this was not so. Mostly the Falāsifa were regarded as heretics, and they tended to form small coteries which kept themselves to themselves, even if occasionally they were in favour with some ruler or minister. This is why they had little influence on the main stream between 850 and 1100.

The chief translators usually also composed original works in which they tried to express the new ideas in a more popular form. Gradually there was a move beyond these popularizing books to works of genuine originality which made a real contribution to the subject. The first person to 'attempt to naturalize Greek philosophy in the Islamic world' was al-Kindī (*c.*800–*c.*868), who is known as 'the *faylasūf* of the Arabs'. He was from the tribe of Kinda and studied in Basra, though his teachers are not known. He made a few translations and corrected some of the previous ones, but his main works were of his own composition. Very few are extant, but over 270 titles are recorded. Some of these works are presumably no more than essays. They range over the whole field of the Greek sciences, and must have greatly encouraged the spread of Greek ideas, since al-Kindī, unlike the later Falāsifa, was still more or less within the main stream. His theological position was close to that of the Mu'tazilites, and like these he enjoyed the favour of al-Ma'mūn and his two successors. Indeed al-Kindī was tutor to a son of the caliph al-Mu'taṣim. After the change of policy under al-Mutawakkil he experienced some adversity. He even had his library confiscated at one point, but eventually recovered it.

The acceptance of a limited number of Greek conceptions into the Islamic universe of discourse was essentially the work of a number of men who were active towards the end of the eighth century. These men were less versed in Greek thought than al-Kindī, but more interested in Islamic theological questions, and they were therefore able to see the relevance of Greek ideas to their theological concerns. Because they were pioneers whose formulations were later superseded, there are no clear accounts of their achievements in the Arabic sources, but recent research has pieced together numerous small items of information to give a convincing picture of their contribution. One man who emerges as of great importance was Hishām ibn-al-Ḥakam, who lived first in Kufa and then in Baghdad, where he became an intimate of the Barmakids. The date given for his death varies between 795 and 815, but a point about the middle of that range is most likely. He is regarded by later Imāmites as one of theirs, but he had also a great interest in physical and metaphysical questions with a bearing on theology, and greatly influenced the Mu'tazilite an-Naẓẓām. About the same time the discussions in Basra were presided over by Ḍirār, who was a contemporary of Hishām ibn-al-Ḥakam. On at least one occasion he argued with the latter and with various scholars in the salon of Yaḥyā the Barmakid. Ḍirār seems to have been a seminal mind, and to have broached many of the questions on the frontier of Greek thought and Islamic theology which were discussed for the next fifty or a hundred years. Some twenty or thirty years later came Bishr al-Marīsī who, though belonging to the Ḥanafite legal school, became notorious as an upholder of the doctrine of the createdness of the Qur'ān.

Discussions of the type in which these men engaged came to be referred to as *kalām*, a word which literally means 'speech' but in this specialized sense is tantamount to 'rational theology'; the people who practise this are *mutakallimūn*. Many of the more conservative scholars looked on all Kalām as abhorrent, whatever the precise doctrinal belief of the individual. It was apparently the custom of these opponents of Kalām in the early ninth century to call all its practitioners 'Muʿtazilites', or collectively, the Muʿtazila. This nickname was certainly applied to Ḍirār. In the generation after Ḍirār, however, there appeared a galaxy of brilliant thinkers who somehow managed to transform 'Muʿtazilite' from being a term of opprobrium into a designation of which one could be proud. Though these thinkers differed among themselves, they came to agree on five principles: God's unity (so conceived as to necessitate the createdness of the Qur'ān); God's justice (implying human freedom); the promise and the threat (implying that God must reward good men in Heaven and punish the wicked in Hell); the intermediate position (*sc.* between belief and unbelief as appropriate to the grave sinner); and commanding the right and forbidding the wrong (or active promotion of social justice). The last two or indeed three principles had political implications; but most of the theological discussions were about the first two. Once there was agreement on these principles, those who accepted them all denied the name of Muʿtazilite to those who rejected one or more; and this included Ḍirār.

In the brilliant generation after Ḍirār, and probably owing much to his teaching, three men were outstanding: Abū-l-Hudhayl (d. *c.*840), an-Naẓẓām (d. *c.*835) and Bishr ibn-al-Muʿtamir (d. 825). The first two reached a great age and are not necessarily younger than the third. All three are said to have been present, along with other men, at a symposium on love on the Socratic model in the house of Yaḥyā the Barmakid, and this cannot have been later than 803. Abū-l-Hudhayl is reckoned the head of the Muʿtazilites of Basra, and was the chief teacher of Kalām there after Ḍirār. An-Naẓẓām was also at Basra and showed more interest than Abū-l-

Hudhayl in the Greek sciences. Bishr ibn-al-Muʿtamir was the head of the Muʿtazilites of Baghdad who, probably because they lived in the capital, were more involved in the politics of the day. Bishr was one of those who was present at al-Ma'mūn's court in the east when the document was signed making ʿAlī ar-Riḍā heir to the caliphate. Even more powerful at court was his pupil Thumāma. It was under the influence of such men that al-Ma'mūn instituted the Inquisition, for the doctrine of the createdness of the Qur'ān was part of Muʿtazilite teaching. After the change of policy under al-Mutawakkil the Muʿtazilites were out of favour at court, but they continued as a school of academic theologians.

The Muʿtazilites of the ninth century claimed that their school had really been founded in the early eighth century by two men, Wāṣil ibn-ʿAṭā' (d. 748) and ʿAmr ibn-ʿUbayd (d. 761), both of whom had been connected with the circle of al-Ḥasan al-Baṣrī. Indeed the respectable interpretation of the name Muʿtazila as 'withdrawers' was said to be due to the fact that they had 'withdrawn' from the circle over the question of the grave sinner being in 'the intermediate position'. There are many discrepancies, however, which make it impossible to regard Wāṣil and ʿAmr as the founders of the Muʿtazila in any important sense. They may certainly be the source of the doctrine of 'the intermediate position' and some of the later political attitudes. The greatness of the Muʿtazila, however, rests on the vast amount of work they did in bringing Greek ideas into Islamic theological discussions; and the two alleged founders do not seem to have contributed anything at all to Muʿtazilism in this respect. The real founders of the Muʿtazila as a school of theology with an infusion of Greek ideas were Abū-l-Hudhayl, an-Naẓẓām and Bishr ibn-al-Muʿtamir, together with other thinkers of about the same period; and in the matters which constituted their greatness these men owed less to the alleged founders than to non-Muʿtazilites like Ḍirār and Hishām ibn-al-Ḥakam.

The Muʿtazilites attracted much attention among European scholars of the nineteenth century. Because they believed in freedom of the will and certain other points, more sympathy was felt for their position than for the standard Sunnite one. They were very far, however, from being free-thinkers and pure rationalists as was sometimes supposed. They belonged to the main stream of Islamic thinking, argued from Qur'ānic verses, had views on 'the roots of law' and so forth. Thus they were in a different position from the Falāsifa, who retained little that was Islamic except belief in God and one or two very general conceptions. The Muʿtazilites were Muslims through and through, engaged both in intra-Islamic debates and in commending Islam to non-Muslims. It was precisely because they found Greek ideas useful in these activities that they studied and adapted them. Only at one or two points had they an interest in the ideas for their own sake or out of intellectual curiosity. Mostly the ideas taken over were relevant to the disputes.

The Greek ideas brought into Islamic discussions by the forerunners like Ḍirār and the great Muʿtazilites like Abū-l-Hudhayl defined the problems of Islamic theology for nearly three centuries. The conceptions introduced in the half-century round about 800 and the problems they raised were worked over with ever greater refinements until about 1100, but virtually no further Greek ideas came in until al-Ghazālī studied the works of the Falāsifa. During these centuries the only further study of Greek ideas was by the Falāsifa in isolation from the main stream.

5

ARAB SELF-ASSERTION IN THE HUMANITIES

The first ʿAbbāsid century was the beginning of the great creative period of Arabic literature, but the full significance of the various developments can be appreciated only if they are seen, not in a purely literary context, but as part of the process by which, in contrast to Greece and Rome, conquering Arabia made the conquered culture still further captive.

Early prose and the Shuʿūbites

A certain amount of prose was gradually produced in the general religious movement. The *Risāla* of al-Ḥasan al-Baṣrī has already been mentioned; and some scholars wrote down Traditions and other historical material during the Umayyad period. In contrast to this religious writing, however, there was also a secular literary movement. This arose from the interest of the Umayyad caliphs and their court officials in learning how other men had ruled empires. The caliph Hishām is said to have had works on the subject of politics translated from both Greek and Persian; and the last caliph, Marwān II, is described as reading about Persian kings. Some epistles are extant from the 'secretary' ʿAbd-al-Ḥamīd ibn-Yaḥyā (d. 750), which incidentally show how the secretaries were becoming aware of themselves as a distinct class with a special role in society.

The change of dynasty in 750 brought more power to men of the secretary class in Iraq, who were nearly all either Persians or natives of Iraq who had become persianized. The most prominent was Ibn-al-Muqaffaʿ (*c.*720–56), the son of a Persian who was a tax-collector under the Umayyads. As mentioned above (p. 111), he was cruelly put to death about 756, either because of being involved with rebels, or because he was a *zindīq* and had written a book in criticism of Muḥammad and the Qur'ān. Despite his youth he produced a number of translations of books which had been circulating in the Persian court in Pahlevi. One of these, *Kalīla wa-Dimna*, is extant, though the text may have been revised lightly at a later date. These translations are in a simple but elegant prose style, which justifies one in regarding Ibn-al-Muqaffaʿ as one of the creators of Arabic prose. *Kalīla and Dimna* consists of tales about animals which incorporate much worldly political wisdom. Other works extolled the glories of ancient Persia, or gave practical information about court ceremonial and the duties of various officials. Ibn-al-Muqaffaʿ was far from being the only writer of this type. The famous book-list of Ibn-an-Nadīm, written in 988, has the names of many other Persian romances, presumably produced at this time or shortly afterwards.

In all the works of Ibn-al-Muqaffaʿ and even in the imitations of Persian romances there was a serious challenge to Islamic society. In the cities of Iraq there was a middle class, now with greater wealth and leisure, and consisting partly of Arabs and partly of the older Persian or persianized inhabitants. Some of these were doubtless attracted to religious matters, but others were certainly more interested in light entertainment. Paper manufacture had come to Baghdad about 800 and had made it possible for many people to have their own copies of entertaining works. The danger in all this was that this class of educated persons, as it increased in numbers, would become more this-worldly and more out of sympathy with the Arabs and their religion. As Sir Hamilton Gibb has phrased it, it was not a question of literary fashions, but of whether Islamic society 'was to become a re-embodiment of the old Perso–Aramaean culture into which the Arabic and Islamic elements would be absorbed, or a culture in which the Perso–Aramaean contributions would be subordinated to the Arab tradition and the Islamic values'.

The oppressive measures of the ʿAbbāsids against *zandaqa* discouraged the secretaries and like-minded persons from the more extreme criticisms of Islamic religion; and thereupon appeared the milder Shuʿūbiyya or Shuʿūbite movement. This was primarily a literary movement, in whose productions the vices of the Arabs were held up to scorn and the merits of other peoples extolled. It was not confined to Persians and persophiles, for there were books in praise of Nabataeans, Daylamites, Copts and others. It was relatively easy for the Shuʿūbites to find material to use against the Arabs, for much Arabic poetry came under one of the two headings, *mafākhir* and *mathālib*, that is, praising of one's own tribe and satirizing of rival tribes – the latter including references to all sorts of disgraceful and dishonourable matters in their past history.

Among Shuʿūbite writers the best known is the blind poet Bashshār ibn-Burd (*c.*714–84), who lived first in Basra but spent the last twenty years of his life in Baghdad. He seems to have been very poor, and this made him an opportunist, who often said things, not because they were firm convictions, but because they were expedient at the moment. This makes it difficult to be certain about what he really believed. There is no doubt, however, that he wrote many bitter verses about Arabs and even accused the Companions of the Prophet in general – and they were nearly all Arabs – of unbelief. His death may have been a punishment for satirical verses about the caliph al-Mahdī, but there was also an accusation of *zandaqa*. All this is in line with his father's east Persian origin. Yet the amazing thing is that he had such a command of the Arabic language and of the techniques of Arabic poetry that he was the outstanding poet of his time in Iraq, now the centre of the Arabic literary world. This shows the contradiction inherent in the Shuʿūbite movement. It is very understandable as a reaction to the arrogant pride of the Arabs, and it gave frustrated non-Arabs an outlet for their feelings; but as a challenge to the Islamic state it was much less serious than the *zandaqa* of Ibn-al-Muqaffaʿ. Its internal weakness was that it could not avoid using the Arabic language and thereby admitting an important aspect of Arab superiority.

Grammar and philology

It is strange that it should be thought appropriate to have a section on the study of grammar in a work of general history, even one that is paying attention to cultural factors. The unusual importance of grammar and philology in the Islamic world, however, is an aspect of the remarkable process by which the language of a relatively uncultured people became that of a highly sophisticated civilization, capable of expressing all shades of emotion and adequate to the highest flights of abstract speculation.

Two practical needs impelled men to the study of grammar. Some agreement about general grammatical principles was needed if men were to make any headway in their arguments about the interpretation of passages from the Qur'ān, and also some agreement about the meanings of obscure words. This matter became urgent in so far as the Qur'ān became the basis of the functioning of the state. In the construing and understanding of passages Qur'ānic Arabic offers a wider range of possibilities than a comparable English text; and it is thus all the more important to know what is admissible grammatically and what inadmissible. The second need was for the accurate use of the language after it had been adopted by many persons whose native language was some other. The non-Arab secretaries would be among the first who were required to write in Arabic, and professional pride doubtless made them want to avoid solecisms. In the background of these practical concerns, too, there was the deep feeling of the desert Arab for his language which led him to find in it his chief mode of aesthetic expression.

The honour of founding the philological disciplines in Arabic goes to Basra. The beginnings are shadowy, but the men whose names are mentioned were also concerned with the study of the text and interpretation of the Qur'ān, so that it was probably the religious need which led to their interest in philology. There was also, of course, a very mixed population in Basra, and many would have only an imperfect knowledge of Arabic and would be confused by the different dialects found in such a city. The first two figures who emerge clearly from the mists, and whose works are in part still extant, are the Arab from Oman, al-Khalīl ibn-Aḥmad (d. *c.*791), and his Persian pupil Sībawayh (d. 793 or later). Sībawayh had a short and somewhat unfortunate life, but his brilliant systematic exposition of the grammatical principles he had learnt from al-Khalīl became the foundation of all Arabic grammatical science and in some respects has never been superseded. In their formulation of principles these two scholars of Basra owed something to the logical teaching of the philosophical and medical college at Gondeshapur. In Kufa also there was a group or school of scholars of philology, perhaps originally dependent on Basra, though later contrasted with it and reckoned to be less speculative.

Grammatical principles were not the only concern of the philologists. Arabic had a huge vocabulary, and there were some dialectal variations in the meaning of words, while non-Arabs living a century and a half after the Hijra found a few Qur'ānic words mysterious. Lexicographical studies were therefore an essential, and one of the works of al-Khalīl is a dictionary arranged not alphabetically but according to a curious phonetic principle. Other scholars wrote such works as *The Book of the Horse*, containing all the words applied to horses. It gradually came to be accepted as a principle that the purest and most correct Arabic was that of the desert tribes. Phrases would be included in the word-books to show the correct usage, and then verses from poems. From this it was a short step to the systematic collection of poems, especially the pre-Islamic poetry of the desert, which up to the late eighth century had been orally transmitted. From this time onwards the collection and study of the older poetry became a major occupation of some philologists. Among the achievements of al-Khalīl was the working out of a metrical scheme suited to the complexities of this poetry. Even such a scheme of prosody was linked with Arab self-assertion, for the metres of Arabic and the accompanying music were felt to be different from those of the Persian tradition.

History and other prose writing

It is probably not accidental that the first branch of historical studies to produce a work of real maturity was the biography of the Prophet. During the eighth century there was a growing interest in the sayings and doings of Muḥammad, especially from a juristic standpoint. Though it was not necessary for legal purposes to assign a precise date to each incident recorded in the Traditions, it was desirable to know something of the chronological order of events. In the Umayyad period scholars like az-Zuhrī had been working on this. It is thus not surprising that what has remained the fundamental work on the life of Muḥammad, the *Sīra* or *Biography* by Ibn-Is'ḥāq (d. 768), was produced at the beginning of the ʿAbbāsid period. This has come down to us chiefly in the edition made by Ibn-Hishām (d. *c.*833); but his editorial work consisted in shortening the preliminary section which did not deal directly with Muḥammad, removing one or two stories which he considered objectionable or dubious, and adding brief notes giving additional items of information or criticizing the authenticity of verses. Thus even after editing the work is essentially that of Ibn-Is'ḥāq.

Another scholar in the same field from the school of Medina was al-Wāqidī (d. 823), whose book on Muḥammad's expeditions is extant and contains more material than the corresponding sections of Ibn-Is'ḥāq. Al-Wāqidī also collected a vast amount of material about other aspects of the career of the Prophet and about the period of the conquests. His pupil and secretary Ibn-Saʿd (d. 845) published the further material about the Prophet, including the text of some letters and treaties, and added to this biographies of the three hundred or so Muslims who fought at the battle of Badr and shorter notes about a thousand or two later scholars in the various centres who were responsible for handing on information about the earliest age of Islam.

During the first ʿAbbāsid century there were a number of historians who were concerned with aspects of the period from the death of Muḥammad to their own time. Their works have not come down to us *in extenso*, but there are many quotations from them in the works of later historians, especially aṭ-Ṭabarī, and some idea can be formed of their character. They all tended to glorify the Arab past and the glories of the conquests. More particularly, however, each in his own way introduced modifications in his presentation of events so that the final picture was acceptable to the outlook of the milieu in which he lived. Thus al-Wāqidī, who after leaving Medina had a good relationship both with Yaḥyā the Barmakid and later with al-Ma'mūn, adopts views which would be in harmony with the general policy of the latter; he shows an anti-Umayyad tendency, he rejects extreme interpretations of ʿAlī's actions, but he is moderately favourable to ʿAlī himself.

A similar interest in the Arab past led to the study of pre-Islamic Arabia. Abū-ʿUbayda (d. *c.*825), a philologist of the school of Basra, specialized in the collecting and interpreting of pre-Islamic poetry and in the course of his studies obtained such a store of knowledge that he was able to boast 'no two horses ever met in battle in pagan or Islamic times, but I had knowledge of them and their riders'. He appears to be the actual source of nearly all the traditional information that has been preserved about the Arab tribes before Islam. Abū-ʿUbayda was sometimes called a Shuʿūbite by later writers, but this seems to be because Shuʿūbites made use of his materials about the seamier side of Arab life, and not because he himself was anti-Arab. It is certain, however, that he had moderate Khārijite sympathies. Another authority on ancient Arabia of about the same period was Ibn-al-Kalbī (d. 819), in whose case it is interesting to note that he went beyond the field of purely Arab interests and began to write about Persian history on the basis of translated works.

Together with the serious study of the Arab past there was a beginning of the use of Arab materials for works of entertainment. This was one aspect of Arab self-assertion against the Persians and Shuʿūbites. Much of the work of one of the greatest of Arabic prose-writers, al-Jāḥiẓ, must have been done before 850 since he was over ninety when he died in 869; but it will be more convenient to speak of him in the next chapter as part of the development of a new secular prose. Apart from the persophile and Shuʿūbite writers, most of the prose of the first ʿAbbāsid century was either religious or technical. The religious works were either theological polemics or juristic discussions or collections of Traditions and other anecdotes, such as the *Muwaṭṭa'* of Mālik and the *Musnad* of Aḥmad ibn-Ḥanbal. By technical prose is meant the translations and the first original works in the fields of science and philosophy. In this case, too, it will be convenient to treat of the Arab achievement as a whole at a later point.

Poetry

The writing of poetry was much cultivated in all classes of the population and reflected all the varying shades of opinion. The leisured rich found delight in verses set to music, and the ability to compose verses was an accomplishment expected of everyone with a claim to being cultured. In such circumstances there was wide variety in the types of poem. There were courtly love-lyrics, lusty drinking-songs and songs of the hunt, coarse satires and fulsome panegyrics. The greatest exponent of most of these forms was the half-Persian Abū-

Nuwās (d. *c.*803), and not far behind him in reputation was that other earlier Persian, Bashshār ibn-Burd, who has been mentioned for his Shuʿūbite leanings.

In all this there was the promise of a new and vigorous poetic movement, but the promise was not fulfilled and the movement lost its living character. The reason would appear to be that when the philologists received wide-spread recognition from the upper strata of society it was difficult for the would-be poet not to adhere to the canons of language and style they established. This led to artificiality, with the emphasis on the manner of saying a thing rather than on the meaningful content. One who escaped from the net of the philologists was Abū-l-ʿAtāhiya (d. 826). He was an Arab from a humble background who by his poetic talents gained the favour of the caliphs al-Mahdī and Hārūn ar-Rashīd. The story goes that his love for a slave-girl of the former caliph was not returned and that in dejection he adopted the life of an ascetic. There is a sadness in much of his poetry as it dwells on human mortality, but this melancholic note, coupled with the simplicity of his language, gave him a wide popular appeal, and his poems may be taken to express the religious and moral outlook of ordinary men, which is in sharp contrast to the frivolity of the court.

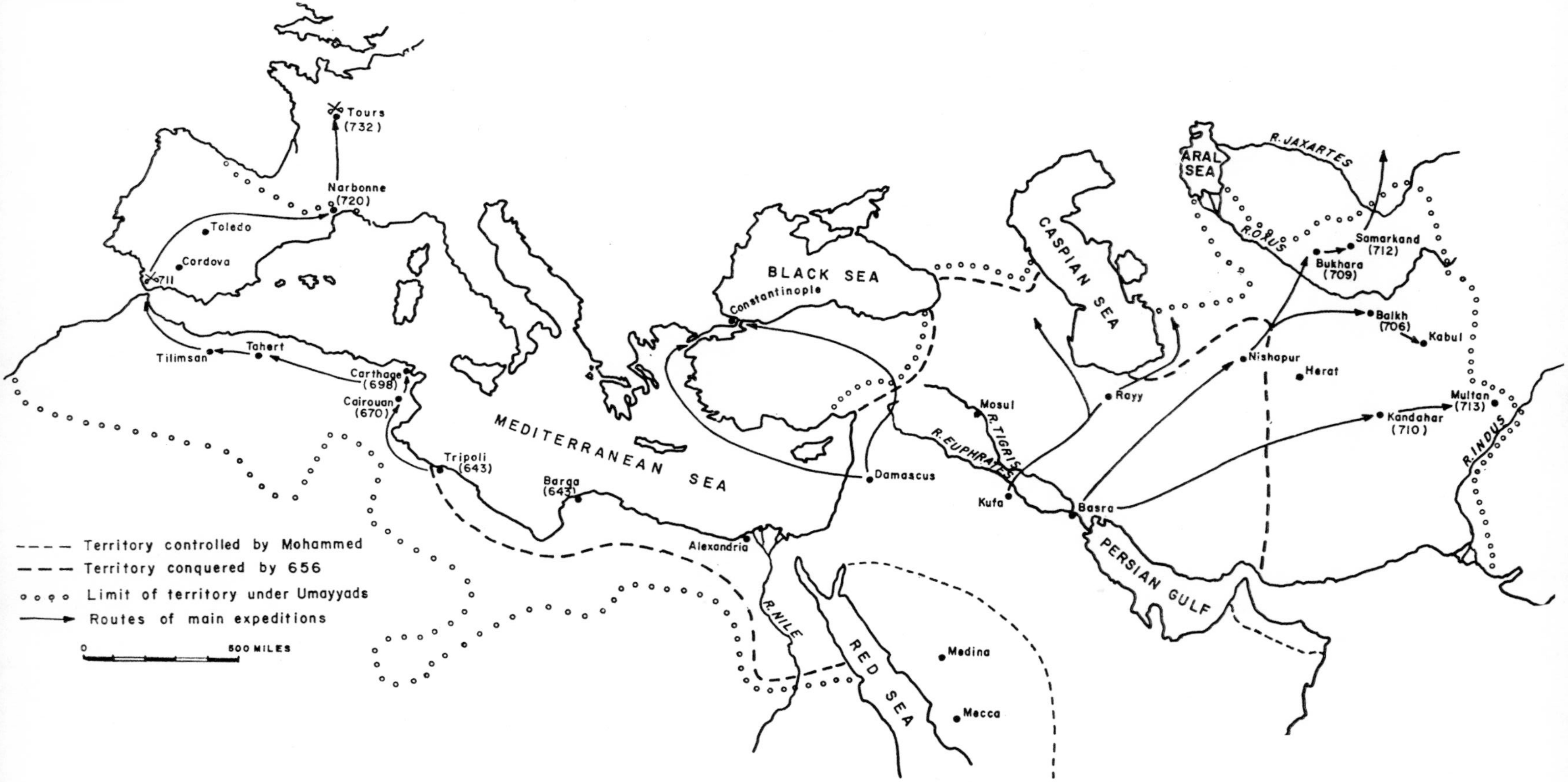

THE UMAYYAD EMPIRE

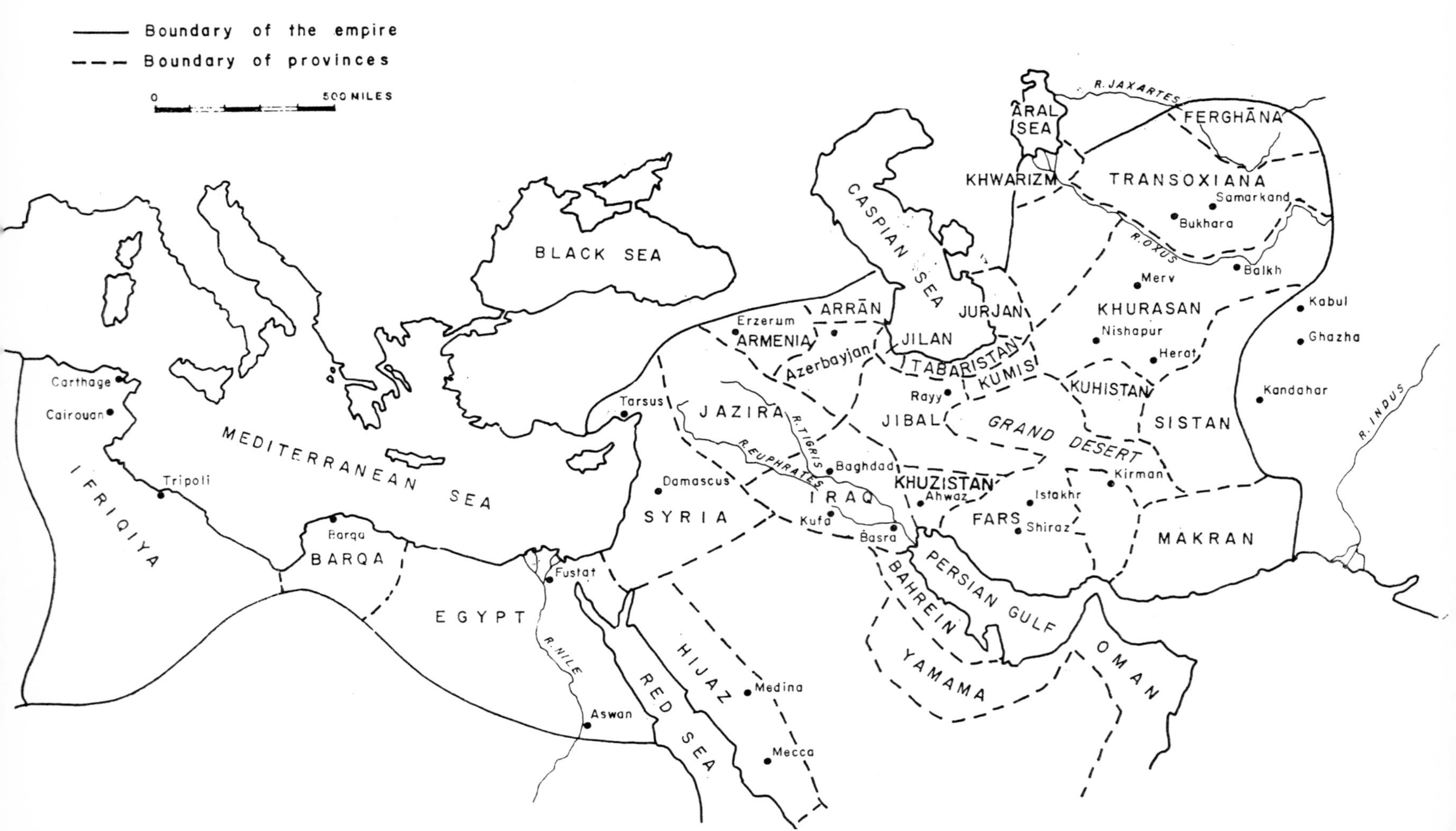

THE PROVINCES OF THE 'ABBĀSID EMPIRE

III

The ʿAbbāsid Decline

850–945

ʿABBĀSID CALIPHS

847	al-Mutawakkil
861	al-Muntaṣir
862	al-Mustaʿīn
866	al-Muʿtazz
869	al-Muhtadī
870	al-Muʿtamid (and al-Muwaffaq)
892	al-Muʿtaḍid
902	al-Muktafī
908	al-Muqtadir
932	al-Qāhir
934	ar-Rāḍī
940	al-Muttaqī
944–6	al-Mustakfī

THE ʿABBĀSID DYNASTY (2)

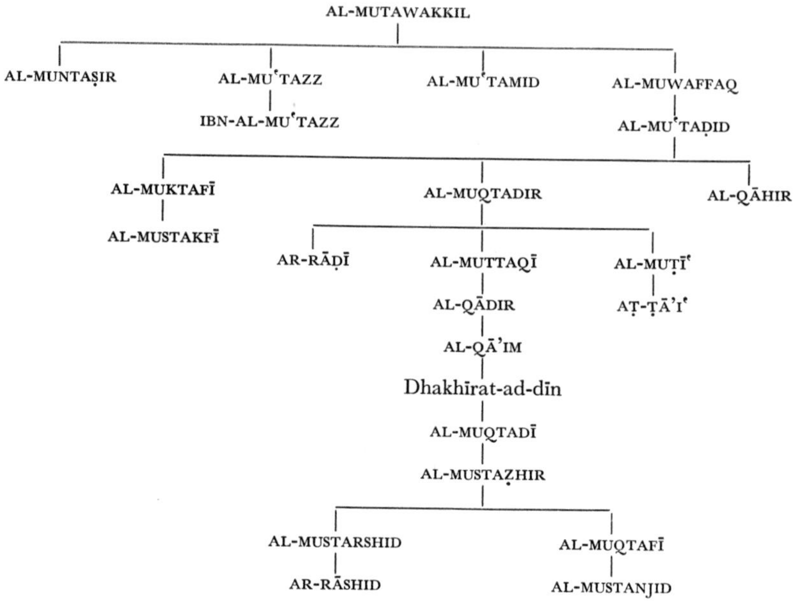

Note: Names of caliphs are in small capitals.

1

THE STRUGGLE AT THE CENTRE

The caliphate of al-Mutawakkil and 'the change of policy'

The caliph al-Wāthiq died in July 847 without having made any arrangements for the succession. Some half-dozen of the most influential men in the court therefore met to decide who should succeed. The vizier and several others wanted to appoint the son of al-Wāthiq, but he was rather young, and they were prevailed upon to accept the late caliph's brother Ja'far, who was aged twenty-seven and took the throne-name of al-Mutawakkil. Al-Mutawakkil was the nominee in the first place of a group of Turkish officers, and his assumption of the caliphal dignity is thus a sign of the increasing influence of the Turks. There was no solidarity among the Turks, however, and at least one important general took the same line as the vizier. The reign of al-Mutawakkil was marked by internal and external peace, and was generally felt to be a time of prosperity, security and happiness.

Several references have already been made to 'the change of policy' near the beginning of the reign, and something further must now be said about this change. Unfortunately the politics of the next quarter of a century is complex and obscure, and has not yet been fully studied in detail, so that the account to be given has something of a provisional character. It seems possible, for example, that the group responsible for making al-Mutawakkil caliph gradually came to control the policy of the empire; but in the present state of our knowledge this cannot be stated with certainty. Two things are clear, however: firstly, that the change did not come about all at once, but occurred in several stages spread over three or four years; and secondly, that it was not the establishment of an out-and-out Sunnite policy but something more subtle and *nuancé*.

The change of policy is sometimes identified with the ending of the Inquisition, but in Egypt at least the Inquisition seems to have continued until 851 or later. Then again it may be that the key event which led to the whole series of changes was the execution, some four months after al-Mutawakkil's accession, of the former vizier, who had been in power through most of the period of the Inquisition. On the other hand, the Muʿtazilite chief judge, Ibn-Abī-Du'ād, was not removed from office until 852. It is sometimes stated by modern writers that in 849 it was decreed that the Qur'ān was the uncreated speech of God; but the older sources speak of the decree as being somewhat different, namely, a decree forbidding everyone to argue or hold discussions about the Qur'ān. This was far from being a clear adoption of the position of Aḥmad ibn-Ḥanbal, but it was much more acceptable to him than to the Muʿtazilites. Actually Aḥmad ibn-Ḥanbal was still under suspicion for the first four years of the reign, apparently because of his association with Arab elements in Baghdad who had links with ʿAlid activists hostile to the government, though Aḥmad himself had no direct association with these activities.

The official attitude to Aḥmad altered abruptly after the fall of Ibn-Abī-Du'ād. He was now summoned to the court at Samarra and shown the highest respect and honour. It was hoped that he would consent to become the tutor of the young prince al-Muʿtazz, so that the latter would have Aḥmad's great public influence behind him in any struggle for power. It appears that different groups among the chief secretaries and generals were 'jockeying for position' over the question of the succession, since the group whose candidate gained the throne would virtually rule the empire. Aḥmad had no great liking for political power under any circumstances, refused the post of tutor and was given leave to return to Baghdad, where he died in 855. He was also moved to withdraw by the fact that some influential men at court held a doctrine which he detested almost as much as the doctrine that the Qur'ān was created. This was the view that, when a man recites the Qur'ān, his utterance of it is created. This view presumably involved some political compromise, but what that is remains obscure. Despite this coolness on the part of Aḥmad ibn-Ḥanbal the general line of policy under al-Mutawakkil was favourable to a moderate Sunnism. The caliph also took measures against the more extreme forms of devotion to ʿAlī and his family; in particular he destroyed the tomb of al-Ḥusayn at Kerbela and stopped the pilgrimages to it. The introduction of new regulations against Christians and Jews, or the enforcement of old regulations, was in part at least a protest against the favour shown at court during the previous reigns to Christians versed in Greek science and philosophy.

The period of anarchy, 861–70

The new policy associated with al-Mutawakkil was not endorsed by all the influential persons at court. Some of his attitudes to ʿAlī and al-Ḥusayn were specially disliked. This group of opponents had as their figurehead the caliph's son and heir apparent, al-Muntaṣir, whereas the supporters of the official policy were rallied behind another son, al-Muʿtazz, who was personally more gifted. At one time it looked as if there would be an attempt to secure the succession for al-Muʿtazz, and this led al-Muntaṣir and his advisers to form a plot which culminated in the assassination of his father in December 861. During the six months of al-Muntaṣir's reign the general line of al-Mutawakkil's later policies was followed, but al-Muntaṣir showed himself more favourable to the admirers of ʿAlī and to his descendants. Pilgrimages to the tomb of al-Ḥusayn were once again permitted. The cause of al-Muntaṣir's death is not clearly known. A chill is said to have developed into a fever, but it is more probable that he was poisoned by enemies for personal reasons. The group which supported him, however, managed to prevent the succession of al-Muʿtazz, and instead placed on the throne a grandson of al-Muʿtaṣim to be known as al-Mustaʿīn.

The general policy during the reign of al-Mustaʿīn was similar to that of the previous six months, though he had to suppress a rising, nominally Zaydite, under an ʿAlid pretender in Kufa. In 865, owing to a quarrel between the senior Turkish generals, al-Mustaʿīn and the general who supported him had to flee to Baghdad, where he took certain pro-ʿAlid measures to gain further popular support. Meanwhile al-Muʿtazz was proclaimed caliph in Samarra. The situation became hopeless for al-Mustaʿīn and he abdicated in January 866. Under al-Muʿtazz a policy like that of al-Mutawakkil was followed, and a strict watch was kept over the more prominent ʿAlids. Though al-Muʿtazz was deposed by the Turkish officers in 869 and replaced by al-Muhtadī, a son of al-Wāthiq, there was little change in policy, and in any case the reign lasted only until 870 when al-Muhtadī was killed fighting a Turkish-led opposition force. The weakness of the central government at this point is shown by the ease with which in 869 a body of insurgent negro slaves of East African origin, known as the Zenj, gained control of the region round Basra and defeated several caliphal armies.

The ʿAbbāsid recovery under al-Muwaffaq and his successors

Al-Muhtadī was succeeded as caliph by a third son of al-Mutawakkil known as al-Muʿtamid, whose reign in contrast to the last four lasted over twenty years until 892. Al-Muʿtamid appears to have chosen as his first vizier a man who had served under his father – a fact which suggests continuity of policy. The most notable feature of the reign, however, was the gradual withdrawal of the caliph from the direction of affairs in favour of his brother Abū-Aḥmad Ṭalḥa, who became first governor of Iraq and Arabia and then viceroy of the eastern part of the empire and second in succession to the throne with the name of al-Muwaffaq by which he is commonly known. The caliph was not always completely passive, and from time to time there was friction between the two brothers; but in general it was al-Muwaffaq who was in control of events until his death in 891. He was succeeded as viceroy and regent by his son, who in turn became second in succession to the throne with the name al-Muʿtaḍid. He was a young man of some energy, however, and before the death of al-Muʿtamid in 892 had been named heir apparent, so that he reached the caliphal throne without opposition.

Al-Muwaffaq had to deal with various troubles in the east and in Egypt, which will be described in the next section. Nearer home he effectively ended the rebellion of the Zenj, though not until 883.

The centre of the rebellion was in the flat lands of southern Iraq where sugar cane was cultivated by slave labour on large estates. The numerous canals made access difficult for an army. The Zenj had erected two cities in strong positions, and from this relatively secure base had pillaged Basra, threatened Wasit and raided Khuzistan, the province to the east. Large armies with suitable boats were brought to the scene, but even so the final siege of the Zenj capital lasted two years.

An important event in the reign of al-Muʿtamid was the death of al-Ḥasan al-ʿAskarī, the eleventh imam of the Imāmite Shīʿites, together with the real or alleged disappearance of the twelfth imam. This led to the formulation of the Imāmite doctrine of the twelve imams and the organization of Imāmism – matters to be considered later in the chapter. Another point of interest is that the vizier from 878 to 885 was Ṣāʿid ibn-Makhlad, only recently converted to Islam from Nestorian Christianity, and with a brother who was still a leading person in the Christian community. The vizier seems to have supported an attempt to improve the position of Christians by referring to the terms of the Prophet's treaty with the Christians of Najrān in the Yemen. In 892 shortly before the end of the reign Baghdad became once more the capital and seat of government and Samarra was abandoned. Some of the government offices had indeed been moved back to Baghdad as early as 883. This was perhaps in part due to a realization that in Samarra it was more difficult to find checks and counterbalances to the power of the Turkish officers.

During the reign of al-Muʿtaḍid there were one or two insurrections, but these were relatively minor and were easily suppressed. More serious was the movement of the Carmathians or Qarāmiṭa which began during this reign and became a major preoccupation during the following reign. Otherwise the chief interest is in the attempts by al-Muʿtaḍid to broaden the basis of support for the caliphal government. The general line of al-Mutawakkil was maintained, and there was no question of a return to the Muʿtazilite compromise; but there were some measures aimed at getting the support of the Ḥanbalites on what might be called the extreme right. At the beginning of the reign it was forbidden to sell books on rational theology or philosophy; and later the caliph remedied an abuse in connection with inheritances of which the Ḥanbalites specially complained. On the other hand, to appease the moderate left, that is, those of (roughly) Imāmite sympathies, he gave important posts to men of this persuasion, notably putting Ibn-al-Furāt in charge of the finances of the empire. He even thought of having the first Umayyad Muʿāwiya publicly cursed, a procedure demanded by some on the left and resisted by the Ḥanbalites. His prohibition of meetings to listen to popular preachers affected chiefly the Ḥanbalites, but was perhaps chiefly intended to prevent the politico-theological temperature from rising. Altogether al-Muʿtaḍid seems to have been aiming at justice and a balance of interests.

The reign of al-Muktafī from 902 to 908 was largely taken up with the Carmathian problem. In 900 and 901 they had had some successes in the neighbourhood of Basra and Kufa and also in Syria. Syria was at this date the responsibility of the Ṭūlūnid governor of Egypt, but he was too weak to cope with the Carmathians and during the next year or two they were able to pillage most of the cities of Syria, probably including Damascus. It was after 906 before the caliphal government was able to suppress the Carmathians in Syria and Iraq, and it proved unable to expel them from the area of Bahrein in the Persian Gulf, where they had established a small state. The central government seems to have been very efficient during this reign, and the finances were in a healthy condition. A strong vizier was able to assert his authority over the generals and to give unity of direction to civil and military affairs.

The final loss of control

Al-Muktafī died in 908 without having made arrangements for the succession. The chief members of the administration were divided in their counsels. The vizier al-Jarjarā'ī, with his lieutenant, another Ibn-al-Furāt (ʿAlī, brother of Aḥmad already mentioned and now dead), and others of Imāmite sympathies, wanted the throne to be given to the thirteen-year-old brother of al-Muktafī, so that they themselves would have most of the power. Another group favoured a more experienced member of the family, usually known as Ibn-al-Muʿtazz. The vizier's party proved stronger, and the boy of thirteen became caliph in September 908 with the throne-name of al-Muqtadir. The rival group, however, mounted a conspiracy and in

December of the same year proclaimed Ibn-al-Muʿtazz caliph. It soon became apparent that the conspiracy was going to fail, and the unfortunate 'one-day caliph' was abandoned by his supporters and shortly afterwards executed.

The caliphate of al-Muqtadir lasted for twenty-four years. From 908 to 924 may be reckoned the great period of the vizierate, though the caliph retained the power of dismissing the vizier and calling him to account, and there were in fact five changes during the sixteen years. Since al-Jarjarā'ī had been killed in the fighting at the time of the conspiracy, Ibn-al-Furāt was the first of these viziers, and he held the office three times in all. His position was left of centre, that is, moderate Imāmite. His chief rival, who held the vizierate on two occasions, was ʿAlī ibn-ʿIsā, who was slightly right of centre (Sunnite), but disapproved of the Ḥanbalites on the extreme right. During this period the viziers managed to keep the finances in order. They ensured that the sums due from the provinces under their control were in fact received, more or less in full. Sometimes they had to have recourse to loans from financiers belonging to their family or partisans. With adequate sums of money to pay the armies they were in a position to exercise a central direction of military operations.

A change came in 924 with increased military activity on the part of the Carmathians with their state at Bahrein. They were now strong enough to pillage Basra (923), and later they threatened Baghdad (927) and removed the Black Stone from the Kaʿba at Mecca (930). After an attack on the caravan returning from the pilgrimage of March 923 there was consternation in Baghdad, and the vizier Ibn-al-Furāt was forced to recall from the north the Turkish general Mu'nis, with whom his relations had become strained. He realized that he was probably signing his own death-warrant, and a few days later (June 924) he and a son were in fact executed after torture. During the eight remaining years of the reign of al-Muqtadir there were eight vizierates, but none of the viziers was able to assert his authority over the military power, represented by the emir who controlled both the army and the police. The emir, however, did not have all the authority in his own hand, but had to co-operate with the vizier. This produced a difficult situation, especially as financial troubles grew worse and the troops often had to mutiny for pay. In one crisis in 929 al-Muqtadir was deposed for a few days in favour of his brother al-Qāhir, but was then restored. In another crisis in October 932 al-Muqtadir was persuaded by his advisers to resist the demands of the general Mu'nis, the emir, who was virtually in revolt against him. Al-Muqtadir went at the head of his troops to meet Mu'nis, and, knowing he was going to his death, proudly wore the cloak of the Prophet with his sword and its red sword-belt.

The two-years reign of al-Qāhir, who succeeded, was occupied by a struggle for power between the caliph, the emir and others. At one point the caliph was strong enough to have Mu'nis executed, but at length he himself succumbed to the intrigues of a former vizier, Ibn-Muqla, and was imprisoned and blinded, this last being to make it impossible (illegal) for him to hold the office of caliph. The new caliph was a son of al-Muqtadir with the throne-name of ar-Rāḍī. For much of the short reign Ibn-Muqla was vizier, but power was rapidly slipping from his grasp. In April 936 Ibn-Muqla was arrested by a hostile officer and ceased to be vizier, but none of the other men to whom the caliph entrusted the post was able to retrieve the financial situation, since several provincial governors were refusing to send any money to Baghdad. In November 936 the caliph decided to accept the conditions offered by Ibn-Rā'iq, the governor of Basra. He was to be the head of the army, the police and the civil administration with the title of 'chief emir' (*amīr al-umarā'*); he was also to be mentioned in the Friday prayer along with the caliph. This was the end of the attempt to maintain a balance between the civil and the military power. The civil power was now completely under the domination of the military, and the caliph had no longer any temporal authority but only certain religious functions.

Though temporal power had now slipped from the hands of the caliphs, it was not firmly in the grasp of anyone else. Ibn-Rā'iq had several rivals. One was his own lieutenant, Bachkam, the leader of a group of Turkish mercenaries, who served him for a year or two and then turned against him. Another Turkish leader who was chief emir for a time was Tūzūn. Yet another contender for supreme power was the Ḥamdānid ruler of Mosul, known by the honorific title of Nāṣir-ad-dawla. He too occupied the position of chief emir for a time; but he differed from the Turks in that, when he had to relinquish the office, he had a strong position in Mosul on which to fall back. Mention might also be made of Abū-'Abd-Allāh al-Barīdī, who came from a Persian family of Shī'ite sympathies and with some expertise in finance. After making a fortune in tax-farming he became governor of a province, and reached the rank of vizier in Baghdad, though not that of chief emir. Each of these men was playing for his own hand, and according to where he saw his own advantage would combine with some of the others or oppose them. Meanwhile Aḥmad ibn-Buwayh was growing stronger in the region east of Basra. When Tūzūn died in August 945, no leader was left capable of resisting Aḥmad ibn-Buwayh. Some officials entered into communication with him, and about the end of the year he entered the capital without opposition. The caliph came out of hiding, welcomed him and gave him the title of Muʿizz-ad-dawla (with similar titles for his two brothers), while he declared his loyalty to the caliph. This is taken as the beginning of the Buwayhid period.

Between 936 and 945 the caliphs tried to play a minor part in the game of power politics, but it usually turned out to their own disadvantage. Ar-Rāḍī died from natural causes in 940 at the age of 33. He was succeeded by his brother al-Muttaqī, whose attempts to gain a little power led to his being blinded by Tūzūn in 944. Only sixteen months later the same fate befell the next caliph al-Mustakfī, a son of al-Muktafī, at the hands of Muʿizz-ad-dawla who suspected him, despite the conferment of titles, of being on too friendly terms with several Turkish generals.

Reasons for the ʿAbbāsid decline

The course of events which has just been described is primarily the decline of the power of the ʿAbbāsid family. It is far from being the end of the Islamic empire, though it signifies a transformation of the character of the empire. It is not even an end of prosperity, though all the fighting meant that for a time there was great hardship. Intellectual life continued to flourish, as it often does in an era of decentralization. So the decline, whose causes are to be discussed, was above all the failure to keep a vast empire together as a single political unit.

One obvious factor is the mere size of the territory to be controlled, especially when the slowness of communications is remembered. This is not in itself an insuperable obstacle, but one of the necessities in holding together a widely extended empire is that there should be a high degree of mutual trust among the chief rulers and administrators. In the Islamic world by the tenth century such trust had largely disappeared. It was noticed in the previous chapter that the Sharīʿa was never applied to the relations of ministers and high officials to one another and to the caliph. The rewards of office were enormous, but the chances of enjoying them in a leisurely old age were slight. Execution, often after torture, was common treatment for dismissed viziers; imprisonment and confiscation of goods almost normal practice. In such circumstances it was almost inevitable that everyone should seek his own advantage at the expense of other men; and the corollary was that it was becoming impossible for the caliph to find men to appoint to provincial governorships who could be relied on to send to Baghdad the surplus from the taxes.

A second factor was the increasing reliance on mercenaries, and this in turn was probably linked with developments in military technology. The caliphs were aware of the problem, but they seem to have ruled out as impossible any return to a civilian militia of townsmen. It became very important for a caliph or governor to keep his troops favourably disposed towards himself by paying them wages regularly. The use of mercenaries also made it roughly true that, the more money one spent, the more military strength one acquired. Thus to maintain his position a caliph would have required sufficient military strength to deal with several unruly provincial governors at once; but this made financial demands that were more and more difficult to meet. The mercenaries, too, probably through *esprit de corps*, were much more attached to officers of similar racial origins than to 'foreigners' in positions of authority; so that it was really only money that could keep them loyal.

The third and perhaps most important factor was thus finance. We know from a budget statement that has been preserved that as late as 919 vast sums were still being sent annually to the central government in Baghdad. It was becoming usual, however, to collect these sums through a system of tax-farming. Sometimes, too, the right to collect taxes in a region seems to have been farmed out to the leader of mercenaries, who presumably collected taxes efficiently. In other cases there was collusion between the tax-farmer and the governor, since it was difficult to collect the taxes without military backing. In either case, once the caliph's military power declined, he was unable to enforce the remission of taxes to Baghdad, and so his revenues fell; and this meant either trouble with the soldiery or a further reduction in his military strength and so in his ability to collect taxes. Because there were no banks from which the caliph could borrow, almost his only course in a financial emergency was to take large sums as fines, or simply confiscate them, from wealthy individuals, much of whose fortune was probably ill-gotten in any case.

Various other points are also mentioned which contributed to the deterioration in the finances. Soldiers were given land instead of money, and this reduced the amounts due to the treasury. To avoid confiscation individuals made property into religious trusts (*awqāf*), and these could be primarily for one's own family. The expenses of the court were enormous, though this may not have been serious until the finances were in a bad condition.

The three factors mentioned are the most obvious ones contributing to the 'Abbāsid decline. Since the matter has not been fully studied, however, there may well be other factors, in particular some factors of a more general character. The whole course of events is worthy of being deeply pondered. One may ask, for example, whether the decline means a failure of the Islamic vision of a theocratic state, or whether the post-945 polity is simply a new application of that vision.

2

GROWING AUTONOMY IN THE PROVINCES

What was happening in the provinces was closely connected with what was happening at the centre. Weakness at the centre led to greater autonomy on the periphery, and this in turn produced financial stringency at the centre and greater weakness. Events in the provinces during the century of ʿAbbāsid decline were very complex, and all that can be attempted here is to give a general outline.

The eastern provinces

As noted in the previous chapter the first family in the east to gain some measure of autonomy were the Ṭāhirids, who ruled in Khurasan with Nishapur for their base. The last of the line, Muḥammad ibn-Ṭāhir II, was expelled from Nishapur in 873 by the founder of the Ṣaffārids, and this marked the end of the dynasty. Though in 885 Muḥammad was nominated governor again by the caliph, he lacked the military power to make himself governor in fact.

The Ṣaffārids were the family of Yaʿqūb ibn-Layth, known as aṣ-Ṣaffār, the coppersmith. He belonged to the province of Sistan or Sijistan, which covered part of eastern Persia and south-west Afghanistan. Defeated insurrectionaries from other parts of the empire had found refuge here and had turned to brigandage; and there was also local discontent. To make life tolerable an army was formed of volunteers from the local population, and Yaʿqūb was the leader of this. By about 867 Yaʿqūb had pacified Sistan, and was moving on the city of Herat which then belonged to the Ṭāhirids, and on to Kabul which was apparently still pagan. Because of his growing power the caliph assigned various governorships to him, and he sent rich presents to Baghdad. He defeated the governor of the province of Fārs in 869 and occupied Shiraz, the capital, but was unable to maintain himself there. In 873, as already mentioned, he occupied Nishapur and most of the remaining Ṭāhirid territory. In 875 he was once again in Fars, and after successes there moved on towards Baghdad. Only twelve miles from the capital he suffered a severe defeat at the hands of al-Muwaffaq, the regent (876). Yaʿqūb died in 879 before his negotiations with al-Muwaffaq were complete, but almost at once the regent recognized his brother ʿAmr, who succeeded him, as governor of all the territories he actually controlled.

This Ṣaffārid empire was short-lived, however. In 900 ʿAmr, trying to extend his rule into Transoxiana, was defeated and captured by the Sāmānid Ismāʿīl ibn-Aḥmad. The various conquests were lost, and only Sistan itself remained to the Ṣaffārids, though even that was under Sāmānid suzerainty and was sometimes occupied. In a remarkable way, however, the Ṣaffārid family maintained itself until nearly the end of the fifteenth century, and produced men who ruled Sistan as governors under Sāmānids, Ghaznavids, Seljuqs and Mongols, and who sometimes were almost autonomous.

The Sāmānids who thus replaced the Ṣaffārids were descended from a landowner in the district of Balkh called Sāmān-Khudā, who became a Muslim. Four grandsons served under al-Ma'mūn in the east, and were appointed governors of four parts of Transoxiana. In 875 the son of one of these, Naṣr ibn-Aḥmad, became governor of the whole of Transoxiana and worked hard at the defence of the whole fertile region against the attacks of Turkish tribes from the steppes. A successful expedition into the steppes in 893 by Ismāʿīl (who had succeeded his brother Naṣr) made it clear to the tribesmen that they could not attack Transoxiana with impunity. With secure provincial frontiers against the pagans and good internal government the Sāmānids had a strong basis for their rule. Though autonomous in practice, they loyally supported the ʿAbbāsid caliph, and were acknowledged by him as rulers of a large part of the Islamic east. After their capture of ʿAmr ibn-Layth in 900, the Ṣaffārids were reduced to the status of local rulers and became their subordinates, while their empire extended from the Indian border to Khurasan. The Sāmānid capital Bukhara became an important centre of Islamic learning (in Arabic) and at the same time contributed to the revival of the Persian language. The Sāmānid family regarded themselves as Persian, and claimed descent from the Sasanian dynasty; and they therefore encouraged writers to give expression to a new sense of Persian identity within Islam.

Apart from these powerful dynasties there were various families which for a time managed to rule a limited district with some measure of autonomy. One such family, the Ziyārids, were mountaineers from Daylam at the south-west of the Caspian Sea. The first of this family, Mardāvīj ibn-Ziyār, managed about 927 by the use of Turkish troops to gain control of much of northern Persia and of the west as far as Ispahan; but most of this was lost when he was assassinated in 935. Among his lieutenants were three Daylamite brothers, sons of Buwayh, ʿAlī, al-Ḥasan and Aḥmad, who then set about creating positions of power for themselves. ʿAlī already held Ispahan and extended his control over the province of Fars. Al-Ḥasan had Jibāl, the western highlands of Persia including Ispahan and Hamadhan. The third Aḥmad ruled Khuzistan (east of Basra), and, as already described, was able – acting in concert with his brothers – to enter Baghdad at the end of 945 and become *de facto* ruler of the centre of the caliphate. Thus was founded the Buwayhid dynasty.

Syria and northern Iraq

The Ḥamdānids were an Arab family from the tribe of Taghlib who rose to positions of influence through their skill as military commanders. Abū-l-Hayjā', a son of the Ḥamdān from whom the dynasty took its name, was appointed governor of Mosul by the caliph in 905, and served in this and other capacities until his death in 929. When his duties took him away from Mosul, he left the city in the charge of his son al-Ḥasan, and in 929 al-Ḥasan succeeded him. He received the honorific title of Nāṣir-ad-dawla and, as already mentioned, became one of the most influential men in the heartlands of the empire. After the establishment of the Buwayhids in Baghdad he contented himself with being ruler of the region of Mosul, except that he also extended his sway westwards into Syria. The Ḥamdānid forces there were commanded by his brother, known as Sayf-ad-dawla, who conquered Aleppo and Homs from the Ikhshīdids of Egypt. Sayf-ad-dawla held his court in Aleppo and became noted as a patron of literature. These Ḥamdānid princes were reckoned to be of Shīʿite sympathies, but their Shīʿism, whatever it comprised, must have been moderate, and there is no evidence that it affected their general policy.

Egypt

The date at which provincial governors attempted to become autonomous varied roughly according to their distance from Baghdad. Thus the first attempt at autonomy in Egypt is later than that in Tunisia and earlier than that in Mosul. In the ninth century it had become normal for the governor of Egypt to remain at the court in Baghdad or Samarra (and take part in the intrigues there) while the actual work of governing was left to a deputy. In 868 a Turkish officer Aḥmad ibn-Ṭūlūn was sent in this way to Egypt as deputy-governor. Because he was efficient, popular and determined to stay in Egypt, subsequent governors found it impossible to replace him. He soon gained control of the financial administration as well as the army, and merely paid a fixed sum as tribute each year to the central treasury. About 869 the caliph asked him to bring back Palestine to its due allegiance, and in 877, while the regent al-Muwaffaq was occupied with the rebellion of the Zenj, he took advantage of the death of the governor of Syria to add that province to the territories he controlled. The position of Ibn-Ṭūlūn was now such that in 882 the caliph al-Muʿtamid, wishing to free himself from the domination of his brother al-Muwaffaq, made an unsuccessful attempt to escape from Samarra and join Ibn-Ṭūlūn's army at ar-Raqqa on the Euphrates. This did not help relations between Ibn-Ṭūlūn and the regent, but the latter seems to have realized that Ibn-Ṭūlūn was too strong to be challenged.

When Ibn-Ṭūlūn died in 883 and was succeeded by his son Khumārawayh, al-Muwaffaq made several attempts to recover Syria and Palestine but, despite some successes, proved unable to maintain control there. In 886, therefore, he made a treaty assigning the governorship of Egypt and Syria together to the Ṭūlūnids for thirty years in return for a light tribute. Just before the death of Khumārawayh in 896 his daughter was married to the caliph al-Muʿtaḍid with great magnificence. Egypt had been remarkably prosperous under Ibn-Ṭūlūn, but it has been thought that his son dissipated his wealth by extravagance and brought the family into difficulties. Certainly the dynasty crumbled rapidly after 896, partly through internal quarrels. The failure of the régime to deal with the Carmathian rebels in Syria gave the caliph a reason for intervening in Syria, and his army after dealing with the Carmathians went on to occupy Egypt (905). This was the end of the Ṭūlūnids.

For some thirty years Egypt was now ruled by a governor duly subordinate to Baghdad, but in 935 another Turkish officer, Muḥammad ibn-Ṭughj, was appointed to the post, and in the difficult circumstances of the times managed to entrench himself securely as ruler of Egypt. A sign of his special position was the title of Ikhshīd conferred on him by the caliph, which apparently implies a degree of autonomy. The title was used in Central Asia in the sense of 'prince' or 'ruler'. Ibn-Ṭughj and his successors to 969 are known as the Ikhshīdids, though they hardly merit the name of 'dynasty'.

Though we now place Egypt and Syria in separate continents, it is worth noting that frequently in past history Syria, or at least the southern part of it, was united with Egypt under a single ruler, usually the ruler of Egypt. This may be due to the fact that the fertility of the Nile valley and the delta made this area potentially the basis of a powerful state, for which Syria was the most advantageous area of expansion. There was no comparable basis in Syria in the 'pre-industrial' world, though at times Iraq (which also had good fertility) was strong enough to make a bid for Syria.

North Africa and Spain

The position in North Africa in the year 850 was that the Aghlabids ruled the province of Ifrīqiya (Tunisia) and part of Sicily in the name of the ʿAbbāsids, though virtually independent. Further west were the Rustamids in western Algeria and the Idrīsids in Morocco, while Spain was under the surviving branch of the Umayyads. All these dynasties proceeded until 909 with the usual ups and downs as local problems worsened or grew less serious. In 909, however, a dynamic new factor entered the North African situation and completely changed the situation. This new factor was the establishment of a Fāṭimid state in Tunisia.

The movement which established this state was an underground one, whose earlier history, just because it was underground, is obscure. The Fāṭimid movement was a branch of the Ismāʿīlite form of Shīʿism which is so called because, while recognizing the same first six imams as the Imāmites – the sixth being Jaʿfar aṣ-Ṣādiq (d. 765) – it differs about the seventh. For the Imāmites he was Jaʿfar's son Mūsā al-Kāẓim, whereas for the Ismāʿīlites he was another son Ismāʿīl. It may be that during his lifetime Ismāʿīl was associated with underground revolutionary elements (and perhaps thereby incurred his father's displeasure); but it is more probable that the connection with Ismāʿīl was introduced at a later period, after the wide acceptance of the Imāmite theory of the twelve imams. In the first decades of the ʿAbbāsid period there was no unitary Shīʿite movement to be divided into followers of Mūsā and followers of Ismāʿīl. There were numerous people who could be described as being 'of Shīʿite sympathies', but they almost certainly held a great variety of different views on points of detail. We simply do not know how the group or groups out of which the Fāṭimid movement developed were related during the eighth century to other groups 'of Shīʿite sympathies', or indeed what they themselves believed. The name 'Fāṭimid' is not an obvious one to describe followers of Ismāʿīl, and might indicate that the movement split off from Zaydism rather than Imāmism.

Whatever may have been the earlier course of the movement, it emerged into the light of history at the end of the ninth century. An agent or missionary for the movement, called Abū-ʿAbd-Allāh, began work among the Kutāma Berbers of Tunisia about 893. By 909 he had so much support that he was able to expel the Aghlabid dynasty from their capital and make himself master of the province. Meanwhile a man called ʿUbayd-Allāh (and also Saʿīd), who was the recognized imam of the movement, made his way from Syria to Egypt to join the missionary, but was prevented from doing so, and found himself instead in Sijilmasa, perhaps as a prisoner. Abū-ʿAbd-Allāh, however, after his military successes had no difficulty in bringing ʿUbayd-Allāh to the former Aghlabid capital, where he was acknowledged as imam in January 910 with the titles of al-Mahdī ('the guided one' or messiah) and 'the commander of the faithful' (*amīr al-mu'minīn*).

This latter title marked a difference between the Fāṭimids and all the other local dynasties so far considered, even the Khārijite Rustamids. The Fāṭimids not merely rejected ʿAbbāsid rule but claimed that they themselves were the rightful rulers of the whole Islamic empire. Moreover they had certain resources for making a serious bid for universal empire. In Syria, the Yemen and other parts of the ʿAbbāsid domains there were underground groups belonging to their movement or not far removed from it in outlook. In North Africa their power soon became formidable. In 909 they expelled the Rustamid dynasty from Tahert, and in the first dozen years of their rule there were two unsuccessful expeditions against Egypt and a successful one against the Idrīsids of Morocco. There were many difficulties, however, in maintaining their control of these vast areas of North Africa; and in the period up to 945 they met with some reverses. The rest of the story belongs to the following chapters.

During the first half of the tenth century Umayyad Spain was at its zenith. In 912 a young man of twenty-one came to the throne as ʿAbd-ar-Raḥmān III, and by his energy and statesmanship solved the chief of the outstanding problems he had inherited and ushered in an era of internal peace and prosperity. From the very beginning of his reign ʿAbd-ar-Raḥmān must have been aware of the threat from the Fāṭimids. One dissident actually professed allegiance to them; and to begin with there was much discontent from which they might have profited, though there is nothing to show that they were ever a serious menace to the Umayyads in Spain itself. In Morocco and Algeria, however, their presence interfered with the diplomatic game which ʿAbd-ar-Raḥmān was increasingly able to play. In 929, therefore, ʿAbd-ar-Raḥmān assumed the titles of 'caliph' and 'commander of the faithful' and took the throne-name of 'an-Nāṣir li-dīn-Allāh'. This was not a claim to be ruler of all the Islamic lands but an assertion that he was independent of all higher Muslim authority. The local emirs of North Africa were given some grounds for acknowledging his suzerainty; and he himself and his court could feel that this new dignity was in keeping with his military and political achievements.

3

NEW FORMS OF SHĪʿISM

As has already been indicated at various points, an understanding of the growth of Shīʿism into its later forms is extremely difficult to acquire, since the later Shīʿites rewrote earlier history in the interests of their propaganda. In doing so they incorporated the assumption that the outlook of earlier times was identical with that of later times. The present section attempts to give a possible account of the development; but it must be emphasized that much in the account is provisional and that further critical research on the sources is required.

The Imāmites

Let us commence this account of the transformation of Imāmism in the decades round the year 900 by repeating some of the points already made.

Firstly, until the eleventh imam, al-Ḥasan al-ʿAskarī, died on or about 1 January 874, there was nothing to make people expect that the number of imams would be limited to twelve or that the twelfth would go into concealment. It follows that the theory of *twelve* imams was worked out after 874. Since it appears in the work on 'The Sects of the Shīʿa' by al-Ḥasan ibn-Mūsā an-Nawbakhtī, who died after 912, perhaps about 922, it must have been formulated before that date.

Secondly, the persons claimed by later ('Twelver') Imāmites as their spiritual ancestors – and who may have held some of their doctrines, though not the figure of *twelve* – were not revolutionaries, seeking to replace the 'Abbāsids by 'Alids, since they discussed their political views openly in the presence of the vizier and even of the caliph himself. It was argued in the previous chapter that they were advocating an 'autocratic' or 'absolutist' conception of the office of caliph, in which appointment to the office was, as it were, 'from above'.

Thirdly, during the ninth century there was no unified Shī'ite movement, but a large number of groups whose views differed to a greater or lesser extent from one another. An-Nawbakhtī in his book speaks of fourteen different groups after the death of al-Ḥasan al-'Askarī, and that comprises only those who acknowledged his imamate. There were also groups which expected the return of previous imams, and there were groups which were in some sense Zaydites or Ismā'īlites.

A further point which may now be made is that even near-contemporaries had no clear knowledge of the son of al-Ḥasan al-'Askarī. An-Nawbakhtī mentions three views: some held that the eleventh imam had no son; some held that his son was two years old when he died; and some held that his son was born posthumously.

In the light of these points the most likely view of what happened is that a group of astute politicians took advantage of the obscurity surrounding the son of the eleventh imam and also of the doubts about the character of another possible imam, his brother Ja'far. By boldly asserting the disappearance of the twelfth imam these politicians retained the loyalty of the believers in the eleventh imam and at the same time gained for themselves unfettered control of what may now be called the Imāmite movement. They had no longer to reckon with the possibility of interference from an imam whose actual political competence might be slight. In other words the Imāmite theory of twelve imams did not come into being of its own accord, as it were, following upon certain events known to all. The theory was an interpretation of selected events, and was deliberately created by politicians to further their own – perhaps very worthy – ends. The man chiefly responsible for the formulation of the theory and for its intellectual defence against other views was apparently Abū-Sahl an-Nawbakhtī (d. 923), an uncle of the writer of the book on the sects. Other men are mentioned as having in turn occupied the position of 'agent' (*wakīl*) of the eleventh imam. What is most impressive is that this group of men largely came to agree with one another, and also to get most of the moderates 'of Shī'ite sympathies' to accept their doctrine of the twelve imams.

The crucial question, however, is what this theory meant in terms of practical politics. Even in the years from 870 to 908 when the caliph's power still seemed to be intact, there would have been little point in replacing the 'Abbāsid family by that of their imams. Indeed an-Nawbakhtī's statement of Imāmite doctrine makes it clear that the leaders deprecated any attempt to envisage the return of the hidden imam in the foreseeable future. What the theory gave the Imāmite leaders, then, was a political party loyal to the existing régime but capable of being somewhat critical of it. The Imāmites thought of themselves as 'the élite' (*khāṣṣa*) and the Sunnites as 'the common people' (*'āmma*); and this is probably to be linked with the fact that several of the family of Nawbakht were experts in financial matters. It seems very likely therefore that the Imāmite sect was a political party whose aim was to promote the interests of the wealthier members of the community. There is admittedly an element of hypothesis here; but the chances are that a detailed study, with this hypothesis in mind, of the complex web of politics from 870 to 945 will show that its general lines are sound. The significance of Imāmism after 945 will be further considered in the next chapter.

At this period the Imāmites not merely worked out the doctrine of the twelve imams with its corollaries, but also laid the foundations of a distinctive system of law (usually known as Shī'ite or Ithnā-'asharite law). The leading scholar in this field was al-Kulīnī (d. 939), whose major work contains over 15,000 Traditions. The Traditions of the Imāmites differ from those accepted by the Sunnites in that the important name in each *isnād* is always that of one of their imams. Even if the imam heard the Tradition from someone else, it is the imam who is regarded as guaranteeing its soundness. From the Imāmite standpoint most of the Companions respected by the Sunnites were not authoritative, since they had preferred Abū-Bakr to 'Alī. Writers on Islamic law, such as N. J. Coulson, have pointed out important differences between Ithnā-'asharite and

Sunnite law; but further study is required to see whether these can be correlated with the social and class interests of the Imāmites.

Ismāʿīlism

The Imāmite theory of the twelve imams seems a neat and tidy theory until one begins to look into contemporary and near-contemporary material on the subject. If, as has been argued, the imams were not revolutionary leaders seeking to overthrow the ʿAbbāsids, what were they? Were they the heads of 'the family', meaning the descendants of ʿAlī, who had some special privileges and were recognized as a unit? Or had they really no position at all? On the whole, it would appear that there was no clear-cut recognition of the imams by their contemporaries. Consider the position in 765 on the death of Jaʿfar aṣ-Ṣādiq, the sixth imam, as described by an-Nawbakhtī. Some of his followers said that the imam was still Jaʿfar who was alive but in concealment; some said it was his son Ismāʿīl, who had appeared to die but was alive in concealment; some said it was Muḥammad, the son of Ismāʿīl; others said it was one of Jaʿfar's sons, Muḥammad, ʿAbd-Allāh or Mūsā. Some of these views may not actually have been held at the time, but may be later progagandist allegations about what happened in 765. Even so, it may be asserted that the situation in 765 was confused. It follows that the origin of Ismāʿīlism is not to be looked for in a single revolutionary movement which separated off from a unitary non-revolutionary movement acknowledging the imams up to date. One would rather expect that several, at first independent, revolutionary groups later came together.

There is indeed some evidence of this kind. Some groups looked back to a man called Abū-l-Khaṭṭāb, executed in 755, who had claimed to be an agent of Jaʿfar aṣ-Ṣādiq but had been repudiated by Jaʿfar. Other leaders were Mubārak and ʿAbd-Allāh ibn-Maymūn al-Qaddāḥ, who organized potentially revolutionary groups round the person of Muḥammad, son of Ismāʿīl. Another leader was Ḥamdān Qarmaṭ, who gave his name to the Carmathians (Qarāmiṭa). Some of these organized a propaganda mission (*daʿwa*) for their movement, and sent out 'missionaries' (*dāʿīs*). By the end of the ninth century there were groups professing Ismāʿīlism or something like it in Syria, Iraq, Persia, Bahrein and the Yemen, and known as Carmathians. Their mutual recognition of one another was doubtless the result of the work of the 'missionaries'. For example, there was a time when the revolutionary group in Bahrein looked to an imam from the descendants of the non-Fāṭimid son of ʿAlī, Muḥammad ibn-al-Ḥanafiyya.

The tensions which arose between the Carmathians of Bahrein and the Fāṭimids, especially after the conquest of Egypt by the latter, may be due to the fact that the Fāṭimids had greater responsibilities and took them seriously, but it may also reflect the independence of the two movements at an early period. It is not even clear what precise claims ʿUbayd-Allāh al-Mahdī made for himself in 909. All these points go to suggest that in 909, perhaps in 969, Ismāʿīlism was still in a fluid and embryonic state, and that the development of its definitive intellectual form was the work of scholars living under the Fāṭimids. Since the Fāṭimids accepted the first six imams of the Imāmites (though sometimes treating ʿAlī as higher in rank and making Jaʿfar aṣ-Ṣādiq fifth instead of sixth), it is possible that they were partly influenced by Imāmite theory. The most important early scholar was al-Qāḍī an-Nuʿmān (d. 974), from whose works one may gain some idea of Ismāʿīlite doctrine at this period, though he was mainly concerned with working out a system of law.

At various times and places – mainly where it was working as an underground movement – Ismāʿīlism established a kind of hierarchy of 'missionaries', where the chief *dāʿī* in a region had some control over the precise form of the propaganda there. We also hear of grades of initiation. In the lowest grade the teaching was at the level of ordinary men and not unlike Sunnite teaching. At the higher grades, however, philosophy was introduced, and educated men had the fullest scope for the use of their intellects in religious matters. In this way Ismāʿīlism made a contribution to the intellectual life of the Islamic world, even though Ismāʿīlite works were rarely read by Sunnites.

Zaydism

Shortly after the middle of the ninth century two small states were formed, one in Daylam at the south-west corner of the Caspian Sea and the other in the Yemen, which are classed as belonging to the

Zaydite branch of Shīʿism. The establishment of these states, however, implied a transformation of Zaydism from being a doctrine for the whole Islamic world to being one which gave a distinctive character to a small isolated community and marked it off from its neighbours. It was at this period that Zaydism was elaborated doctrinally and given a legal system. The founder of the state in the Yemen, al-Qāsim ibn-Ibrāhīm ar-Rassī (d. 860), also made an important intellectual contribution. It is not clear, however, how this developed form of Zaydism is related to the earlier and vaguer forms.

4

THE CONSOLIDATION OF SUNNISM

The period from 850 to 945 saw a process taking place which may be called 'the consolidation of Sunnism'. It was a complex process, which is perhaps best described as the extension of areas of agreement. There was no single set of theological doctrines or legal principles which was generally accepted; nor was there any single body or organization which resulted from the process. There was not even a word for 'Sunnites' at this period. The nearest was a phrase like 'Ahl as-Sunna' (the people of the Sunna), or elaborations of this like 'Ahl as-Sunna wa-l-Istiqāma' and 'Ahl as-Sunna wa-l-Jamā'a' (the people of the Sunna and uprightness, ... and the community). The last, however, was still being used as a party designation about the year 1000. In other words, various groups were moving closer together in fact, but none was yet ready to acknowledge the others as fellow-Sunnites.

The doctrines of the creed

Creeds occur in the Islamic world, but their function is different from the function of Christian creeds. There is no body in Islam comparable to the Christian ecumenical councils, which is capable of legislating on doctrinal matters. The Islamic creeds are therefore the statements of individuals, even though they may come to be regarded as authoritative within the man's theological or juristic school. Of those translated and discussed in *The Muslim Creed* by Arent Jan Wensinck, the *Waṣiyya* and *Al-Fiqh al-akbar II*, though ascribed to Abū-Ḥanīfa, were almost certainly composed by his followers at a much later date, possibly about 850 and 925 respectively. We possess another Ḥanafite creed of the same time, that of aṭ-Ṭaḥāwī, who died in 933 at the age of eighty. Credal statements by Aḥmad ibn-Ḥanbal have been preserved in a biographical dictionary, and there are two versions of the creed of al-Ashʿarī (d. 935). Thus the material is plentiful.

At first sight one is struck with the differences between these creeds, even between creeds from the same school. This is only natural, since these documents came from groups of theologians who were busy arguing with other groups of theologians; and thus the points in dispute were bound to be mentioned. Further examination, however, shows that there is also an area of agreement; and this area of agreement might be said to express the heart of Sunnism. Thus they are all agreed that the Qur'ān is the uncreated speech of God, though they differ over whether man's utterance of the Qur'ān is created or uncreated. From this some go on to discuss the attributes of God, such as his speech, power or omnipotence, will, hearing; and though they disagree in details, they agree that God has attributes distinct from his essential being and is not a bare unity. They are also agreed that God must in some sense will everything that happens, but the Ḥanafites tend at the same time to place more emphasis on man's responsibility than does al-Ashʿarī.

In some ways the most important article in the creed is one we occidentals would not regard as theological at all, namely, that the best (or most excellent) in the community after Muḥammad is Abū-Bakr, then ʿUmar, then ʿUthmān, then ʿAlī. Yet this is the article which defines Sunnism over against Shīʿism. Both Imāmites and Zaydites say that ʿAlī was best and most excellent, though the Zaydites allow that Abū-Bakr despite his inferiority was truly imam. Until about 850 too, it may be noted, even Sunnites were not agreed that ʿUthmān was third, since some put ʿAlī above him.

The Qur'ānic sciences

The study of the text of the Qur'ān made an important advance in the early tenth century by the official recognition of 'the seven readings' as alone authoritative. To the inexperienced in these matters it may seem strange that seven different ways of reading the text of the Qur'ān should be regarded as equally authoritative, when we would have imagined there ought only to be one. It has to be remembered, however, that when the Qur'ān was first written down, perhaps in part during the Prophet's lifetime, or perhaps shortly afterwards, the system of writing used was defective in various ways. For one thing it represented consonants only without any vowels, except that sometimes letters like W and Y might represent a long vowel or diphthong. It is as if one were given the letters BRD and had to decide whether this was BiRD, BoReD, BRooD or BuRieD. To make matters worse, in the oldest writing of all, two or more consonants might be represented by the same sign. Thus writing down was, to begin with, little more than a mnemonic device to help one to remember exactly what one already knew by heart.

Though the Qur'ān may have been written down in part in Muḥammad's lifetime, devout Muslims normally knew by heart large sections of it, and did not rely on writing. This led to the existence of the variants which were excluded by the text produced about 650 on the authority of the caliph 'Uthmān. This text was written down, but in the most defective form of script. Gradually the script was improved, as we can now illustrate from the earliest copies of the Qur'ān. Dots were added to distinguish letters, signs were added for short vowels, and various diacritical marks were used to indicate the doubling of consonants and other varieties of pronunciation. It was towards the end of the ninth century before a complete script was in use. By this time, however, other variant readings had appeared. Most (but not all) of these followed the authoritative text in respect of the consonants but differed in the vowels; and this led to divergences, which were usually trifling as far as the sense went, but could be annoying when verses were being repeated together in public worship. Early in the tenth century a scholar called Ibn-Mujāhid (d. 935) realized that it was no longer possible to have complete agreement, and selected seven sets of readings which seemed to be equally acceptable. These sets of readings were the work of earlier scholars, three from Kufa and one each from Mecca, Medina, Damascus and Basra. Ibn-Mujāhid's seven readings were not immediately accepted by all scholars, but before his death a court gave support to his views by condemning another scholar who claimed that he might read the consonantal text in any way that accorded with grammar and gave a reasonable sense. Thus the early tenth century saw the wide acceptance of a more or less uniform text of the Qur'ān – a consummation of the work of several generations of textual scholars.

About the same date there appeared a massive work which in a slightly different way summed up the achievements of the interpreters and exegetes of the Qur'ān during the previous centuries. This is the *Tafsīr* or 'Commentary' of aṭ-Ṭabarī, which in one printed edition occupies thirty volumes. It deals separately with every verse and with nearly every phrase, giving full accounts of the occasion on which a passage was revealed and of the incidents referred to, and mentioning important textual variants. The bulk of it, however, is occupied by the quotation, with full references, of the interpretations of a verse given by the leading scholars of the past. It is now thought that aṭ-Ṭabarī derived most of this information from written sources. He is far from being a mere compiler, however, for he has been selective in the choice of sources, rejecting much unsatisfactory material altogether; where earlier scholars differ, he shows how their views may be reconciled or else gives reasons for preferring one of the views. In short, he has made a distinctive personal contribution and at the same time preserved most of what was worth preserving of the work of previous scholars.

The career of this remarkable man deserves a brief mention. More fully his name is Muḥammad ibn-Jarīr aṭ-Ṭabarī, and he was born in 839 in the province of Ṭabaristān at the south of the Caspian Sea. He studied in Syria and Egypt, as well as in Basra, Kufa and Baghdad, eventually settling in the last. He is said to have heard lectures by Aḥmad ibn-Ḥanbal, which is just possible chronologically, but in law he first belonged to the school of ash-Shāfiʿī. After a time, however, he diverged from that school and founded his own school, known as the Jarīriyya, but it lasted for only one or two generations. He is even said to have made some study of the 'foreign sciences' of medicine and mathematics. His major work, however, probably more important than his Qur'ān-commentary, was a vast *History of the World*. This included Biblical history, traditional Persian history, some material about pre-Islamic Arabia, the life of the Prophet, and then – by far the greater part of the work – all that was most significant in the records of the affairs of the Muslims and the Islamic state. He died in Baghdad in 923.

The Traditions of the Prophet

In the study of Traditions also the period from 850 to 945 was one of consolidation. By the year 850 many thousands of anecdotes about Muḥammad were in circulation, and scholars like Aḥmad ibn-Ḥanbal were well aware of the need for a critique of these anecdotes to distinguish those which were sound and authentic from the false. As indicated in the previous chapter, the critique practised was one based essentially on the credentials of the transmitters. By about 850 there was a wide consensus of scholars that this type of critique was satisfactory, and some men therefore set about making collections of 'sound Traditions'. Among the early collections were two of the greatest, those of al-Bukhārī (d. 870) and Muslim (d. 875). Each is called *Al-Jāmi' aṣ-ṣaḥīḥ*, which might be rendered 'The Sound Collection', and is divided into 'books' or chapters, each of which contains the sound Traditions relevant to a topic of concern to the jurists (though this, of course, includes questions of ritual and theology).

During the next half-century four other collections were made which came to be regarded, along with the first two, as specially reliable. There were *Al-Jāmi' aṣ-ṣaḥīḥ* of at-Tirmidhī (d. 892), and three, by Ibn-Māja (d. 886), Abū-Dāwūd (d. 888) and an-Nasā'ī (d. 915), each called *Sunan*, that is, the Sunnas or practices, sc. of Muḥammad. These were by no means the only collections that were made about this time, but these, often called 'the six books', came to be highly regarded by large numbers of scholars. They are sometimes referred to by European scholars as 'canonical', but there was never any official statement to this effect, and indeed no body capable of making such a statement. The six books approved themselves gradually by their own merits; even in the fourteenth century there were a few scholars who questioned the complete reliability of Ibn-Māja.

In the nineteenth century European scholars liked to point out that among the 'sound Traditions' there were many which were almost certainly unhistorical according to modern ideas of objective history. This is possibly true, but for many purposes it is irrelevant. It is more important to ask what was contributed to Islamic society by this great effort of transmitting and criticizing Traditions. To this question the answer is that the corpus of Traditions contained in the 'six books' is the basis of the laws, practices and modes of conduct found acceptable by the Islamic community of the heartlands in the earlier part of the ninth century. This documentary basis gave a certain stability to Islamic practice and so to the structure of Islamic society. It allowed for some variation in detail, though it discouraged change. Above all, however, it excluded undesirable deviations. It thus determined to a great extent the character of the day-to-day life of Sunnite Muslims, and encouraged the trend to homogeneity. The difference between Sunnite Islam and the forms of Shīʿism mentioned is perhaps more in this practical field than in the doctrinal.

The legal schools or rites

The period from 850 to 945 witnessed the last attempts to form new legal schools. Although Aḥmad ibn-Ḥanbal died in 855, the Ḥanbalite school does not seem to have taken shape until after that date. Mention has also been made of the Jarīrite school, founded by the historian and Qur'ān-commentator aṭ-Ṭabarī (d. 923), which lasted only for about a couple of generations. Less ephemeral was the school founded a little earlier by Dāwūd ibn-ʿAlī (d. 884) and known as the Ẓāhirite school. It was so called because it claimed that particular rules should be based only on the *ẓāhir*, the 'literal and evident' meaning of Qur'ān and Traditions. Latterly it is chiefly in Spain that we hear of the Ẓāhirite school, but there were one or two adherents of it in Syria and Egypt until the fourteenth and fifteenth centuries.

The ending of the formation of new legal systems among the Sunnites may perhaps be taken as the beginning of another process by which the various schools or systems or rites came to be regarded as equally valid. In Arabic the Ḥanafites, Mālikites, Shāfiʿites, Ḥanbalites and the minor groups are each spoken of as a *madhhab*, and the word has so far usually been rendered as 'school'. This is appropriate in so far as each is based on a slightly different view of the principles of jurisprudence. Each *madhhab*, however, also has its distinctive practices, from detailed rules for inheritance to the details of the ritual words and acts of public worship or prayer; and from this point of view it is conveniently called a 'rite'. Nowadays, as has been the case for some centuries, each individual belongs to a specific rite (of the four named above), performs the prayer according to the forms of this rite, and when he dies has his inheritance distributed according to the rules of this rite. Usually the people of a region belong to the same rite; but in cosmopolitan cities men of different rites rubbed shoulders and became embroiled in disputes, which had to be brought before the courts. There were then further rules about which rite was to be the basis of the court's decision; and judges became qualified to give decisions according to more than one rite.

Mutual acceptance of one another by the various rites came about only slowly. The classical statement on mutual recognition is taken to be one by ash-Sha'rānī written about 1530. His basic point is that God permits 'latitude of interpretation' in that the fundamental principles have to be elaborated and applied to particular situations by the exercise of man's independent judgement; and thus the rules in the various Sunnite rites are permissible expressions of the same Sharī'a. Long before this, however, a saying had been attributed to Muḥammad (though not in the canonical collections) to the effect that 'diversity in my community is a mercy [from God]'. Indeed this statement, though not ascribed to Muḥammad, occurs in a short creed probably composed by Abū-Ḥanīfa himself. At that date it could not apply to the legal rites, but might be attempting to say that the differences on points of law between the schools in the various cities were better than the legal uniformity which the central government seems to have tried to impose.

The mutual recognition of the rites doubtless went hand in hand with the development of the concept of Sunnism, and the mutual recognition of different groups of Sunnites. It was aided also by the common acceptance of 'the six books' and of the discipline of 'the roots of law' (principles of jurisprudence). To some extent, then, the legal aspect of Sunnism was beginning to assume its definitive form by 945.

5

INTELLECTUAL CURRENTS OF THE AGE

The period of nearly a century being considered in this chapter, though marked by the decline of caliphal power and by political troubles of various kinds, was one of advance and achievement in intellectual life and is not unfittingly at the centre of what has been called the Golden Age of Arabic literature. Here it is possible to mention only the main features of the period.

The maturing of Arabic prose literature

Though philology continued to be studied, the great achievement of the philologists had been accomplished before the middle of the ninth century, namely, the creation of a linguistic vehicle worthy of a great civilization. The next step was to find appropriate contents for works in the language. In the early ʿAbbāsid period there had been many translations from Pahlevi or adaptations of Persian material, and, had this trend become dominant, it would have threatened the specifically Arab basis of Islamic civilization. The reversal of the trend is due above all to two men, al-Jāḥiẓ and Ibn-Qutayba.

Abū-ʿUthmān ʿAmr ibn-Baḥr, known by the nickname of al-Jāḥiẓ, 'the goggle-eyed', was born in Basra, probably a little before 780. His blood was largely African, but he was a client of the Arab tribe of Kināna and felt himself an Arab. He studied under the most distinguished philologists then lecturing in Basra, though study may have been difficult because of his poverty – he is said for a time to have made a living by selling fish. It is not clear, however, how he acquired all his learning or how he embarked on a literary career. In later life he lived in Baghdad for a time and was in touch with court circles. This last may have been achieved through his association with certain Muʿtazilites. He himself was reckoned a Muʿtazilite and a pupil of the Basran Muʿtazilite an-Naẓẓām, and he and his followers are sometimes said to constitute a sub-sect. He was in Baghdad during the period of Muʿtazilite ascendancy at court, but managed to retain his position even after al-Mutawakkil's change of policy. He retired to Basra and died there in 869.

A number of his writings deal with questions in theology from a Muʿtazilite standpoint, and others with related political questions, including the defence of the ʿAbbāsids against ʿAlid and other opponents. Because of these he may have received a monthly pension from the caliph. The most important part, however, of the voluminous work of al-Jāḥiẓ consists of his cultivation and extension of the category of *adab*. This has been described as a literary genre comprising works which combine entertainment and instruction. The word *adab* meant originally something like 'manners'; and the books of *adab* by earlier writers like Ibn-al-Muqaffaʿ aimed primarily at giving guidance to members of the secretarial class in the performance of their duties. The contents ranged from general maxims for administrators and information of practical importance to details of court ceremonial, but the whole was in a very readable form with abundance of anecdotes. The trouble with the earlier works of *adab* was that most of the material came from the Persian tradition. One of the great services of al-Jāḥiẓ was to produce books of *adab* in which Arab materials were predominant, though he was also ready to borrow from the other traditions known to him – Persian, Indian and Greek. At the same time he extended the genre to include works mainly for entertainment, such as his seven-volume *Book of Animals*, which is not a treatise on zoology, but a collection of anecdotes, proverbs, verses and items of folk-lore about the various animals.

Ibn-Qutayba came from an arabized Persian family and was born at Kufa in 828. He studied under various distinguished philologists, Traditionists and jurists, and from about 851 to 870 was judge of

Dīnavar, a town to the east of Baghdad in the Zagros mountains of Persia. He may have owed this appointment to the fact that he had become the literary spokesman for the type of theologico-political view most in favour in court circles after 'the change of policy' at the beginning of al-Mutawakkil's reign. His views were not far from those of Aḥmad ibn-Ḥanbal, but he differed on the question of the 'utterance' of the Qur'ān. While his contributions to theology may have been underestimated by recent writers, it remains true that his chief achievements were in the field of *adab*. His greatest work is usually reckoned to be *The Fountains of Story*, a collection of literary materials not unlike *The Book of Animals*, but arranged under such headings as sovereignty, war, the greatness of great men, fasting, friendship, food and women. As in the writings of al-Jāḥiẓ Arab materials were predominant, but Ibn-Qutayba's style had greater simplicity and clarity and became the model for most later Arabic prose. Despite his Persian origin he opposed the Shuʿūbites and wrote an essay in praise of the Arabs. For the secretaries he produced a manual of philology, a biographical anthology of Arabic poetry, and a handbook of history which is almost exclusively Arab and Islamic. He settled in Baghdad about 871 and lectured there until his death in 889.

The end-result of the work of al-Jāḥiẓ and Ibn-Qutayba was that the Shuʿūbite movement faded away, and it seemed to be tacitly agreed that Islamic religious thinking should have as its complement or perhaps rather substructure an Arabic humane literature which gave a picture of the secular world as seen through Arab (including Muslim-Arab) eyes. Such was the success of Arab self-assertion in the humanities. It is not surprising that it was in ultra-Arab Umayyad Spain that a work was produced parallel to, and in popular favour even in the east superseding, *The Fountains of Story*; this was *The Unique Necklace* by Ibn-ʿAbd-Rabbihi (860–940). One can see the influence of *adab* even in a historical compilation like *The Golden Meadows* by al-Masʿūdī (d. 956). Though most of this book follows the order of the caliphs reign by reign, giving a chapter to each, the author is more interested in anecdotes and quotable verses than in history in any more restricted sense.

Perhaps it was because so much creative effort was going into prose writing that there was no outstanding poetry in this period. There was argument about the respective merits of the 'ancients' and the 'moderns', and attempts to find some sort of synthesis. The 'Abbāsid prince, caliph for a day, Ibn-al-Mu'tazz wrote, besides a book on poetics, a great quantity of verse in which he experimented with innovations in technique; but in the end the conventions of Arabic poetry were little changed.

History and geography

Historical writing was one of the branches of study in which there was a significant advance during the period under survey, and this was particularly the case with histories of the Islamic state and world histories. Mention has already been made of the great *History* of aṭ-Ṭabarī, of which the main part deals with the Islamic state or states and preserves a judicious selection of the divergent accounts of previous historians. In the case of most events aṭ-Ṭabarī's own view is discernible, but the reader is not forced into accepting it. Like his Qur'ān-commentary this history is a kind of consummation of all the previous work on the subject.

Two older men, however, are also historians of importance. Of the life of one, al-Balādhurī, little is known. He was probably born before 820 and is thought to have died in 892. He spent most of his life in Baghdad, and mixed in court circles in the reign of al-Mutawakkil. Apart from a large collection of historical and biographical materials genealogically arranged, he is known for his account of the Islamic conquests. This is arranged province by province, beginning with Arabia and Syria, then dealing fairly fully with the conquests westwards to North Africa and Spain, southwards into Nubia, and finally eastwards, but only as far as the western provinces of Persia.

The other, al-Ya'qūbī (d. 897), lived as a young man in Armenia, then had offices under the Ṭāhirids in Khurasan until they lost power, and finally settled in Egypt. His *History* is of great interest as being a history of the whole world. A longish opening section deals with Biblical history from Adam to Jesus. Then come lists of kings of Nineveh, Babylon, India, the Greeks, the Romans, China, Egypt and several minor places or peoples. In the middle of this is a long account – almost as long as all the lists of kings together – of Greek science and scientific works. The first part, which is about a third of the whole, concludes with material about pre-Islamic Arabia. The second part is a sketch, without mentioning sources, of Islamic history from the birth of Muḥammad until about the year 872.

The interesting thing here is that the Muslims are now forming an idea of their own significance in world history. Because Islam came into being on the periphery of the regions influenced by Judaism and Christianity, and then conquered some of the main lands where these religions flourished, it was natural to take over Biblical history and make this the basis of the earlier part of world-history. Aṭ-Ṭabarī had a wider knowledge of Persian history and fitted this into the chronological scheme provided by Biblical history. For the rest of the world no clear chronological scheme was available, and on the whole Muslims had little interest in these 'lesser breeds without the Law'. For the Roman empire they mentioned only the names of the emperors and the length of their reigns; the latter was presumably for chronological comparisons. The centre of attention was the Qur'ānic picture of world-history, arranged and expanded according to the Bible and other Jewish and Christian books. The pre-Islamic tradition of Persia was doubtless included because the Persians had become Muslims and constituted a prominent section of Islamic society. Above all, however, the Islamic state is seen as the culmination of world-history, with Islam as the final form of religion and the Islamic community as the leading part of all mankind.

The study of geography began in the ninth century, and indeed the historian al-Yaʿqūbī is sometimes reckoned as primarily a geographer. It was clearly necessary for men responsible for running a vast empire to have some knowledge of the various provinces and of the relative positions of the main centres of population. There was also, however, some genuine curiosity. To al-Yaʿqūbī's account of the kings of China, for example, he adds some strange facts about the land and the people. Several travel books appeared in the tenth century and were widely read. About 916 there was published a book allegedly based on a voyage to India and China made by a merchant called Sulaymān about 851. In 921–2 an ambassador was sent by the caliph al-Muqtadir to the prince of the Volga Bulgars, and this man, who was keenly observant, wrote an account of his journey. In 942 the Sāmānid ruler in Bukhara detailed one of his court to accompany a Chinese embassy back to China; and he too wrote an account of his journey and of his return through India. The book of *The Marvels of India*, written about 953 by a Persian sea-captain and based on the tales of other tenth-century sailors, also deals with the East Indies. In such ways the Muslims were forming an idea of their position not only in time but also in space.

The maturing of rational theology

The beginnings of Kalām or rational theology were described in the previous chapter (pp. 137–140). By 850 the most creative thinkers among the Muʿtazilites were dead, and the group was on the point of losing its special position at court as a result of 'the change of policy', especially the abandonment of the Miḥna. In both Basra and Baghdad, however, the Muʿtazilites continued to exist as a group, but their theology was now much more academic. At the same time there was strong opposition, mostly in Traditionist and Ḥanbalite circles, to the whole discipline of Kalām and the application of reason to doctrinal questions; and in justification of this opposition it has to be admitted that from a strict Sunnite point of view some of the *doctrines* of certain rational theologians were objectionable as well as their methods. During the ninth century, however, a number of men were attempting to use the rational methods of Kalām to defend doctrines which were more or less Sunnite, although in the absence of a concept of development it was difficult for later Muslim scholars to appreciate the contribution of such men, and hence little detailed information about them has been preserved.

What came to be the standard account was that the application of the methods of Kalām to a Sunnite doctrinal position was primarily the work of al-Ashʿarī. This al-Ashʿarī was born in Basra about 873 and studied among others under al-Jubbā'ī (d. 915), the head of the Muʿtazilites of Basra at the time. Al-Ashʿarī was one of his best pupils, and it was thought he might have succeeded his master (though al-Jubbā'ī also had a very intelligent son). At some point, however – reputedly at about the age of forty, but that may be a conventional figure – al-Ashʿarī experienced a 'conversion'. He is said to have become dissatisfied with the Muʿtazilite attempt to explain rationally all the vagaries of human destiny, and to have challenged his master with the problem of the three brothers, of whom one was good, one wicked and one died as a child. The usual Muʿtazilite view was that the first was in Heaven, the second in Hell, and the third in a kind of limbo, since he had had no opportunity to perform good works and acquire merit. Some Muʿtazilites tried to say that God caused the third to die as a child because he knew that, if he had grown up, he would have become wicked and gone to Hell; but this lays them open to the retort, 'Why did not God cause the second to die before he became wicked?'

The actual 'conversion' is said to have come about during the month of Ramaḍān through three dreams. The accounts vary in detail, but there seem to have been three stages. In the first dream the Prophet appeared to him and told him to follow true Traditions. The second dream may have had something to do with doubts about particular doctrines. After it al-Ashʿarī abandoned Kalām completely. The Prophet appeared for a third time, however, and said that he had not told him to give up Kalām but only to follow true Traditions. Al-Ashʿarī then devoted the remainder of his life – he died in 935 – to the defence by the methods of Kalām of a Ḥanbalite form of Sunnite doctrine. Though he admired Aḥmad ibn-Ḥanbal and claimed to follow him, the Ḥanbalites in their hostility to the use of reason would having nothing to do with him.

At about the same time in distant Samarkand a theological school consisting of men of the Ḥanafite legal rite were moving towards a somewhat similar result. The leading figure here was al-Māturīdī (d. 944), who was almost an exact contemporary of al-Ashʿarī. The two men are often spoken of as the joint founders of Sunnite rational theology, and from what we possess of the works of the two men it is clear that there is much justification for this idea. The two men had been dead for centuries, however, before the idea of their parallel roles found expression. Before the year 1000 the Māturīdites in Samarkand knew something of the teaching of the Ashʿarites in Iraq, though considering it inferior to their own. The Ashʿarites at the centre of the empire, however, did not deign to pay any attention to the 'provincials'; and the first references to the two men together seem to come about the middle of the fourteenth century.

Despite silences and disparaging remarks due to *odium theologicum* or some such feeling these two men really made important contributions to the intellectual life of Islam. The Greek concepts and methods of argument which had been taken over by the Muʿtazilites and their predecessors were now mostly brought into the main stream of Sunnite thinking, and rational theology had established its *droit de cité* within Islam. As will be seen later, however, in connection with al-Ghazālī, this was not the final stage. Indeed already al-Fārābī (d. 950), a contemporary of al-Ashʿarī and al-Māturīdī, had committed himself to the philosophical system of Neoplatonism, and was giving an original presentation of it in Arabic in a semi-Islamic form; but this will more conveniently be dealt with later.

Ṣūfism

From the very beginning asceticism – the attempt to attain a certain moral perfection through strenuous efforts of self-discipline – had had a strong attraction for Muslims. The most distinguished ascetic during the first Islamic century was al-Ḥasan al-Baṣrī, but there were many others. Towards the middle of the ninth century there developed out of the ascetic movement an interest in mysticism proper, that is, in experiences which might be described as ecstasy, union with God, 'passing away [*fanā'*] into God', and the like. Al-Muḥāsibī (d. 857), who is primarily an ascetic who laid emphasis on self-examination, had had profound experiences of the love of God and could speak of him as 'the Beloved'. A little later Abū-Yazīd al-Bisṭāmī (d. 875), who possibly knew something of Indian mysticism, was so carried away by his ecstatic experiences that he burst into 'intoxicated' utterances (identifying himself with God) such as 'Glory be to Me! How great is my Majesty!' Another 'drunkard' was al-Ḥallāj (d. 922), who said 'I am the Truth' (or 'the ultimate Reality'); it has been vigorously maintained that this can be given a 'sober' or non-blasphemous meaning, though the first impression is that it is tantamount to saying 'I am God'. Al-Ḥallāj travelled widely and had great success as a popular preacher, so that some of the authorities were alarmed and had him arrested and tried. The charge was apparently *zandaqa* in the sense of 'false belief prejudicial to the state', and he was eventually condemned and executed by crucifixion.

By about 900 there was a group or school of mystics in Baghdad with associates elsewhere. The word *ṣūfī* came to be given to such persons and developed into the normal Arabic word for 'mystic'; it was derived in the first place from the wearing of garments of wool (*ṣūf*). The ṣūfī movement spread to most parts of the Islamic world, and from the thirteenth century was organized in the dervish or ṣūfī orders. The movement was thus an important aspect of Islamic society. In the early period especially it also contributed to theological thinking, since their personal experiences gave the ṣūfīs greater confidence in approaching fresh theological problems. Al-Muḥāsibī was one of the first to attempt a refutation of the Muʿtazilites.

It is also of interest to consider why there should have been this outburst of mysticism in the ninth century. One possible reason is the deterioration of the quality of political life at the centre with the coming of the Turkish troops. It might be thought that, because men were no longer able to engage meaningfully in political activity, they turned to the cultivation of the inner life. It seems more likely, however, that this was a reaction to the success of the Islamic religious institution in controlling the whole of a Muslim's outward life, and even much of his thinking. Religion, by offering Muḥammad as an exemplar, controlled the ordinary man's daily conduct; and religion, at least to all appearances, controlled the highest political authority. Yet this very success meant that religion had become this-worldly and had lost the aspect of transcendence. Al-Ma'mūn's Inquisition had showed that the ulema were subordinate to the politicians. Aḥmad ibn-Ḥanbal's refusal to accept a position at court even under al-Mutawakkil was probably not just a political gesture but an assertion that religion was something more than the this-worldly. Thus there are grounds for thinking that in its origins ṣūfism was essentially an assertion of the dimension of transcendence.

List of Illustrations

We are grateful to the following for permission to reproduce the illustrations:

Popperfoto 1, 2; Paul Elek 3, 7a, 7b, 21, 22; Edinburgh University Library 4; A. F. Kersting 5, 14, 18; Librairie Larousse 6; Institut Francais d'Archeoligie de Beyrouth 9, 10; Israel Dept. of Antiquities and Museums 8; Dayton International 11, 24, 28; Editions Arthaud 12, 13, 20; Photo Hassia 15; Harrison 16; John Hilleson 17; Aerofilms 23, 25; Staatliche Museen zu Berlin 26; Library and Archives, Weidenfeld and Nicolson Ltd 27; Productions du Dragon 31; Roger-Viollet 29, 30, 33; John Donat 32; Hamlyn Group Picture Library 34.

Fig. 1. The Kaʿba

Fig. 3. The mosque at Medina

Fig. 5. Damascus – the interior of the Umayyad mosque

Fig. 6. Detail of mosaics in the Umayyad mosque

Fig. 7a. The Syrian desert

Fig. 7b. A nomadic encampment in the Syrian desert

a. detail from a floor

b. window decoration

Fig. 8. Decorations from Umayyad palaces

c. ceiling decoration

Fig. 9. An Umayyad palace (Kasr al-Hayr)

Fig. 10. Aleppo – the citadel

Fig. 11. Aleppo – the mosque

Fig. 12. The mosque at Hebron

Fig. 13. A typical view of Egypt

Fig. 14. The mosque of Ibn-Ṭūlūn in Cairo

Fig. 15. The nave of the mosque of Ibn-Ṭūlūn

Fig. 16. Cairouan – a minaret

Fig. 18. Cairo – a Fatimid gate and wall

Fig. 20. Medinat az-Zahr

Fig. 19. Minaret at Rabat

Fig. 21. The mosque of Cordova – the mihrab

Fig. 22. The mosque of Cordova – oratory of al-Ḥakam II

Fig. 23. Ctesiphon

Fig. 24. Ukhaydir

Fig. 25. Aerial view of Samarra

Fig. 26. The minaret at Samarra

Fig. 27. Samarra – ruins of a palace

Fig. 28. The Mustansiriyya at Baghdad

Fig. 29. The dome of Malik-Shah at Isfahan

Fig. 33. Qanat (underground water-channel)

Fig. 35. (opposite) An astro

Fig. 34. An Umayyad bronze ewer

'ig. 30. (opposite) *Gunbad-i-Kabus*

Fig. 31. Bukhara – the Mausoleum of the Samanids

Fig. 32. A Persian landscape

Fig. 36. A piece of Buwayhid silk

Fig. 37. A bronze griffin (Fatimid)

Fig. 38.
Medallion of Caliph al-Mutawakkil – with dromedary

Fig. 40. The Caliph ʿAbd-al-Malik

39. Medallion with
e and effigy of Caliph al-Mutawakkil

Fig. 41. Effigy of Heraclius and his sons

Fig. 42. Effigy of King Khôsro

Examples of Arabic calligraphy

Fig. 43. 'Praise be to God' in a 'chessboard' arrangement

Fig. 44. The Bismillah and the Shahada

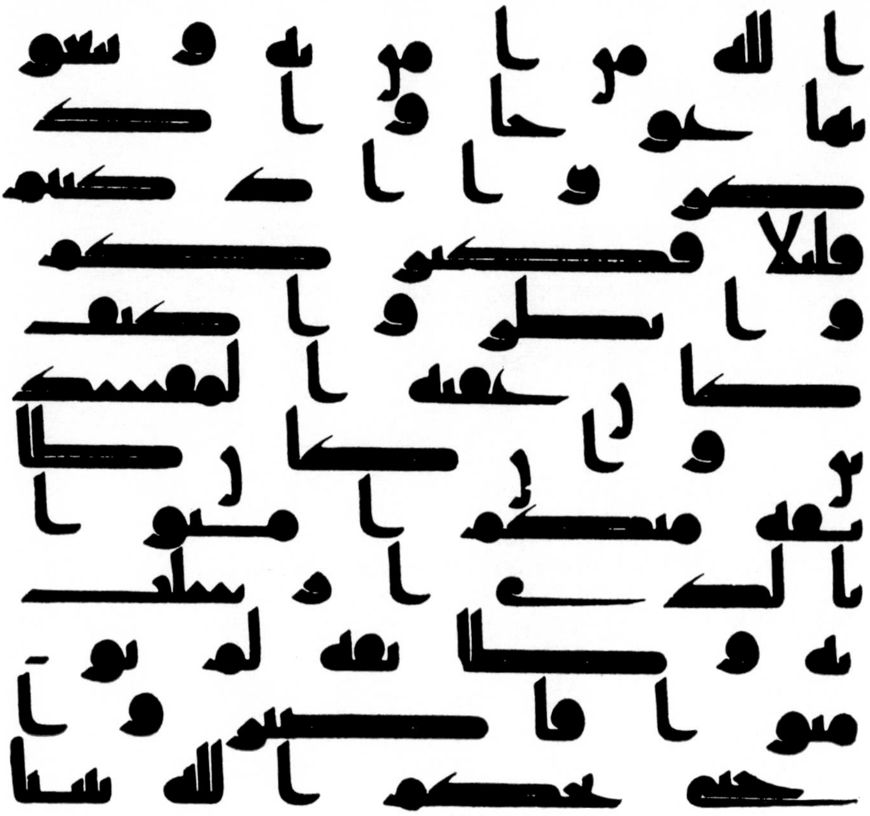

Fig. 45. An early form of writing without diacritical marks

الحمد لله وحده عشرة معجزات من النبي صلى الله عليه
وسلم من علق في بيته لم تحترق بالنار وان وضعها في النار
خمدت باذن الله تعالى اولها لم يظهر ظله على الارض
قط وثانيها لم يظهر بوله على الارض قط وثالثها لم يتثوب قط
ورابعها لم يحتلم قط وخامسها لم ينزل عليه الذباب
قط وسادسها تنام عيناه ولا ينام قلبه وسابعها يرى من خلفه
كما يرى من امامه وثامنها لم تنفر منه الدواب اذا ركب
وتاسعها ولد صلى الله عليه وسلم مختونا وعاشرها اذا جلس بين
قوم كان كتفه اعلاهم صلى الله عليه وعلى اله اجمعين
الفقير السيد الحاج احمد العارف غفر له لسنة اثنا عشر وثلثمائة

Fig. 46. Alternate lines in the styles known as Thuluth and Naskh

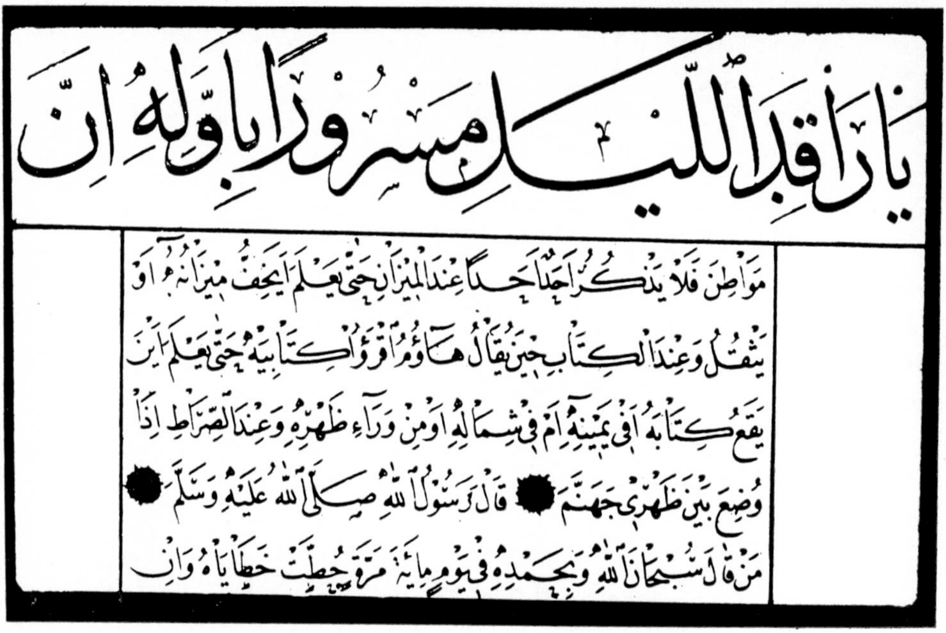

Fig. 47. Another combination of the Thuluth and Naskh styles

Fig. 48. A verse about wisdom in decorative form

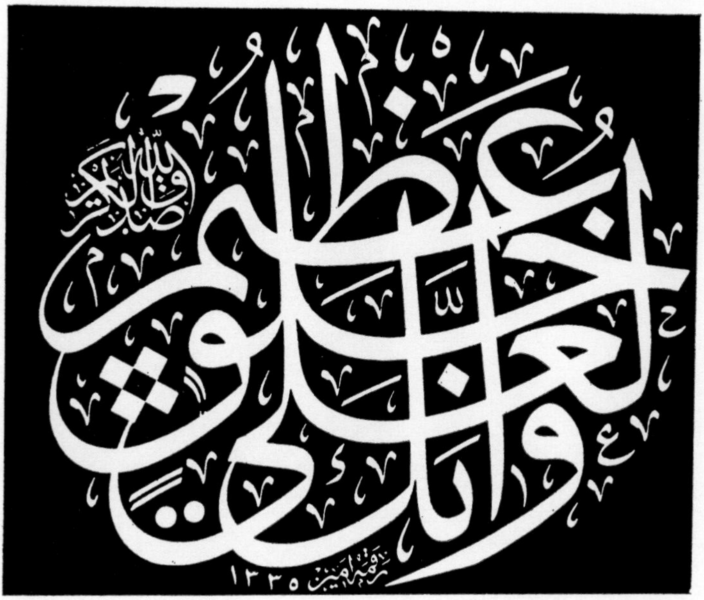

Fig. 49. A verse of the Qur'an arranged decoratively

Fig. 50. The names of God and Muhammad

IV

The Buwayhid Period

945–1055

ʻABBĀSID CALIPHS

944	al-Mustakfī
946	al-Muṭīʻ
974	aṭ-Ṭā'iʻ
991	al-Qādir
1031–75	al-Qā'im

BUWAYHID EMIRS IN IRAQ

945	Muʻizz-ad-dawla Aḥmad
967	ʻIzz-ad-dawla Bakhtiyār
978	ʻAḍud-ad-dawla
983	Ṣamṣām-ad-dawla
987	Sharaf-ad-dawla
989	Bahā'-ad-dawla
1012	Sulṭān-ad-dawla
1021	Musharrif-ad-dawla
1025	Jalāl-ad-dawla
1044	ʻImād-ad-dīn Abū-Kālījār
1048–55	al-Malik ar-Raḥīm

THE BUWAYHIDS

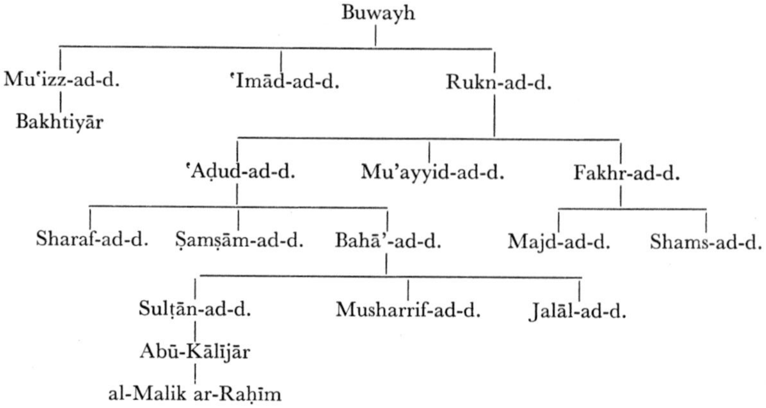
Buwayh
Mu'izz-ad-d.
'Imād-ad-d.
Rukn-ad-d.
Bakhtiyār
'Aḍud-ad-d.
Mu'ayyid-ad-d.
Fakhr-ad-d.
Sharaf-ad-d.
Ṣamṣām-ad-d.
Bahā'-ad-d.
Majd-ad-d.
Shams-ad-d.
Sulṭān-ad-d.
Musharrif-ad-d.
Jalāl-ad-d.
Abū-Kālījār
al-Malik ar-Raḥīm

1

THE 'EMPIRE' OF THE BUWAYHIDS

The period from 945 to 1055 has been designated the Buwayhid period because Baghdad at this time was under Buwayhid domination. On the other hand, Buwayhid power even at its greatest was far less than that of the Umayyad caliphs or the earlier ʿAbbāsid caliphs, since it controlled only Iraq and western Persia. Eastern Persia, Transoxiana and Afghanistan were at first under the Sāmānids and then under the Ghaznavids. From 969 the Fāṭimids were securely based in Egypt and usually in control of much of Syria as well, while everything west of Egypt was either under the Fāṭimids or under independent dynasties. Nevertheless the Buwayhids deserve special consideration in that Baghdad was still the centre of the Islamic world and the residence of the ʿAbbāsid caliph.

Muʿizz-ad-dawla and his brothers

The Buwayhid dynasty came to power through the parallel efforts of three brothers who managed to co-exist in tolerable harmony with one another. Indeed Buwayhid power always remained a family affair, with brothers and other relatives ruling in various provinces and districts and giving a degree of recognition to one another. This was both a strength and weakness for the Buwayhids. While family loyalty was strong, their dominions were comparable to a single state; but once this loyalty declined and brothers were ready to fight against brothers, each was no better than a petty princeling.

The three brothers who founded the dynasty were ʿAlī, al-Ḥasan, and Aḥmad, the sons of Buwayh or Būyeh. They were Daylamites, members of the fierce highland peoples from the area south-west of the Caspian Sea who in the early tenth century were rivalling the Turks as providers of mercenary troops for the Islamic world. The brothers began in the service of the Sāmānids, and then transferred to that of Mardāvīj, an individual not unlike themselves who, finding himself in command of a considerable body of troops, tried to make himself into an independent ruler. The three brothers all showed gifts of leadership. When Mardāvīj was assassinated in 943, ʿAlī, the oldest of the three, was master of Ispahan and in process of making himself independent. In the confusion of the next year or so, the three brothers extended the area they controlled to most of western and south-western Persia. In particular Aḥmad, the youngest, was in Khuzistan and al-Ahwāz, the area immediately to the east of Basra and Wāṣit, and was thus in a position to march on Baghdad in 945 when appealed to by a party at court after the death of the general Tūzūn. At Aḥmad's approach in December 945 the caliph went into hiding, but Aḥmad's agent al-Muhallabī persuaded him to meet the Daylamite general. Aḥmad professed loyalty to him, but in January 946, since court intrigues against himself continued, had al-Mustakfī deposed from the caliphate and replaced by a son of al-Muqtadir with the throne-name of al-Muṭīʿ who had for some time been a rival of al-Mustakfī.

At his first meeting with al-Mustakfī financial control of Iraq was given to Aḥmad ibn-Buwayh and his name was to be put on the coinage, so that he became in effect ruler of Iraq, though he does not seem to have received the title of 'chief emir' (*amīr al-umarāʾ*). He received an honorific title, however, Muʿizz-ad-dawla ('strengthener of the state'), and his brothers ʿAlī and al-Ḥasan the titles of ʿImād-ad-dawla and Rukn-ad-dawla ('pillar' and 'support of the state'). They may all have received the title of 'chief emir' from al-Muṭīʿ, though this is not quite certain. One of the difficulties was that, though Aḥmad was at the capital, Baghdad, he was the youngest, and ʿAlī, the oldest, regarded himself as the senior member of the triumvirate.

Muʿizz-ad-dawla ruled in Baghdad for over twenty years, while to the east his brothers increased the area under their control. ʿImād-ad-dawla died in 949 and was succeeded at his own wish, since he had no son, by his nephew, son of Rukn-ad-dawla, who is best known by the title he received in 962, ʿAḍud-ad-dawla. Muʿizz-ad-dawla had to work hard to restore order in Iraq; when he first entered Baghdad, for example, the eastern half was in the hands of the Ḥamdānid prince of Mosul, Nāṣir-ad-dawla. Once order had been restored he set about making good the material damage suffered by Baghdad during the troubles of the last dozen years or so. The struggle against the Ḥamdānids of Mosul continued for most of the reign. On at least three occasions Muʿizz-ad-dawla occupied Mosul for a time, apparently as a way of imposing his terms on the Ḥamdānid prince. In 952 a joint attempt of Carmathians and Omanis to take Basra was repulsed by the Buwayhid forces. Towards the end of his reign Muʿizz-ad-dawla made some gestures of support for the Shīʿites; in 962 he had Muʿāwiya publicly cursed, and in 963 he commanded mourning for al-Ḥusayn on the tenth of Muḥarram. As Daylamites in general had a reputation for excessive lamentation, it is possible that they may have contributed to the form of the Shīʿite observance of mourning for al-Ḥusayn. The effect of the Shīʿism of the Buwayhids on their policies will be considered later.

Bakhtiyār and ʿAḍud-ad-dawla

Just before his death in March 967 Muʿizz-ad-dawla appointed as his successor his son ʿIzz-ad-dawla, more commonly known by his own name of Bakhtiyār. The latter was easy-going and pleasure-loving, and left most of the administration of the regions under him to viziers, and badly chosen viziers at that. He was on terms of hostility both with the Ḥamdānids of Mosul and with ʿImrān ibn-Shāhīn, who had established himself as an independent ruler in the Baṭīḥa or Marshes of southern Iraq. When the Fāṭimid threat from Syria became serious, he tried to reach an understanding with the Carmathians there. Meanwhile to the south-east his cousin ʿAḍud-ad-dawla was growing in strength, and to his original province of Fārs had added Oman (in Arabia), Kirmān and Makrān (on the northern shore of the Persian Gulf), as well as becoming overlord of Sijistan and for a time subduing the Baluchi tribesmen.

A crisis came in 974 when during the absence of Bakhtiyār in the south-east a Turkish general seized power in Baghdad, after a quarrel between the Turkish and Daylamite troops in which the Sunnites in the populace sided with the Turks and the Shīʿites with the Daylamites. The caliph al-Muṭīʿ was deposed (5 August) and replaced by his son with the name of aṭ-Ṭā'iʿ. ʿAḍud-ad-dawla now persuaded his father, Rukn-ad-dawla, the recognized head of the Buwayhid family, to allow him to go to the aid of Bakhtiyār. In January 975 he defeated the Turks and entered Baghdad; but when in March 975 he brought pressure to bear on Bahktiyār to give up his appointments, his father intervened and insisted that Bakhtiyār should remain in control of Iraq. On the death of Rukn-ad-dawla in September 976, however, ʿAḍud-ad-dawla proceeded with his plan to make himself ruler of Iraq. Bakhtiyār advanced to meet him, but was defeated at al-Ahwāz (July 977), and then, after entering into alliance with the Ḥamdānid prince of Mosul, his former enemy, was defeated again at Samarra and killed in the battle (May 978).

Much of the remaining five years of the life of ʿAḍud-ad-dawla was spent in dealing with those who had helped Bakhtiyār or showed some inclination to do so. The ruler of the Marshes was forced to pay tribute, and likewise the sons of a Kurdish chieftain Ḥasanwayh. Two other sons of Rukn-ad-dawla had received territories from their father. One, Fakhr-ad-dawla, was not prepared to be subservient to his brother, and tried to get help from Qābūs ibn-Washmgīr, prince of Jurjān and Ṭabaristān. The other brother, Mu'ayyid-ad-dawla, was willing to co-operate, and was first made governor of Hamadhan and then appointed by the caliph to rule Jurjān and Ṭabaristān, from which territories in due course Qābūs was driven. Both Qābūs and Fakhr-ad-dawla took refuge at the Sāmānid court until after the death of ʿAḍud-ad-dawla, when they recovered their domains. By the time of his death, then, in 983 ʿAḍud-ad-dawla had brought under his control what may properly be called an empire, though it began to split up immediately after his death. His closing years are generally reckoned the high-water mark of Buwayhid power. He was even appealed to for help by a pretender to the Byzantine throne. His position was marked by certain special privileges of the kind appreciated at this period, such as marrying the caliph's daughter and having a second name of honour – Tāj-al-milla, 'crown of the community'.

The sons of ʿAḍud-ad-dawla

The death of the great man at the early age of forty-seven was something of a shock to most of the people. A group of ten philosophers emulated the sayings of ten Greek philosophers on the death of Alexander, and tended to feel that in his pursuit of worldly power he had lost his soul. For the politicians the problem was how to effect a transfer of power peaceably. The death was concealed until one of his sons – to be known as Ṣamṣām-ad-dawla, 'scimitar of the state' – had been appointed his deputy by the caliph, ostensibly at the request of ʿAḍud-ad-dawla himself. This kept matters quiet in Baghdad. Another son, however, Sharaf-ad-dawla, managed to install himself in Shiraz as ruler of the province of Fārs, while two other sons jointly occupied al-Ahwāz and Basra for about three years. Mu'ayyid-ad-dawla, uncle of the new ruler of Baghdad, retained his provinces but died in June; it is said that he had been planning to take the position of ʿAḍud-ad-dawla, but this may merely mean that he hoped to assert his position as head of the family. On his death the area he ruled passed into the hands of his brother Fakhr-ad-dawla.

Ṣamṣām-ad-dawla was strong enough to quell an insurrection at Mosul and to inflict a severe defeat on a Carmathian force which attacked and pillaged Kufa; but in 987 his difficulties had increased and he lost his nerve and surrendered to his brother Sharaf-ad-dawla, who thus became ruler of Iraq. Unfortunately a form of dropsy afflicted Sharaf-ad-dawla, and he died after about two-and-a-half years, aged twenty-seven. Before he died he gave orders for the blinding of Ṣamṣām-ad-dawla, who had been imprisoned at Siraf on the Persian Gulf south of Shiraz. Shortly afterwards, however, in 989, Ṣamṣām-ad-dawla was released and became ruler of the province of Fārs, where with the aid of a competent vizier he was able to maintain himself until 998, when his Daylamite troops mutinied and in the ensuing disturbances he met his death. He was thirty-four.

After Sharaf-ad-dawla supreme power in Iraq passed to yet another son of ʿAḍud-ad-dawla who came to be known as Bahā'-ad-dawla. He may be said to have reigned for over twenty years, from 989 until his death in 1012, but his authority fluctuated considerably. There were constant struggles for power between rival military leaders, and frequent reversals of fortune. To the north Mosul passed from the Ḥamdānids to the nomadic Arab family of the ʿUqaylids, who at times acknowledged Buwayhid suzerainty. In the east the Sāmānid state was disintegrating and being taken over by the Ghaznavids and the Qarakhanids. The death of Fakhr-ad-dawla in 997 led to the division of western Persia between two young sons, while Qābūs regained Jurjān and Ṭabaristān.

For a time Bahā'-ad-dawla was under the influence of a cruel and unwise adviser, usually known as the Muʿallim ('teacher'). On the suggestion of this man and in the hope of gaining considerable wealth, in November 991 he deposed the caliph aṭ-Ṭā'iʿ and replaced him by a cousin with the throne-name of al-Qādir bi-llāh, 'the powerful through God'. The Muʿallim was responsible for so many actions of this kind that in the following year the army revolted and refused to be satisfied except by the death of the Muʿallim. So things continued until nearly the end of the reign when the threat from the Fāṭimids began to take more serious proportions. The Fāṭimids had nearly always had some hold over Syria, but there were signs that their propaganda was having some effect further afield. In 1010 Qirwāsh, the ʿUqaylid emir of Mosul, used a Fāṭimid form of introduction to the Friday address instead of the usual one mentioning the caliph al-Qādir. The caliph called the attention of Bahā'-ad-dawla to the seriousness of this act, and the latter sent an army which forced Qirwāsh to recant and ask pardon. In the following year a document was published challenging the Fāṭimid claim to be descended from ʿAlī and Fāṭima; the signatories included Imāmite scholars and the document was probably instigated by the caliph.

The decline of Buwayhid power

The remaining forty-three years of Buwayhid rule in Baghdad were shared by three sons of Bahā'-ad-dawla and the son and grandson of the first of these. Much effort and energy were spent in fighting other members of the family. Thus Sulṭān-ad-dawla, who ruled Iraq from 1012, became involved in a war with his brother Musharrif-ad-dawla and other princes in the region of Diyarbekr about 1019, and was so severely defeated in 1020 that he agreed to retire to the provinces of Khuzistan and Fārs, while Musharrif-ad-dawla ruled in Iraq until his death in 1025. With names of honour, even second names of honour, becoming very common Musharrif-ad-dawla went a step further and styled himself Shāhinshāh or 'king of kings', an ancient Persian title.

A third brother, Jalāl-ad-dawla, was nominated as 'chief emir' in 1025 but was not at first strong enough to move from his governorship in Basra and assert his authority in the capital. Indeed most of the next twelve years was spent in fighting between him and his nephew Abū-Kālījār (also known as 'Imād-ad-dīn al-Marzubān), the son of Sulṭān-ad-dawla who had succeeded to his father's provinces on the latter's death in December 1024. Sometimes one, sometimes the other, was 'chief emir' in name, but neither was able effectively to fill the office. The Turkish troops, especially in Baghdad, gave constant trouble with their demands for more money. Eventually in 1037 the two made peace with one another, and this was sealed by the marriage of a daughter of Jalāl-ad-dawla to a son of Abū-Kālījār.

When Jalāl-ad-dawla died in 1044, Abū-Kālījār succeeded to such power as remained to the Buwayhids. A new menace, in the shape of the Seljūqs, had been increasing rapidly in the east since about 1030. Abū-Kālījār tried to avert the danger by making a treaty with Ṭughril-Beg, the Seljūq leader, coupled with a twofold marriage alliance, but this gave only a limited breathing-space. When Abū-Kālījār died in 1048 and was succeeded by his eldest son with the title al-Malik ar-Raḥīm, the Seljūqs were again moving forward. Chaos reigned in Iraq. The Turkish troops were as often as not out of control, there was rioting between Sunnites and Shī'ites, and various local groups throughout the country tried to gain some advantage for themselves. Alliances were constantly changing, while the more far-sighted politicians were trying to make friends with the Seljūqs. The one person who stands out as competent was a Turkish military leader al-Basāsīrī, who gave much useful service to Jalāl-ad-dawla and later to al-Malik ar-Raḥīm; but by 1054 or 1055 he was beginning to play for his own hand.

The Seljūqs were a family of chiefs of the Ghuzz or Oghuz Turkish people who, as leaders of bands of mercenaries, entered the Islamic world towards the end of the tenth century and became Muslims. While the Ghaznavid family was devoting most of its attention to its Indian territories and quarrelling within itself, the Seljūqs began to advance into Khurasan on their own account. In 1038 their leader

Ṭughril-Beg proclaimed himself sultan – now the usual title for a military governor – in Nishapur, and in 1040 he expelled the Ghaznavids from Khurasan. After this progress was steady: Jurjān and Ṭabaristān in 1041, Hamadhan and Rayy in 1042; an expedition beyond Mosul in 1043; the treaty with Abū-Kālījār in 1045; the capture of Ispahan in 1050 and of Azerbaijan in 1054. It is not surprising that, with the Buwayhids less and less able to maintain order in their shrinking domains, some men in Baghdad began to look to Ṭughril-Beg. As early as 1041 the caliph al-Qā'im (who had succeeded his father al-Qādir in 1031) is said to have officially appointed Ṭughril-Beg to the governorship of the provinces he had conquered, and some titles of honour followed in 1050. By 1055 affairs were so desperate that the caliph's vizier Ibn-al-Muslima invited Ṭughril-Beg to come to Baghdad to his help, though the caliph apparently disapproved. Ṭughril-Beg eventually entered Baghdad on 19 December 1055, after having on the previous Friday received the mention in the prayers which marked him out as next to the caliph. After a disturbance in the city al-Malik ar-Raḥīm was arrested, and he died in prison some three years later. Baghdad and Iraq were not securely in Seljūq hands for another five years, thanks to men like al-Basāsīrī, but 1055 is taken as the end of the Buwayhid era and the beginning of that of the Seljūqs.

The strengths and weaknesses of the Buwayhid régime

The Buwayhid régime was originally based on the military power of the Daylamite mountaineers. They were good fighting men and loyal to their leaders. As time went on, however, they ceased to be entirely satisfactory as soldiers, and the Buwayhid emirs came to rely more and more on Turkish mercenaries, that is, men who had been taken from their homes as slaves at an early age and trained for warfare, so that their main attachment was to their corps and its leaders. Moreover, the Turks were mostly cavalrymen, whereas the Daylamites were infantry. By the later tenth century the running of a province or the maintaining of a small independent state had thus become largely a matter of finance. The more money you had, the more troops you could hire and the more successes you were likely to have against external or internal enemies. Unfortunately the troops became aware of the fact that they were indispensable to their leaders, and began to make demands for higher wages and other donatives. Towards the end of the Buwayhid period the soldiers involved had no interest in fighting except financial, and were forcing the emirs to spend more on their army than the economy could afford. From this point of view alone the position of the Buwayhid dynasty was hopeless.

In the second place the conception of family ties had at first been a source of strength to the Buwayhids. Three brothers, all in positions of power, all competent and able to trust one another, had a great advantage over other forms of leadership. There was a corresponding weakness, however, which became apparent as time went on. It seems to have been contrary to the Buwayhid or Daylamite tradition for power to be concentrated in the hands of one man. ʿAḍud-ad-dawla personally acquired control over a vast area, but he made no attempt to hand his 'empire' as a whole to one of his sons. After more than a generation of a life of wealth, luxury and power there was a decline in fraternal and family loyalty among the Buwayhids, and the dynasty gradually disintegrated.

Thirdly, the earlier part of the Buwayhid century was a period of economic prosperity. This was increased by the strong government of the early Buwayhids and the public works which they undertook. Towards the year 1000, however, trade between the Indian Ocean and the Mediterranean area began to be diverted from the Persian Gulf route to the Red Sea route, perhaps because of the Carmathians and other disturbers of the peace of the Gulf, perhaps because of Fāṭimid policies of encouraging trade through Egypt. The decline of trade through Iraq certainly contributed to the financial difficulties of the later Buwayhids. Some of their own practices, however, also had a bad effect on the economy. Payment of the troops was a perennial difficulty. To make it easier the Buwayhids made great use of an idea first met with earlier – the idea of the *iqṭāʿ*. This was nothing like a 'fief' at this period, though it is sometimes translated in this way. It simply meant that in lieu of pay an officer was given the right to land-tax in a certain district. At first he had, out of the land-tax he received, to pay a tithe on the land (which was a smaller sum); but later he kept the whole amount of the tax. This was a way of giving the recipient a precisely calculated sum of money; but it reduced the degree of control over the finances exercised by the responsible officials and was ultimately unsatisfactory.

Finally there was the question of ideology or creed. What Shīʿism or Imāmism meant in practice to the Buwayhids is a matter yet to be discussed, but Imāmism may be described as a somewhat negative creed, enabling one to maintain a detached attitude towards the régime under which one lives. In the first half of the tenth century this had been the creed of rich bankers and financial experts in Baghdad, and by adopting it the Buwayhids had gained their support. Later, however, they had to meet the forceful propaganda of the Fāṭimids, and some gentler Sunnite propaganda from the Ghaznavids and the Seljūqs; and in these circumstances the negative Imāmite creed was ineffective. The Seljūqs were well aware that, if they gave full support to Sunnism, this would gain them many friends in Iraq and elsewhere. The Buwayhids had not been oppressive in their treatment of the Sunnites, but the caliph and his entourage must have found their tutelage irksome in various small ways, since the caliph had a special responsibility for the administration of Sunnite law and the maintenance of the Sunnite basis of society. These considerations undoubtedly had some weight with Ibn-al-Muslima when he invited the Seljūqs to Baghdad.

2

THE PROVINCIAL 'EMPIRES'

The Buwayhids have been given pride of place in this account because they were in control at the centre of the Islamic world. One of the features of the Buwayhid period, however, is that in other regions of that world there were other dynasties just as powerful as the Buwayhids, perhaps at times even more powerful. The chief of these will now be described briefly, though there were also some minor ones which have to be passed over in silence.

The end of the Sāmānids

At the beginning of the Buwayhid period the great 'empire' in the east was that of the Sāmānids with its centre at Bukhara in Transoxiana and extending over Khurasan and parts of Afghanistan. This 'empire' continued strong for a decade or two after 945, but before the end of the century it had disintegrated for much the same reasons as the ʿAbbāsid caliphate. Some of the more distant areas were under more or less independent rulers, who merely acknowledged the suzerainty of the Sāmānids and made certain payments; but it became increasingly difficult to ensure that the payments were received. The Sāmānids had become largely dependent on Turkish mercenaries, and found the same difficulty in controlling these that was experienced elsewhere. In particular a Turkish officer called Alptigin, who was appointed governor of Khurasan about 955, in 962 considered it desirable after a change of ruler in Bukhara to move eastwards into eastern Afghanistan where he made himself master of the town of Ghazna and the surrounding region known as Zābulistān. He and other Turkish officers who succeeded him were recognized as governors by the Sāmānids and on occasion given military assistance, though they also resisted Sāmānid armies trying to enforce greater subservience.

In 977 the Turkish troops in Ghazna deposed their commander for misrule and chose in his place another Turkish officer called Sebüktigin. He still regarded himself as governor on behalf of the Sāmānids, and in 993 went to the help of the Sāmānid ruler when the latter had to cope with a full-scale rebellion. Sebüktigin and his son Maḥmūd spent about two years chiefly in Khurasan, and Maḥmūd was made governor of Khurasan for the Sāmānids. In 997 a serious quarrel disrupted the Sāmānid dynasty, and Maḥmūd, who became emir of Ghazna in 998 after his father's death and a brother's abdication, took advantage of the chaos to assert his independence. At the same time a Turkish people under the dynasty of the Qarakhānids or Īlek Khāns was invading the Sāmānid domains from Central Asia. By 999 or 1000 the Sāmānid 'empire' had been divided up, Maḥmūd taking Khurasan and the Qarakhānids Transoxiana, with the Oxus as the frontier. This was the end of the dynasty, though a Sāmānid emir managed to hold out in remote spots until 1005.

The Ghaznavids

The foundation of the Ghaznavid 'empire' by Sebüktigin has just been described. In the earlier part of his rule Sebüktigin had more than once invaded the Panjab and gained some fortresses on the Indian frontier. This was an important piece of preparation for the great conquests of Maḥmūd in India. Sebüktigin, though acting with complete autonomy, continued to regard himself as a governor for the Sāmānids; and Maḥmūd seems to have been prepared to do the same until it became obvious that power was slipping from the grasp of the Sāmānids. He then asserted his independence and began to expand his 'empire' at a phenomenal rate. He first secured his hold on Khurasan and the surrounding provinces which had been loosely under Sāmānid suzerainty. In Khurasan he restored the mention of the ʿAbbāsid caliph in the Friday prayers, and in return was appointed the caliph's governor in Khurasan, with the titles of Walī Amīr al-Mu'minīn and Yamīn-ad-dawla. The acknowledgement of the caliph was of course a politic move, but Maḥmūd was also a genuine believer in Sunnite Islam and looked on it as the basis of his state. His campaigns in India were regarded as in some sense wars for the faith and attracted thousands of *ghāzīs* or 'volunteers' from Khurasan (though they may have been moved by desire for plunder as well as by zeal for the faith). The subjugation of Khurasan may be said to have been completed by the defeat of the Qarakhānids near Balkh in 1008, for after this they made no attempt to cross the Oxus.

Part of the importance of Khurasan for Maḥmūd was that, since it was prosperous and wealthy, the taxes from it helped to finance his campaigns in India – he is reckoned to have made seventeen expeditions in all. About the year 1001 he conquered Kabul, Multan and Kashmir. After the final defeat of the Qarakhānids he returned and completed the occupation of the Panjab. This was followed by pillaging expeditions into the valley of the Ganges. In 1025 a great expedition led to the acquisition of Gujerat, as well as the plundering of an extremely wealthy Hindu temple at Somnath. Thus by the time of the death of Maḥmūd in 1030 his 'empire' included the Panjab and the Indus valley in India, and the whole of Afghanistan and eastern Persia, while a belt of small states immediately to the west of his own territories acknowledged his suzerainty. Only south-west and north-west Persia were beyond his influence.

The Persian provinces did not remain for long in the hands of the Ghaznavids. Maḥmūd had apparently wanted his son Muḥammad to succeed him, but Muḥammad was relatively inexperienced and not altogether competent, and was rejected by the army in favour of another son, Masʿūd, who had commanded victorious armies and was his father's governor of the western provinces. Soon after Masʿūd was established as sole ruler of the empire, the Seljūqs began to invade some of his provinces in Persia. At this point Masʿūd rejected the advice of his counsellors and decided to commit the bulk of his resources to a further effort in India. The Seljūqs meanwhile began to spread rapidly through Khurasan. The news of this eventually brought Mas'ūd back from India, but in 1040 at Dandānqān (near Merv in Khurasan) he suffered a decisive defeat at the hands of the Seljūqs, which meant the end of the Ghaznavid 'empire' in Persia. Mas'ūd, himself dispirited, was murdered by his discontented army as he moved towards his Indian capital of Lahore.

This was far from the end of the Ghaznavid 'empire'. From 1040 to 1059 fighting continued between the Ghaznavids and the Seljūqs, but by the latter date it was accepted that western Afghanistan should be under the Seljūqs and eastern Afghanistan under the Ghaznavids. On this basis there was peace between the two empires for half a century. Indeed in the twelfth century a Ghaznavid prince was given military help by the Seljūqs. The Ghaznavid state continued to be strong in its new location until the sack of Ghazna in 1150, and the dynasty did not disappear until 1186.

The Ghaznavids are memorable from several points of view. Maḥmūd was patron of the Persian poet Firdawsī, who was a major figure in the revival of Persian literature, and encouraged architecture and other arts. He contributed to the improvement of the position of the caliph in the eleventh century. And he was perhaps the person chiefly responsible for the expansion of the Islamic religion in the Indian sub-continent.

The Ḥamdānids

The state, or rather two states, of the Ḥamdānids hardly constitute an 'empire', yet they are worthy of some mention. Ḥamdān was an Arab of the tribe of Taghlib, who from 868 to 895 was the leader of a tribal band which took part in various local wars in the province of the Jazīra (which then included Mosul and the upper course of the Tigris as well as the modern Syrian province of Jezireh). Some of his sons followed him in this occupation of freelance commander, and one, Abū-l-Hayjā' 'Abd-Allāh, became the caliph's governor in Mosul in 905 and held this position – with some intervals due to the complex intrigues of the period – until his death in 929. This came about through his implication in an abortive plot to replace the caliph al-Muqtadir by al-Qāhir. His son al-Ḥasan, in the unstable conditions before the loss of power by the 'Abbāsids, made himself master of Mosul in a struggle against his uncles and in 935 was recognized by the caliph as governor of Mosul and of the whole of the Jazīra.

In the period between the appointment of Ibn-Rā'iq as 'chief emir' and the assumption of power in Baghdad by the Buwayhids this Ḥamdānid governor of Mosul joined in the contest for supreme power, received from the caliph the title of Nāṣir-ad-dawla, 'defender of the state', and actually became chief emir for about a year from 942 to 943. When he had to yield this position to a Turkish officer Tūzūn, he retained his provincial governorship and continued to play a part in the struggle for power. When it was clear that the Buwayhids were firmly established in Baghdad, he came to terms with them. On two or three occasions, when he was dilatory with his payments to Baghdad, the Buwayhid Muʿizz-ad-dawla had to use force against him and even occupy Mosul, but he nevertheless retained his control of the province until 967 when he was deposed by his sons. Most of the power eventually passed into the hands of one of the sons, Abū-Taghlib, who maintained a precarious balance until 978 when he was defeated by the Buwayhid ʿAḍud-ad-dawla and became a fugitive. This was virtually the end of the Ḥamdānids of Mosul. Though a little more is heard of some members of the family, their power was gone.

Nāṣir-ad-dawla had a younger brother ʿAlī or Sayf-ad-dawla, 'sword of the state', who had acted as his subordinate in various ways, and who in 944 took advantage of the confusion of the times to occupy Aleppo. He had to fight against the forces of the Egyptian Ikhshīdids who then ruled most of Syria, but by 947 he had made himself master of northern Syria and part of the province of the Jazīra. This new state was nominally under the Ḥamdānids of Mosul, but sometimes was in fact stronger and to all intents independent of both Mosul and Baghdad. Sayf-ad-dawla continued to rule until his death in 967 at the age of fifty-one. Much of his energy was expended in resisting Byzantine pressure directed by the vigorous Macedonian emperors. Nevertheless his court was renowned for his patronage of the arts, especially literature through 'the circle of Sayf-ad-dawla'.

He was succeeded by his son Saʿd-ad-dawla (967–91), who had a difficult time playing off against one another the three major powers surrounding him, the Buwayhids, the Byzantines and the Fāṭimids. In the second half of his reign the Buwayhids could devote little attention to Syria, but Fāṭimid power grew rapidly after their conquest of Egypt in 969, and Ḥamdānid Aleppo had usually to have the support of either the Byzantines or the Fāṭimids. After the death of Saʿd-ad-dawla power was effectively in the hands of Lu'lu', his general and freedman (of unspecified origin), who finally got rid of the Ḥamdānid princes about 1004 and ruled on his own account; but he and his son Manṣūr were not able to maintain themselves for more than a decade or so.

The Fāṭimids

The year 945 saw the Fāṭimids securely established in Tunisia and in control of some of the surrounding regions and Sicily. The next important advances came in the reign of al-Muʿizz (953–75), who had the services of a brilliant general, Jawhar. In the earlier part of the reign Jawhar led a victorious army to the Atlantic, and Fāṭimid suzerainty was asserted over the whole of North Africa. Then al-Muʿizz turned his eyes eastwards. It was really implicit in the Fāṭimid claims that they should attempt to gain possession of the Islamic heartlands; and two of his predecessors had engaged unsuccessfully in campaigns against Egypt. Now, after careful preparations, including political propaganda (which was helped by a severe famine in Egypt), Jawhar penetrated to Old Cairo (al-Fusṭāṭ) without difficulty and assumed control of the country. An Ikhshīdid prince was still nominal ruler, but the Ikhshīdid régime had ceased to function and offered no resistance to Jawhar. The name of the ʿAbbāsid caliph was at once omitted from the Friday prayers, though Ismāʿīlite forms were introduced only gradually. Jawhar immediately began to build a new city for his troops, calling it al-Qāhira, 'the triumphant one', or Cairo. In 973 Cairo became the residence of the Fāṭimid imam or caliph and the centre of his government.

Of the Asian territories which had acknowledged the Ikhshīdids the cities of Mecca and Medina quickly recognized the Fāṭimids, but there were difficulties in Syria. A Fāṭimid general was able to enter Damascus, but it was lost again and was not securely in Fāṭimid hands until 978. Surprisingly enough, much of the fighting was against the Syrian Carmathians who, like the Fāṭimids, professed the Ismāʿīlite form of Shīʿism, but at this point were not prepared to acknowledge the Fāṭimid imam. The Fāṭimids continued to increase their hold on Syria, but were never fully established there as they were in Egypt. Mosul accepted their suzerainty for a year or so about 990; and in 1015 they gained Aleppo but found that the governors they installed there tended to revolt. Such control as they achieved over Syria brought them, as already noticed, within range of the struggle for power in Iraq. With the Fāṭimid ruler and his advisers more and more occupied with the affairs of Syria, the governors in Sicily and North Africa became more and more independent until Cairo had virtually lost all its influence in the western provinces.

In Egypt itself the Fāṭimid era lasted just over two hundred years and was a time of great prosperity. Egypt was spared the disturbances which made life difficult in Iraq and Syria. Trade flourished and was encouraged by the rulers; and it took many directions, to India by the Red Sea, to Italy and to the western Mediterranean, and at times to the Byzantine empire. Because of the tolerant attitudes of the régime the era was one of great intellectual vitality (about which more will be said later). The tolerance showed itself, among other ways, in the fact that the numerous viziers included some Christians, a convert or two from Judaism and even an Imāmite, while Jews held other high offices. This statement is not effectively contradicted by the strange reign of al-Ḥākim, from his coming to the throne in 996 at the age of eleven until his mysterious disappearance in 1021. He was certainly cruel and eccentric and he was possibly mad; but even if the reports about the difficulties he made for Jews and Christians are true and not malicious gossip, they were exceptional in the Fāṭimid period as a whole.

The end of Umayyad Spain

The reign of ʿAbd-ar-Raḥmān III, which had begun in 912 in difficult circumstances, ended in 961 in a blaze of glory, and was followed by the relatively peaceful reign of his son al-Ḥakam II (961–76). In this period Umayyad Spain attained its greatest power and prosperity. The suzerainty of the caliph of Cordova was acknowledged for part of the time by the Christian princes in the north of Spain and by some of the local rulers in North Africa, though the latter at times had to submit to the Fāṭimids instead. Power and prosperity seemed to external observation to continue for most of the reign of the next caliph, Hishām II (976–1013), but the political structure had been altered. Hishām was only eleven when he came to the throne, and power was in the hands of various officials; by 981 one of these, Ibn-Abī-ʿĀmir, an extremely competent but unscrupulous political climber, had made himself dictatorial ruler of Islamic Spain, nominally on the order of the caliph. In the course of rising to supreme power he eliminated his associates and rivals. He had a strong and loyal army, and gave it sufficient to do in numerous expeditions by which he maintained suzerainty over the Christian princes in the north. The most famous expedition was that of 997 in the course of which the shrine of Saint James at Compostela was pillaged and, apart from the actual tomb, destroyed.

In 981 Ibn-Abī-ʿĀmir took the name of honour of al-Manṣūr, more fully al-Manṣūr bi-llāh, 'the one rendered victorious by God', and he was usually known in Europe as Almanzor. By the time of his death in 1002 the name was fully justified, for his authority was unquestioned as far as the Pyrenees in the north and over a wide area in North Africa. He was succeeded by his son with the name of honour of al-Muẓaffar, who had no difficulty in obtaining from the caliph a grant of similar powers to those of his father. For six years he more or less maintained the position of Umayyad Spain, though the Christian princes were becoming restive. After his death in mysterious circumstances in 1008 what happened is best described by saying that Umayyad Spain collapsed like a house of cards. In a few years what had been a flourishing state at the height of its power and glory experienced a complete débâcle, with its structure shattered beyond the possibility of restoration.

Al-Muẓaffar was succeeded by a younger brother who had none of the necessary qualities for the position. He soon antagonized the citizens and lost the loyalty of the army. The result was chaos, since there was no individual or group of men capable of maintaining order throughout the country. Hishām II was forced to abdicate in 1009, though he was restored the following year. Between that date and 1031 he and six other members of the Umayyad family, and three members of a half-Berber family, each held the office of caliph briefly. None had any real power, and in 1031 the council of ministers ruling Cordova decreed the abolition of the caliphate. By about this time the unitary Umayyad state had split up into thirty or so statelets, each centred on one of the towns. The period up to 1091 is known as that of the 'party kings' (*mulūk aṭ-ṭawā'if*, *reyes de taifas*). The period from about 981 to 1009 is sometimes called that of the 'Āmirid dictatorship.

The reasons for this sudden disintegration of an apparently flourishing state have not been adequately studied. Certain factors can be discerned. Difficulties of communication between the regions encouraged a measure of local independence. Two foreign elements had recently increased in numbers and not been assimilated: Berbers as soldiers, and 'Slavs' (or eastern Europeans) as slaves, soldiers or government officials. Al-Manṣūr and al-Muẓaffar as highly successful generals might be compared to some of the Turkish or Daylamite generals in the east, though less is heard in Spain about the troops getting out of hand and demanding more money. With the growing wealth of the recent decades there may have been a lessening of religious zeal and of the capacity of religion to hold men together. Finally, it may be that the ruthless efficiency of al-Manṣūr in destroying potential rivals either removed all the men with the necessary gifts for ruling a large country or deterred them from embarking on a political career and obtaining the necessary experience. The Christians in the north, of course, were gradually becoming stronger and at times more ready to join together, with much support and inspiration from the cult of Saint James of Compostela; but the disintegration of the Umayyad state must have been primarily due to internal factors.

3

POLITICS AND THEOLOGY

The earliest theological discussions in Islam arose out of political disputes, and the above brief account of the political history of the Buwayhid period has required a number of references to Shīʿism and Sunnism. This makes it desirable to look more closely at the relation of these religious beliefs to the political conflicts of the time.

Imāmism or Imāmite Shīʿism

In the previous chapter (§3) it was argued that Imāmism acquired its definitive form only in the half-century or so after the death of the eleventh imam in 874; and it was further suggested that, while it had popular support, it was a party chiefly concerned with the interests of financiers and other wealthy persons. It would also seem likely that by 945 most of the fourteen groups mentioned by an-Nawbakhtī as existing after the death of the eleventh imam had been merged in the Imāmites. When these various points are taken as a basis for further investigation, there are two further questions to be considered: what was the relation of the Buwayhids to Imāmism? and what was the policy of an Imāmite party under the Buwayhids?

We are told that the Buwayhids were already Shīʿites when they first appear in Persia, but it is not stated what their Shīʿism involved. There were Zaydites in the neighbourhood of Daylam, the original home of the Buwayhids, but there is no evidence to show that the Buwayhids were interested in following any particular ʿAlid leader. Nor is there anything to suggest that they were devoted to some hidden imam, or that before 945 they subscribed to the Imāmite creed. Though Imāmism and Ismāʿīlism now had a rudimentary organization, Shīʿism in general, as Sir Hamilton Gibb expressed it, 'was more of a widely diffused emotional or intellectual tendency' which, because it was looser and vaguer, was more acceptable to some men than the organized Sunnism of the ulema. It was probably in this sense that the Buwayhids were Shīʿites; they highly esteemed the descendants of ʿAlī, but the ʿAlids had no special place in their policies. The idea of an ʿAlid caliph could easily have occurred, as the historians report, to men who had made and unmade ʿAbbāsid caliphs; but one of their advisers is then alleged to have said: 'no one seriously believes in an ʿAbbāsid caliph, and no one would object if you ordered his execution; but men would believe that an ʿAlid caliph was divinely inspired, and would obey *him* if he ordered *your* execution'.

Some pro-Shīʿite acts are recorded of the Buwayhids, but these do not appear to be of deep significance. Soon after coming to power in Baghdad Muʿizz-ad-dawla separated the ʿAlids from the rest of the Hāshimites (mainly the ʿAbbāsids) and gave them a separate *naqīb* (perhaps 'dean') – a senior member of the group who could represent its interests and exercise a certain power of jurisdiction. The ʿAlids, however, were probably only vaguely Shīʿite and were almost certainly not Imāmite – why should they look for the return of a deceased relative? In 962 Muʿizz-ad-dawla ordered the cursing of Muʿāwiya and those who oppressed the family of the Prophet; and in 963 he encouraged the celebration of what later became the Imāmite ceremonies of the mourning for al-Ḥusayn and the feast of Ghadīr Khumm (the commemoration of an incident in which Muḥammad assigned a special rank to ʿAlī). These actions seem to be pro-Imāmite, even if the mourning ceremony owes something to Daylamite practice. The Buwayhids in general, however, were not firmly committed to these points, and the two ceremonies were for a time forbidden by ʿAḍud-ad-dawla and two later deputy-governors when it was found that they fomented rioting between the Shīʿites and Sunnites in Baghdad. Apart from the two ceremonies and the Sunnite imitations, this rioting became a constant feature of Baghdad life, but it seems to have been a safety-valve for popular feeling rather than evidence of a serious political divergence.

The Buwayhids, then, do not seem to have been out-and-out believers in Imāmism, but, in so far as the Imāmites were organized, they sought their support and gave them some privileges. They may have found the Imāmite intellectuals with their popular following a useful counterweight to the rigidity of the Sunnite ulema.

What of the firm believers in Imāmism? It was suggested in the previous chapter both that they represented the interests of certain wealthy groups and also that they gave general support to the ʿAbbāsid government, while maintaining a measure of critical detachment. The coming to power of the Buwayhids did not greatly alter the position for them. They supported the Buwayhids and got some recognition from them, but, in that they still expected the return of the 'hidden imam', they preserved some detachment from the actual rulers. It came to be held that about 941 a change had taken place from the 'lesser absence' (*ghayba*) of the twelfth imam, when he still had a representative on earth, to the 'greater absence', when he had no such representative. This may reflect some change of organization within the Imāmites, such as control by a group of scholars rather than a single statesman. The general impression one gets of Imāmism at this period is that it had become a religion without close political implications. In effect it said, 'Wait until God brings back the hidden imam'. Thus it had no clear practical goals to set before men to arouse their enthusiasm for the struggle against the Fāṭimids and was unable to supply the Buwayhids with an effective response to Fāṭimid propaganda.

From all this it is easy to understand that the Buwayhids, though gently supporting the Imāmites, did not make any serious attempt to convert their Sunnite subjects to Imāmism. It is also understandable that they were content to allow the office of caliph to remain in the ʿAbbāsid family. Since most of their subjects were Sunnites, nominal appointment by the caliph to the office of 'chief emir' or something similar counted towards gaining popular support. To give the caliphate to an ʿAlid, had a suitable one been available, might have had the unfortunate consequences envisaged in the story told above, while to abolish the office altogether would have meant losing some popular support; and if some rival managed to set up an ʿAbbāsid caliph in his own capital, this would increase his popular support.

The Fāṭimid form of Ismāʿīlism

From the first the Fāṭimids had claimed that they were the rightful rulers of the whole Islamic world, and their move to Egypt and Syria in 969 was a step towards the realization of that end. In addition to their military effort they mounted an intense propaganda campaign throughout the Asian provinces. This was carried out by a large number of 'missionaries' (*duʿāt*, sing. *dāʿī*) in a hierarchical structure under a chief *dāʿī*. The propaganda was not exclusively a refurbishing of old arguments for popular consumption, though sometimes it might be this. This missionaries operated at different levels, and many aimed at appealing to persons of higher education, especially in the Greek sciences. At its highest level Ismāʿīlism was presented by the Fāṭimids as monotheism expressed in terms of Greek philosophy. Something similar was attempted in a work produced in Basra under Ismāʿīlite (but not Fāṭimid) inspiration, probably in the second half of the tenth century, known as *The Epistles of the Pure Brethren* (al-Ikhwān aṣ-Ṣafā); this was a somewhat crudely executed encyclopedia of the Greek sciences, whose primary aim was to show the individual how to gain happiness in the world to come. The work done under the Fāṭimids was more genuinely scientific and philosophical.

This openness to Greek thought led to some notable scientific achievements in Cairo under Fāṭimid patronage, though otherwise literary production under the Fāṭimids is less than might have been expected where there was an outburst of intellectual activity. Fāṭimid Cairo, however, apart from its own productions, deeply stimulated the thinking of the whole Islamic world by its intellectual energy, its adventurous spirit and its tolerant attitude. To meet Fāṭimid propaganda one had to develop comparable qualities of mind, so that even opponents were greatly influenced. As part of their missionary effort the Fāṭimids founded what may be regarded as the oldest university in the world. This was the mosque of al-Az'har, begun in 970 as the mosque for the new city of Cairo, but gradually transformed into a centre of higher learning, which it has continued to be ever since, though under Sunnite control since the late twelfth century. Another Fāṭimid institution, dating from 1005, was the Dār al-Ḥikma or Dār al-ʿIlm, 'house of wisdom' or 'of science', which formed part of one of the palaces and had a library and meeting-rooms for scholars, as well as giving instruction in Ismāʿīlite doctrine. Despite all this eagerness for spreading the Ismāʿīlite faith, the majority of the population of Egypt remained Sunnite and found life on the whole tolerable, even if at times the government introduced oppressive measures.

Sunnism

In 945 the Sunnites had been moving towards a wide but not precisely defined agreement and also, though rather more slowly, towards mutual recognition. After 945 they had two new problems to deal with: a head of state who was not a Sunnite, and a caliph who was politically powerless. The caliph had indeed some representative functions and some control over the religio-legal side of life; but that was all. The sort of power he still had is illustrated by one or two events recorded from the Buwayhid period. In 1003 Bahā'-ad-dawla tried to make a certain ʿAlid chief judge, as well as appointing him to other offices such as the deanship of the ʿAlids; but the caliph objected to the appointment as chief judge and had his way. We are not told, however, whether he objected because the man was an ʿAlid and so presumably an Imāmite, or because the chief emir had encroached on his prerogatives. In 1011 the caliph al-Qādir, by way of countering propaganda, had a refutation published of the Fāṭimid claims to be descended from Fāṭima's son al-Ḥusayn, and a few years later invited Maḥmūd of Ghazna to join in opposing Muʿtazilites and Ismāʿīlites. In 1018 he had a document formally read which condemned Muʿtazilite doctrines such as that of the createdness of the Qur'ān and also some Imāmite doctrines. This creed or statement of doctrine came to be known as the Qādiriyya after its author. It was given another formal reading in 1041 by his son, the caliph al-Qā'im. The interesting thing is that it seems to be essentially a Ḥanbalite creed.

The simplest way to describe all this is to say that the caliph had ceased to belong to the political institution and become part of the religious institution. At the same time the caliph had become a mouthpiece of Sunnism; and al-Qādir in particular was personally attracted by the most popular and least academic form of Sunnism, namely, Ḥanbalism. All this is not surprising in view of the caliph's loss of political power; but it is important to notice that for the Sunnite ulema he had acquired a new function as a kind of guarantor of the validity of the Sunnite form of law. This partly explains the theologico-juridical treatment of the office of caliph or imam by Sunnite writers like the jurist al-Māwardī (d. 1058) and the theologians al-Bāqillānī (d. 1013) and al-Baghdādī (d. 1037). Just as the Sharī'a is a fact, whether put into force or not – that is to say, it is a fact that God has given certain commands to men, whether they obey them or not – so that the Sharī'a is in effect an ideal law, in the same way the office of caliph is described in ideal terms. It is his function, they say, to command the army, defend the frontiers and manage the state finances as well as to punish wrongdoers and the like.

In an article on al-Māwardī's book Sir Hamilton Gibb suggests that he is not merely stating an ideal but is working towards a recovery of power by the caliphs, and that his method includes a rationalization of past history. An example of the latter point is al-Māwardī's statement that an imam may, after becoming imam, set aside the person nominated by the previous imam as second in succession; this had actually happened several times and is here justified. Such rationalization of the past, however, is not just saying that 'whatever is is good'. While Sir Hamilton's views may be accepted up to a point, it would seem that the practical aim was not the restoration of caliphal power but opposition to the Imāmite conception of the state, in which the fundamental character of the Sharī'a was denied. For the Imāmites the imam, when present, was above the Sharī'a and could overrule it. In the early eleventh century the imam was absent and his return was expected only in the distant future. Thus the Imāmites were somewhat detached from the actual state. For them, too, the Buwayhid ruler, though functioning as head of state, was not an imam, and so was presumably free to pursue his own personal or dynastic interests. To judge from the creed of the Imāmite writer Ibn-Bābawayh (d. 991), they acknowledged that individuals were subject to God's commands and prohibitions, but did not develop this into a theory of the state. In practice this would seem to imply that the basis of the state was human interest. Against this al-Māwardī is saying that 'the state is based on the Sharī'a, which covers every aspect of life, so that in principle all private and public acts are subject to the Sharī'a'. Just as in the ninth century contemporary political problems were discussed in terms of long-past history, so in the eleventh century contemporary problems (especially the nature of the state) are discussed in terms of an idealized caliphate.

While the new problems created by the rise to power of the Buwayhids were thus being tackled, work continued in the other Sunnite disciplines on much the same lines as before. The chief new feature was the development of rational theology, and the production of more comprehensive and systematic treatises. By the beginning of the eleventh century the Ash'arites had become a definite school; or perhaps it might be more correct to say that the school of rational theologians in Iraq had accepted al-Ash'arī as their figurehead. The outstanding member of the school was the *qāḍī* al-Bāqillānī, just mentioned, who extended the scope of theological discussions at various points. He was on good terms with 'Aḍud-ad-dawla and was sent on an official mission to the Byzantine emperor in Constantinople in 982. Rational theology was also cultivated by small groups of Mu'tazilites, but their precise position in the community at this date has been little studied and is not clear. Theologically the Mu'tazilites were not Sunnites, but one, 'Abd-al-Jabbār, of whose writings several have recently been recovered, was a Shāfi'ite judge in Baghdad and Rayy. He died in 1025. The writer known as aṣ-Ṣāḥib ibn-'Abbād (d. 995), who was a vizier under Mu'ayyid-ad-dawla and Fakhr-ad-dawla, is said to have had Mu'tazilite leanings, but is probably to be classified as Imāmite. In general Imāmism accepts much Mu'tazilite teaching. Despite the names mentioned, Mu'tazilism seems to have been declining in support and influence. The Ḥanbalites with their anti-rational theology continued to be active and to have a large popular following, especially in Baghdad. The most influential exponent of Ḥanbalism in the Buwayhid period was probably Ibn-Baṭṭa (d. 997), whose 'profession of faith' has been translated into French.

During the Buwayhid period a new theological sub-discipline established itself, namely, heresiography or the study of heretical sects. There had indeed been some earlier study of such matters, especially among the Mu'tazilites; and one of the surviving works of al-Ash'arī deals with the views of individuals and sects on many points, though without asking how far they are heretical. This is perhaps a kind of residuum from his Mu'tazilite phase, since Sunnites found it difficult to accept such a study as valuable. For

Muslims generally knowledge was essentially the wisdom by which men live, not the information which gives one power over things and persons. There was therefore no point in studying what was *ex hypothesi* false, and to do so might even be dangerous. The heresiographers eventually found a justification for their study in a Tradition, according to which the Prophet said, 'My community will divide into seventy-three sects, of which only one will be saved'. Another Tradition spoke of the Jews having seventy-one sects, the Christians seventy-two and the Muslims seventy-three; and there are many slight variants of both Traditions. In themselves such sayings seem unlikely – sects are not a matter for boasting – and it has been plausibly suggested that they have been derived from a saying about seventy-odd virtues. The importance of the Traditions is that they justified the study of heretical sects by way of explanation of the Prophet's saying; and we find Sunnite heresiographers manipulating their material to produce seventy-two heretical sects. The important figure under the Buwayhids was Abū-Manṣūr al-Baghdādī (d. 1037) whose book of this category is entitled *The Distinction between the Sects*.

4

TRENDS IN LITERATURE

The period from the coming of the ʿAbbāsids to the coming of the Seljūqs has been called 'the golden age of Arabic literature', and the last century of that period was the most productive. All that is possible here is to look at the main trends and to see how they are related to the political history. In particular two matters stand out. One is the way in which writing in Arabic, whether by men of Arab descent or not, came to be dominated by the Arab feeling for words and language; and this is in a sense the outcome of Arab self-assertion. The other is the decentralization of literary activity, following on the growth of provincial autonomy – a process which found its extreme embodiment in the appearance of a new Persian literature.

As part of the background of these literary trends it may be noted that there had been an increase in book-production and the formation of libraries. Books had to be copied by hand, but paper was easily obtainable and relatively cheap, since the first paper-mill had been built in Baghdad about 800 by Yaḥyā the Barmakid. In 990 a minor college in Baghdad had over 10,000 books in its library, while at about the same time the Fāṭimid and Umayyad caliphs in Cairo and Cordova respectively are said to have had collections of over 100,000 volumes. One of the precious surviving documents of this period is the *Fihrist* or *Index* of Ibn-an-Nadīm, written in 988, which contains the titles of a vast number of books, mostly not now extant, together with biographical notes on the authors, and other materials.

The emphasis on language and form

The first of the two trends to be described is the Arab feeling for words and language which underlies pre-Islamic poetry and was an important factor in the acceptance of the Qur'ān by Arabs. As literature in general increased in volume, it was natural that some philologists should discuss the good and bad qualities of writing as literature, in other words should engage in literary criticism. As poetry was the genre with the longest tradition, it was most discussed; and by the end of the tenth century many critics were saying that the difference between good and bad poetry was not in its content but in the manner of expression, that is, in certain formal qualities. These ideas of the critics seem to have affected other genres also, notably that of 'epistles', which in the tenth century were especially popular among members of the secretary class. In particular it became fashionable to write not in ordinary prose, but in a special form known as *saj'* or rhymed prose. The Qur'ān was also said to be written in *saj'*, and that of the tenth and later centuries was not unlike some of the early passages of the Qur'ān with their short verses; but there are also differences.

From literary 'epistles' the use of *saj'* spread to official correspondence. One of the persons greatly addicted to it was the Ṣāḥib Ibn-'Abbād, already mentioned. It also spread to historical writing, especially of the adulatory kind, an important early example being a history of Maḥmūd of Ghazna by al-'Utbī (d. 1036), one of his officials in charge of posts. Such writing was an excellent vehicle to display the author's wit and his command of recondite language, but it encouraged artificiality and a degree of remoteness from ordinary living; and such characteristics came to manifest themselves in other aspects of Islamic civilization.

This trend reached its full development in the creation of a genre which is distinctive of Arabic literature, the *maqāma* or 'assembly'. This was the achievement of a man known as Badī'-az-zamān ('the wonder of the age') al-Hamadhānī (969–1008). He had a great facility for extemporizing verses on a difficult subject or with prescribed rhymes, and possessed a photographic memory. He wrote 'epistles' which demonstrate his capacity for verbal gymnastics, and from these moved on to invent the 'assembly'. This has been described as a 'dramatic anecdote' in which a narrator tells of an incident in which the hero is a witty vagabond. The whole is in rhymed prose interspersed with verse, and is often full of elaborate word-play. Al-Hamadhānī is said to have composed over four hundred 'assemblies', of which only fifty-two have survived. Each is complete in itself, but they are linked together by having the same narrator and hero. This collection of incidents has been described as the nearest Arabic approach to the novel.

Developments in provincial centres

The second main trend was decentralization and the flourishing of literature in several provincial centres. This is a feature which has often been observed in times of political disintegration and is found in Islamic Spain after the break-up of the Umayyad caliphate in 1031.

The most brilliant single centre was possibly Aleppo in the third quarter of the tenth century under the patronage of the Ḥamdānid Sayf-ad-dawla, who ruled this little principality from 944 to 967. To Aleppo for a time came the philosopher al-Fārābī (to be mentioned in the next section) and the literary historian from Baghdad, Abū-l-Faraj al-Iṣfahānī (d. 967), whose great *Book of Songs* (*Kitāb al-aghānī*) is the source of most of our knowledge of pre-Islamic Arabia. It was the poets above all, however, who brought fame to 'the circle of Sayf-ad-dawla'. Of these the greatest was al-Mutanabbī (915–65), whose life reflects the troubles of the times. He was born in Kufa of Arab stock, but spent much of his early life in Syria. He appears in the Syrian desert as leader of a band of discontented nomads, apparently basing his leadership on some kind of religious basis, since from this episode he is said to have received the nickname by which he is known, which means the 'prophetaster' or 'would-be-prophet'. In 948 he found his way to Aleppo, where he sang the praises of Sayf-ad-dawla and was richly rewarded; but in 957 for an unknown reason he left Aleppo for the protection of the hostile Ikhshīdids in Egypt. By 961, however, trouble developed there also; instead of praising the emir Kāfūr he satirized him and had to flee to Iraq and then to Persia. For a time ʿAḍud-ad-dawla received him, but he was killed by robbers on his way back to Iraq from Persia in 965. Some Arab critics have hailed al-Mutanabbī as the greatest of

Arabic poets, though Europeans have been more hesitant. He was a master of the tricks of style beloved by the Arabs, but did not sacrifice content to form. His satire was vigorous and could be devastating, and his reflections on life in general provided many quotable lines.

Another important poet from the school of Aleppo, though he came too late to be one of the 'circle', was Abū-l-'Alā' al-Ma'arrī (973–1057). He spent most of his life in his birth-place, the small town of Ma'arrat an-Nu'mān in northern Syria, but studied in Aleppo for some years and spent eighteen months in Baghdad about 1007. He has been characterized as 'a great humanist and an incisive, though pessimistic, thinker'. To his pessimism and scepticism the loss of his sight at an early age may have contributed, and also his failure to make his way in Baghdad. He began by following al-Mutanabbī, and was always subject to the stylistic requirements of the time; but he eventually learned how to express his views freely and fearlessly, and in his later years collected round him a large number of students and admirers. One of his prose works, *Risālat al-ghufrān* (*The Epistle of Pardon*), has attracted some attention. It describes a visit to heaven and hell and interviews with heathen poets, imagined to be pardoned and among the blessed, and also with poets accused of *zandaqa*, like Bashshār ibn-Burd, whose views are condemned, though hope for their salvation is expressed.

Islamic Spain was another region which made noteworthy contributions to Arabic literature. At first literary activity was mainly in Cordova, but in the period of the 'party kings' it became diffused through various centres. It was in Spain that the strophe first appeared in Arabic poetry. The Arabic *qaṣīda* or 'ode' consisted of lines all identical in metre and rhyme, though not fixed in number. Perhaps it was some kind of popular song in Spain which led to the invention of the *muwashshaḥ*, the *zajal* and similar forms. A typical rhyme scheme for the *muwashshaḥ* would be: *aa bbb aa ccc aa ddd aa* ... *xxx aa*; but there were permissible variants. The *zajal* was similar, but usually had only a single *a* rhyme after each stanza, though commencing with a couplet. From Spain the *muwashshaḥ* was accepted into the Arabic heartlands in the late twelfth century.

There are various similarities between the poetry of Islamic Spain and Romance lyrics of the twelfth and thirteenth centuries, especially those of the Provençal troubadours; and this has occasioned much discussion and little agreement. Some influence of the Arabic tradition on Romance literature should probably be allowed; but it should possibly be restricted, as has been suggested by Pierre Cachia and the author, to 'imaginative tales, strophic forms of poetry and perhaps the particularly refined lyricism of their love-songs'. In this connection it may be noted how a Spanish Muslim, Ibn-Ḥazm (d. 1064), who developed into a dry and caustic jurist and theologian, in his earlier days was a poet and the author of a delightful account of the various forms of love and experiences of lovers, entitled *The Ring of the Dove*, in which illustrative anecdotes are interwoven with verses by himself and others. Such was the amatory climate of al-Andalus, as the Arabs called their land.

The revival of Persian literature

As a final effect of decentralization may be noted the reappearance of literature in Persian. This is especially connected with the court of the Sāmānids in Bukhara, and to a lesser extent with that of the great sultan Maḥmūd of Ghazna. The Sāmānids came from a family of Persian landowners, and their autonomy enabled them to foster what is most conveniently called 'national' feeling. This was in line with the outlook of the Persian Shuʿūbites, but it was a positive assertion of Persian values and not a mere denial of Arab claims. Encouraged by the Sāmānids, a poet called Daqīqī undertook the composition of an epic to be called the *Shāh-nāmeh* or *Book of Kings*; and after his murder the work was taken up (about 980) by another poet, Firdawsī of Ṭūs, and brought to completion in 994, it would seem, though he went on revising it until 1010. In its final form the *Shāh-nāmeh* is mostly concerned with the early legendary kings, but it also has a section on Sasanian history. It was probably about 1004 that Firdawsī, apparently in financial difficulty, went to Ghazna in hopes of receiving a handsome reward when he presented the work to Maḥmūd. There are conflicting stories of what happened at Ghazna, but the most likely version is that he received a reward but not nearly as much as he had expected. He went back to Ṭūs and died in or around 1020, aged about eighty.

The *Shāh-nāmeh* has become the 'national' epic of Persia. The conception of 'nation' was, of course, still in the future, but the poem by giving expression to the feeling of what it was to be Persian, and by bringing together and welding into a unity different strands of local tradition, helped to form a common consciousness and sense of identity. Essentially it shows the Persians their place and function in world-history, for it begins with the creation of the world. The Persians (Iran) are the forces of light and good, who have to fight against the forces of evil and darkness (Turan), especially in the shape of the barbarian Turkish invaders from the steppes of Central Asia. This view of history found a deep echo in Persian hearts, for it was in line with the theological dualism of good and evil in their former religion, Zoroastrianism. Yet it is formulated in such a way that it does not contradict Islamic dogma, since the struggle may be regarded as that of God against the devil (Satan or Iblīs). In this way the Persians began to find their distinctive vocation within the Islamic world; and the manner in which they did so both accorded with their own deepest feelings and gave them some compensation for the sense of inferiority produced by Arab self-assertion.

5

SCIENCE AND PHILOSOPHY

This is a convenient point at which to survey the whole achievement in science and philosophy of the Muslims writing in Arabic, since many of the leading figures were active during the Buwayhid period. Such a survey is the more necessary since there still remains a certain tendency to belittle the work of the Arabs (in the sense of Muslims writing in Arabic), and to regard them as no more than transmitters of Greek ideas. Even one who was well aware of the Arab contributions, Baron Carra de Vaux, writing on 'Astronomy and Mathematics' in *The Legacy of Islam* (1931), felt compelled to begin by disparaging the Arabs: 'We must not expect to find among the Arabs the same powerful genius, the same gift of scientific imagination, the same "enthusiasm", the same originality of thought that we have among the Greeks. The Arabs are before all else the pupils of the Greeks; their science is a continuation of Greek science which it preserves, cultivates, and on a number of points develops and perfects.' A moment later, however, he concedes that 'the Arabs have really achieved great things in science', and he goes on to enumerate some of the points to be mentioned here.

There is, of course, no denying that the Arabs were the pupils of the Greeks. Science and philosophy in Arabic came into existence through the stimulus of translations from Greek, together with the presence in Iraq of colleges where there was still a living tradition of

Greek thought, even though the medium of instruction was Syriac. In contrast to the teachers in these colleges, however, the Arabs, once they had assimilated what was to be learnt from the Greeks, went on to make important advances; and it is these contributions of the Arabs which will be emphasized here.

Medicine

Medicine was probably the first Greek science to attract the Arabs because of its obvious practical importance. Not merely was it taught in the colleges of Iraq, but the teaching was accompanied by a flourishing medical service. At first teaching and practice were in Christian hands, but after the chief works of Galen and Hippocrates had been translated into Arabic many Muslims also became proficient in medical science. In the period from 800 to 1300 medical writings in Arabic have been preserved from the pens of over seventy authors, mostly Muslims, but including a few Christians and Jews. Rulers, viziers and other wealthy men began to found hospitals, providing as well as the buildings endowments for the payment of the staff. The first hospital in Baghdad was founded by a Christian physician about 800 on the initiative of the caliph Hārūn ar-Rashīd; and records have been preserved of the founding of four other hospitals there in the first quarter of the tenth century. A thirteenth-century hospital in Cairo is said to have had accommodation for 8,000 persons. It was lavishly appointed, and had separate wards for male and female patients, as well as for different categories of ailment. The staff included physicians and surgeons, pharmacists, attendants of both sexes and administrative officers; and besides store-rooms and a chapel there were facilities for lecturing and a library.

The first important physician was Abū-Bakr Muḥammad ibn-Zakariyyā' ar-Rāzī (d. 923–32), known in Europe as Rhazes. He was active both in Baghdad and in his native town of Rayy (near Teheran). He wrote voluminously on many scientific and philosophical subjects, and over fifty of his works are extant. His greatest work is one translated into Latin as the *Continens*, 'the Comprehensive [Book]'. It was an encyclopedia of all medical science up to that time, and had to be completed by his disciples after his death. For each disease he gave the views of Greek, Syrian, Indian, Persian and

Arabic authors, and then added notes on his clinical observations and expressed a final opinion. The excellence of this work was widely recognized, but it was too bulky for general use and was to some extent replaced by a shorter work, *The Complete Art of Medicine* by ʿAlī ibn-al-ʿAbbās al-Majūsī (d. 994), the court physician of ʿAḍud-ad-dawla. The Latin translation of this was usually known as the *Liber regius* and the author as Haly Abbas.

The greatest writer on medicine was Ibn-Sīnā or Avicenna (d. 1037). He exemplifies a common feature of the Muslim scholars of this period, namely, excellence in more than one discipline, for he was at the same time one of the two greatest Arabic philosophers. His eminence in medicine was due to ability to combine extensive theoretical knowledge and systematic thought with acute clinical observation. His vast *Canon of Medicine* was translated into Latin in the twelfth century and was used much more than the works of Galen and Hippocrates. It dominated the teaching of medicine in Europe until at least the end of the sixteenth century. There were sixteen printed editions of it in the fifteenth century, one being in Hebrew, twenty editions in the sixteenth, and several more in the seventeenth. Roughly contemporary with Avicenna was the chief Arabic writer on surgery and surgical instruments, Abū-l-Qāsim az-Zahrāwī (d. after 1009), usually known in Latin as Abulcasis.

While Arabic medicine thus reached its highest point in the early eleventh century, it continued for many centuries longer. Indeed books in the Arabic tradition continued to be written until the seventeenth century, though by this time they were repetitive and not original. The gift of careful observation did not disappear, and some fourteenth-century Arab doctors in Spain wrote about the plague as they had experienced it in Granada and Almeria.

Mathematics and astronomy

Astronomy was a practical science for the Arabs, partly because they believed in astrology, and partly because they had to know the direction of Mecca from every Islamic city, in order to face in this direction in their prayers. In astronomy as in medicine fruit was borne by the talent for accurate and patient observation. Al-Khwārizmī (d. after 846) produced for the caliph al-Ma'mūn an abridgement of some Indian astronomical tables; and about 900, in an effort to smooth out discrepancies between tables from Indian, Persian and Greek sources, al-Battānī or Albategnius drew up some extremely accurate tables. The Ptolemaic system was, of course, universally adopted, but Arab astronomers were increasingly aware of the weaknesses of that system, even if they failed to discover a satisfactory alternative.

Some branches of mathematics were closely associated with astronomy, and it was probably in this field that the Arabs made their greatest contribution to human knowledge. Our ordinary numerical notation, often called 'Arabic numerals', certainly came to us from the Arabs. Though there are some gaps in the evidence, it is now generally held that the Arabs derived the 'ten signs' from Indian sources. It was the practical bent of the Arabs, however, which was quick to grasp the advantages of this system over the clumsy Roman numerals, and the slightly less clumsy Greek system. It was not enough, however, to express numbers in decimal notation; it was also necessary to show how to use this notation to perform simple arithmetical operations. Al-Khwārizmī (just mentioned) and his successors went so far as to show how to find the square root of a number. The beginning of decimal fractions is traced to a work written about 950 by a man called al-Uqlīdisī, 'the Euclidean'. Al-Khwārizmī also wrote a book which may be reckoned the foundation of algebra, and indeed our word 'algebra' is derived from its title, from the word *al-jabr* meaning 'restoration'. Later Arab mathematicians went on from algebra to pioneer the field of analytical geometry, and the Arabs are also the inventors of trigonometry. About the middle of the twelfth century a mathematician-astronomer of Seville greatly contributed to the development of spherical trigonometry.

Another distinguished mathematician was Ibn-al-Haytham (d. 1039), known in Latin as Alhazen. In giving a solution of what is still known as Alhazen's problem he performed an operation which was tantamount to solving a quadratic equation. He was unrivalled in what was then called 'optics', but would now mostly be included in physics, *inter alia* producing a theory of light superior to that of Euclid and Ptolemy. He conducted numerous experiments, and as a result of his work with spherical and parabolic mirrors and in respect of the refraction of light in passing through a transparent medium was able to give a calculation of the height of the earth's atmosphere.

Other sciences

The same painstaking attention to detail also led to advances in botany, where numbers of plants were described and listed. Curiosity was here supported by a medical or pharmacological interest. The fundamental work appears to have been the *Book of Plants* of the well-known historian Abū-Ḥanīfa ad-Dīnawarī (d. 895); though this book is now lost, most of what was important in it seems to have been preserved in the works of a thirteenth-century pharmacologist of Malaga.

Alchemical studies may also be said to have been pursued for a practical reason, namely, the procuring of gold. Some work in alchemy was directed to the mystical and allegorical interpretation of chemical changes, but there were also men who were genuinely interested in understanding the chemical constitution of matter, and who employed what was essentially the experimental method of modern science. Among the latter were several of the great scientists of the Islamic world whose chief competence was in another discipline. The physician ar-Rāzī wrote some important treatises on alchemy. The hypothesis of the transmutation of the elements was rejected by the philosopher-physician Avicenna, and also by another great scholar not so far mentioned, al-Bīrūnī (d. 1048?). The latter is known mainly as an expert on India, but his studies included Indian science. In the field of alchemy he himself measured the specific gravity of many substances and attained a high degree of accuracy.

Works were produced which might be classified as zoology or mineralogy, but the interest, especially of the books on animals, is literary rather than scientific.

Philosophy

The specific Arabic contribution to philosophy is difficult to assess, but one general consideration is important, namely that philosophy cannot be kept alive by merely translating and repeating the thoughts of other men. Indeed to translate philosophical works adequately into any language is possible only when there has been some original thinking in that language. In this way the early translations of Greek philosophy were frequently revised and improved. Something has already been said about the first original Arabic thinker, al-Kindī, and about the acceptance of many Greek ideas into Kalām or rational theology. While these ideas were being incorporated into their systems by Sunnite rational theologians like the Ashʿarites, other men were working towards a more thoroughgoing acceptance of Greek philosophy with relative disregard for Islamic doctrine. Of the latter two men stood head and shoulders above their contemporaries, al-Fārābī and the physician Avicenna.

About the life of al-Fārābī little is known. He was born in Turkestan, probably about 870, but came to Baghdad and studied philosophy and the Greek sciences, in the main with Christian teachers. It is not known how he gained a livelihood, for he was neither an official nor a secretary, but his wants were probably few, since he lived as an ascetic. He died in 950, having spent the last ten years or so of his life in the entourage of Sayf-ad-dawla at Aleppo. His philosophy was essentially a form of Neoplatonism, though adapted to Islamic doctrine at least in respect of monotheism. He tried not to offend Muslim susceptibilities gratuitously, but made no secret of his conviction that philosophical truth is universally valid, whereas religious symbols are an inferior way of conveying truth, suited to the less rational of mankind. With his metaphysics he linked a political theory, considerably influenced by Plato's *Republic* and *Laws*. Just as all existing things emanate from God, so in the ideal or virtuous state there is a hierarchy of command with the head of state at its summit. This fits in well with certain Shīʿite ideas and would be acceptable in Ḥamdānid Aleppo, but he also seems to make some concessions to Sunnism.

Avicenna was born in 980 near Bukhara, and spent the early part of his life there. He had some teachers, but much of his vast learning was obtained by his own undirected reading. In his autobiography he records that he had some difficulty with Aristotle's *Metaphysics* until he came across a small book on the subject by al-Fārābī. When he was twenty-two his father died and he had to seek employment as an official in the local administration. In the troubled circumstances of the times he frequently had to move to a post in another centre. From about 1015 to 1022 he was in Hamadhan and for part of the time had the onerous and dangerous position of vizier to the local Buwayhid emir. There were experiences of imprisonment and flight.

Later he was in Ispahan with the founder of a minor dynasty. He died in 1037 on an expedition to Hamadhan. While, as he acknowledges, he was under the influence of al-Fārābī, he seems to have given more attention than the earlier thinker to metaphysics and logic, and less, despite his involvement in political life, to political theory. He was also something of a mystic. While his metaphysics is clearly in the Neoplatonic tradition, he is just as clearly an original thinker of great power.

It is often stated that in the eastern Islamic world there was no philosophy after Avicenna. If philosophy is taken in a restricted sense, this is true; on the other hand, there were some distinguished writers in the east, especially in Persia, whose teaching combined philosophy with theosophy. In the Islamic west there was a flowering of philosophy in the twelfth century, culminating in Ibn-Rushd or Averroes (1126–98), the great commentator on Aristotle, who had a great influence on European Christian thought but little on that of the Islamic heartlands.

Islam and Hellenism

This brief survey of science and philosophy in the Islamic world is sufficient to show that there was an intellectual current among Muslims capable of responding to Greek thought and of being more fruitfully and creatively stimulated by it. Arab science and philosophy in their turn contributed greatly to developments in Europe. What is strange and in need of some investigation is the failure of Arab science to maintain its advance, and its actual decline from about the twelfth century onwards, at a time when Europe was progressing rapidly.

One point to be emphasized is that the devotees of philosophy and science in the Greek tradition were never more than a small minority even among the intellectuals of the Islamic world. They were a class apart from the ulema, and often had no contact with them. In Baghdad in the late tenth and early eleventh centuries there was a philosophical coterie in which Muslims and Christians met and discussed with a degree of freedom; but this was exceptional. The situation was probably better in Fāṭimid Cairo, since Ismāʿīlites had usually been interested in science as well as religion; but their religious heresies were a barrier between them and the Sunnites. Sometimes rulers other than the Fāṭimids – notably the caliph al-Ma'mūn – gave encouragement to Hellenizing scholars.

Another matter to notice is that the great majority of the ulema, and *a fortiori* the ordinary people, were shut off from philosophy and the other 'foreign sciences'. It was only at one or two isolated points that Greek conceptions came into the main stream of Islamic thought. One such point was the late eighth and early ninth centuries, when a number of Greek ideas were taken over, used and discussed by the rational theologians. After the reign of al-Ma'mūn, however, there was no further absorption of Greek ideas for about two and a half centuries, until al-Ghazālī (1058–1111) began to study philosophy for himself. He concluded that there was nothing in mathematics or natural science (physics) which was contrary to the Islamic faith, but saw that they could lead to false attitudes. Logic he held to be very useful to the theologian, and he wrote some books commending it to the ulema. Metaphysics, politics and ethics he thought should in general be rejected since they frequently contradicted Islamic doctrine.

Al-Ghazālī well expresses the final attitude of Islam to the 'foreign sciences', namely, that they are to be judged by their conformity to religious doctrine or lack of it. In other words, reason was to be tolerated only in so far as it was completely submissive to faith. This is an attitude which is basically in opposition to the Greek philosophic trust in reason – following the argument whithersoever it leads – and it does not provide an atmosphere in which science is likely to flourish. If such was the attitude of the *rational* theologians, then, when one remembers that there were also anti-rational theologians with much popular support, it is not surprising that science declined.

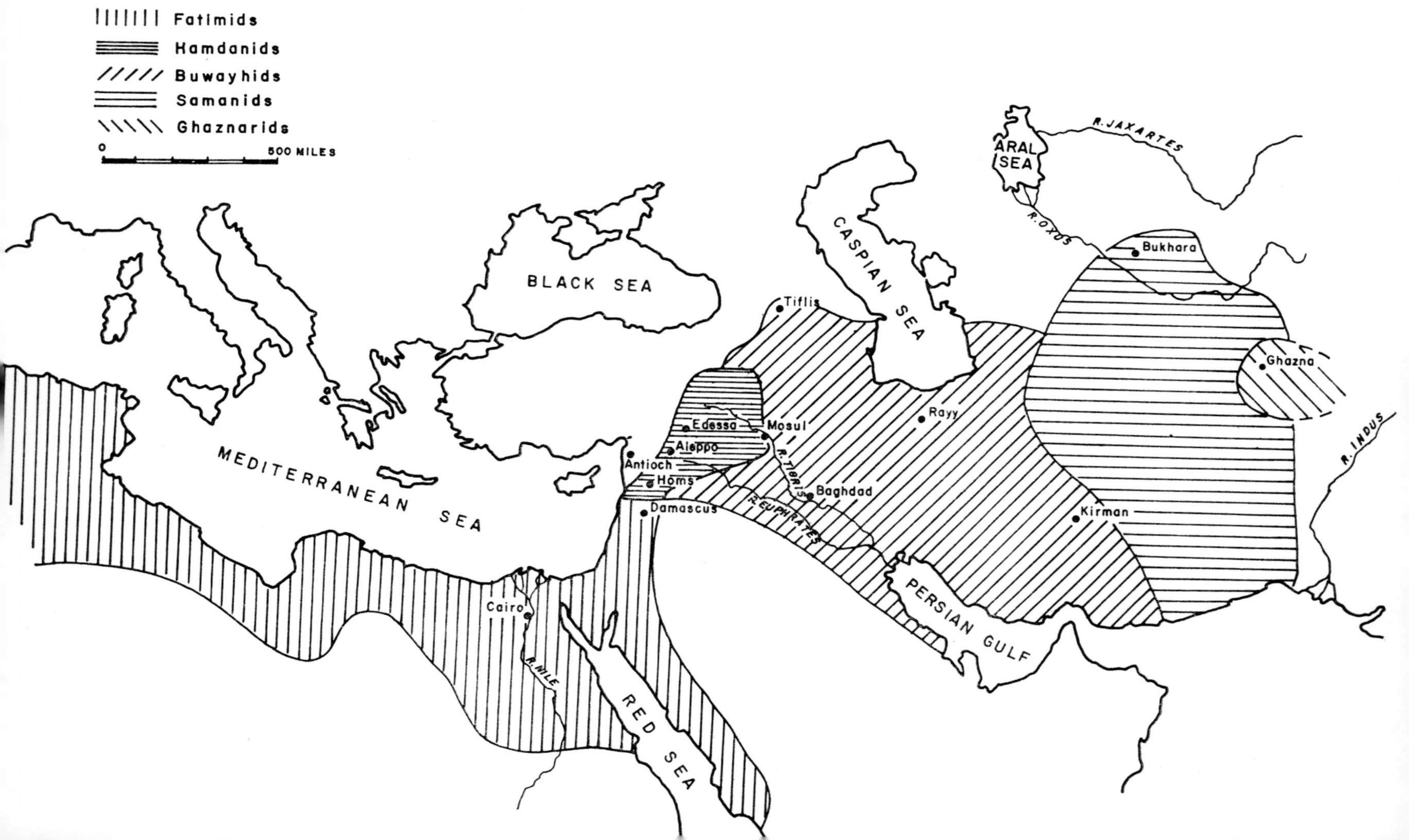
Fatimids
Hamdanids
Buwayhids
Samanids
Ghaznarids
0
500 MILES
BLACK SEA
CASPIAN SEA
ARAL SEA
R. JAXARTES
R. OXUS
Bukhara
Ghazna
R. INDUS
Tiflis
Edessa
Mosul
Rayy
Aleppo
Antioch
Homs
R. TIGRIS
Baghdad
Damascus
R. EUPHRATES
Kirman
MEDITERRANEAN SEA
Cairo
R. NILE
RED SEA
PERSIAN GULF

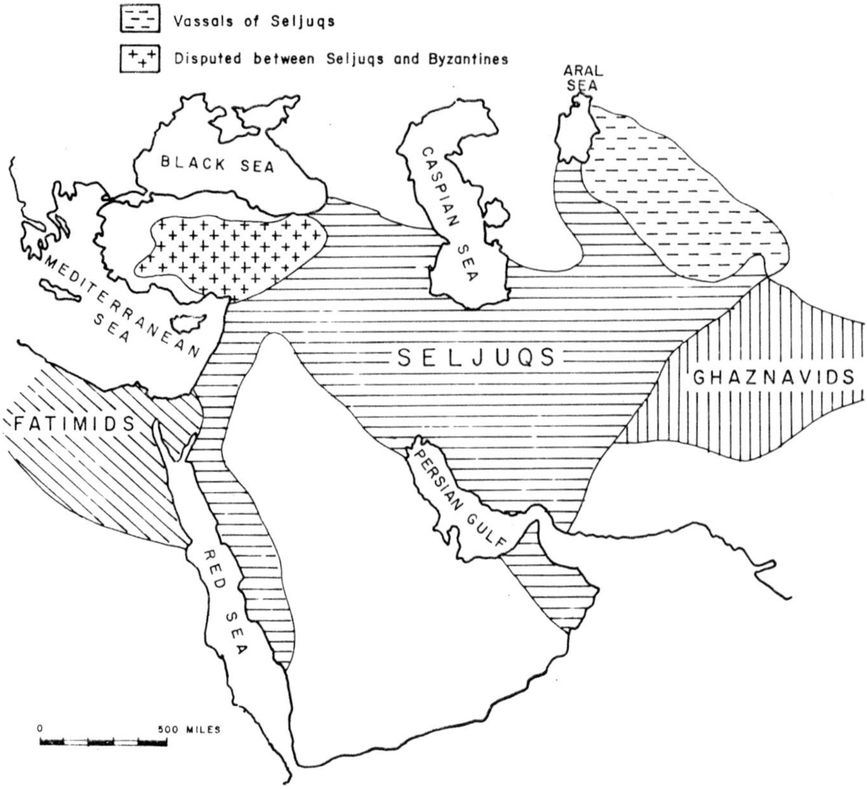

THE SELJUQ EMPIRE ABOUT 1090

V

The Earlier Seljūq Period

1055–1100

ʻABBĀSID CALIPHS

1031	al-Qā'im
1075	al-Muqtadī
1094–1118	al-Mustaẓhir

GREAT SELJŪQS OF BAGHDAD

1055	Ṭughril-Beg
1063	Alp-Arslān
1072	Malik-Shāh I
1092	Maḥmūd
1094–1105	Barkiyāruq

THE GREAT SELJŪQS

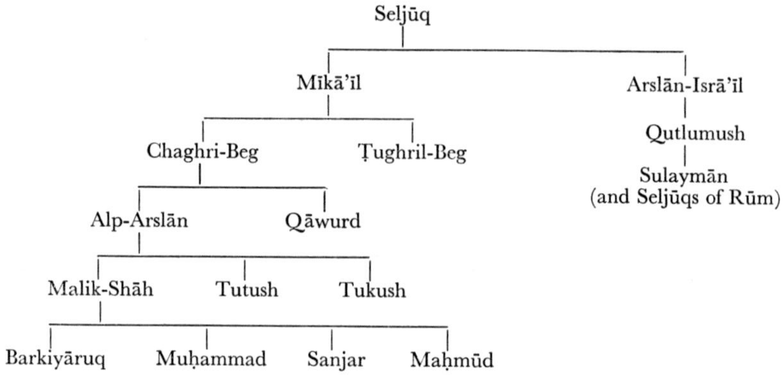

1

THE 'EMPIRE' OF THE GREAT SELJŪQS

The successors of Ṭughril-Beg as holders of the supreme power in the Seljūq domains are usually referred to as the Great Seljūqs to distinguish them from their own subordinates and from the independent though related dynasty of the Seljūqs of Rūm, who ruled in Asia Minor. The power of the Great Seljūqs declined rapidly after the death of Malik-Shāh in 1092 owing chiefly to internal squabbles, but one of his sons, Sanjar, who ruled in Khurasan, continued to be recognized as supreme sultan from 1118 to 1157. The year 1100 is in some respects an arbitrary date at which to conclude this study, but it is by no means unsuitable, especially when interpreted with some elasticity.

Ṭughril-Beg

The entry of Ṭughril-Beg into Baghdad on 19 December 1055, though taken as the beginning of the Seljūq era, did not mean that he was in secure possession of Iraq. For over four years he had to contend with two powerful rivals, the general al-Basāsīrī and his own half-brother Ibrāhīm Ināl, while the struggle was complicated by the presence of several minor figures such as local dynastic rulers and the caliph's vizier, Ibn-al-Muslima. All these leaders, greater and lesser, were seeking their own interests through a maze of intrigues, and were ready to change alliances whenever it seemed advantageous. There are even indications that for a time Ṭughril-Beg's own vizier al-Kundurī, was plotting against him. Ibn-al-Muslima, while described as the caliph's vizier, may also have been playing largely for his own hand; and his attempts to get money to further his policies made him very unpopular, so that few were sorry when he was put to death by al-Basāsīrī in 1059. Ibn-al-Muslima had been hostile for years to al-Basāsīrī and had favoured Ṭughril-Beg (for whose invitation to Baghdad in 1055 he had been responsible); and in this he seems to have diverged from the caliph whose policy, as some have suggested, was to prevent any one military leader from becoming all-powerful.

Ibrāhīm Ināl from about 1042 had had a strong position in north-west Persia, including Hamadhan, and he might well have been the first Seljūq to enter Baghdad. In 1049 he and Ṭughril-Beg quarrelled, and Ṭughril-Beg seized most of his territories but later came to an agreement with him and handed them back. In 1058, when Ṭughril-Beg was confronted by a number of difficulties, Ibrāhīm Ināl again revolted, but his defeat on this occasion involved his death at Ṭughril-Beg's own hands.

Al-Basāsīrī tried various alliances, and from time to time was in a strong position. His most serious move was to profess allegiance to the Fāṭimid caliph in Egypt and in return to receive a large sum of money, though there is no reason to think that he was deeply convinced of the truth of Fāṭimid claims. In all such intrigues the 'Abbasid caliph was a kind of pawn, but the validation of a man's rule which he and he alone could give was so important that all the candidates for power tried to get his support, or better still to gain control of his person. Even when al-Basāsīrī entered Baghdad in December 1058 and had prayers said in the name of the Fāṭimid al-Mustanṣir, he did not send the caliph al-Qā'im to Cairo but saw to it that he was in the hands of one of his own allies. Ṭughril-Beg, however, by various means skilfully managed to get hold of the caliph and to bring him back to Baghdad before marching out to the decisive battle near Kufa on 15 January 1060 in which al-Basāsīrī was defeated and killed.

For the short remainder of his life – he died in September 1063 – Ṭughril-Beg was in undisputed control of his 'empire'. Of two minor figures in the struggle for power one died shortly after al-Basāsīrī and the other submitted. After the troubles of the previous years things moved along quietly. The chief event in Baghdad seems to have been the marriage of Ṭughril-Beg to a daughter of the caliph. Stories are told of the reluctance of the caliph to consent to this union of the blood of the Prophet's house with that of a rough Turk, though it appears that ʿAḍud-ad-dawla had married a daughter of the caliph aṭ-Ṭāʾiʿ.

Alp-Arslān

Alp-Arslān had some trouble with rival claimants to supreme power, but it was not so serious as in the case of his uncle Ṭughril-Beg. The latter, who was childless, had apparently appointed a nephew Sulaymān as his heir, and the vizier al-Kundurī proclaimed Sulaymān as sultan in Rayy. Alp-Arslān, however, who had succeeded his father Chaghri-Beg as governor of Khurasan about 1060, was much too strong; al-Kundurī submitted almost at once, then was imprisoned and eventually after about a year put to death. Another rival, his cousin Qutlumush (ancestor of the Seljūqs of Rūm), met him in battle and was defeated towards the end of 1063. The other contenders for power submitted to Alp-Arslān and became governors under him, except that his brother Qāwurd in Kirmān retained a measure of independence. His position was thus not without problems, but he had a fair measure of control over the 'empire'.

In the east Alp-Arslān maintained peace with the Ghaznavids according to the terms of a truce arranged by his father, and he reasserted his authority in the region of Khwārizm (south of the Aral Sea). Then he turned his eyes westwards, doubtless with the ultimate aim of attacking the Fāṭimids. First, however, he compelled the small Georgian kingdom to make its submission to him. His operations in this area in 1064 and 1068 secured his frontier in Azerbaijan, and at the same time opened the way for the tribal bands of Turkmen, who were loosely attached to him, to go on raiding expeditions into Armenian and Byzantine territory. The Byzantines, provoked by the operations and the raiding parties, attacked the Muslims in turn, but peace was eventually arranged (1069). Alp-Arslān next moved through south-east Asia Minor to force the emir of Aleppo to abandon the suzerainty of the Fāṭimids for that of himself and the ʿAbbāsid caliph. The Byzantine emperor now moved with a very large force to take him in the rear, but Alp-Arslān was able to collect sufficient men to offer battle at Manzikert (Malāzgird) on 26 August 1071. The Byzantine army was annihilated and the emperor taken prisoner in 'the most decisive disaster' ever suffered by the Byzantines. It was only slowly after grave troubles in the capital that the Byzantines recovered. Neither Alp-Arslān nor Malik-Shāh tried to follow up his advantage; but Asia Minor was now wide open to raiding parties of Turkmen and other tribesmen. Raiding passed into settling down and occupying the country, while the Greek and Armenian villagers fled before them. The country passed into Muslim possession much more securely than could have been effected by a series of military victories. Alp-Arslān himself was killed in the east in December 1072 by a prisoner who had been brought into his presence.

Malik-Shāh

There was no difficulty about the succession of Malik-Shāh although he was a minor, partly because he had been designated by his father, but more because affairs were being controlled by a very strong vizier, known by his honorific title of Niẓām-al-mulk, who had been associated with Alp-Arslān while he was still no more than governor of Khurasan. There were the usual intrigues and the signs of disaffection among local rulers, but Niẓām-al-mulk coped with all this for twenty years without much difficulty. His murder in 1092 is usually attributed to the Assassins, but it is possible that it was engineered by the rival who succeeded him as vizier, perhaps with the connivance of Malik-Shāh who by this time was finding that the great power of the vizier seriously restricted his own.

During the reign of Malik-Shāh the eastern frontier of the 'empire' was maintained and even extended; that is to say, the local rulers of governors within this area were made to recognize the suzerainty of Malik-Shāh and to send the appropriate sums of money. Peace was observed with the Ghaznavids, though they did not acknowledge Seljūq suzerainty. It was above all in Syria and Asia Minor that advances were made. In Asia Minor there was not merely the penetration and settlement of Turkmen in tribal groups, as already mentioned, but the establishment of petty states by some of their chiefs with a small town as centre, and the creation of a wider area of control under a Seljūq prince, Sulaymān, the son of Qutlumush. From 1077 he had a measure of suzerainty over most of the lesser rulers in Asia Minor, but he was driven southwards by the Byzantines and defeated and killed near Aleppo in 1086 by a Seljūq army. Later, just after the death of Malik-Shāh in 1092, Sulaymān's son Qïlïch-Arslān managed to gain the allegiance of most of his father's officers and established the dynasty of the Seljūqs of Rūm, which continued to rule in Asia Minor for some two hundred years. The recovery of Syria from the Fāṭimids was largely the work of a general called Atsïz, who conquered Jerusalem in 1073 and Damascus in 1076, but was killed in 1078 by Tutush, brother of Malik-Shāh, when he was put in charge of Syria by his brother. He, like Sulaymān, had a constant struggle to obtain recognition and tribute from the local rulers, and the situation remained confused.

The beginning of Seljūq decline

It is generally agreed that the power of the Seljūqs reached its peak at the end of the reign of Malik-Shāh. The 'empire' stretched from Central Asia and the Indian frontier to the Mediterranean, and from the Caucasus and the Aral Sea to the Persian Gulf, with a slight measure of control over Mecca and Medina. From time to time there was some local recalcitrance here and there, but on the whole the sultan's writ ran. The death of Malik-Shāh, however, led to a renewed struggle for the supreme power – a struggle which on this occasion threw up no individual strong enough to contain the centrifugal forces. It was in the Turkish tradition that the princes of the ruling family should each receive a command, while the senior member of the family had a certain primacy; but with the growth of power and wealth family loyalty weakened and this practice became unsatisfactory. The matter was complicated by the fact that, when the prince was a minor, he was put under the charge of an older and more experienced man known as the *atābeg* or 'father-chief'. This name or title was given to Niẓām-al-mulk in 1072 when Malik-Shāh was a minor. In the twelfth century several of the Atābegs of the

Seljūq princes managed to create little states for their own families. In addition, of course, the Great Seljūqs had to face all the problems which had confronted the Buwayhids.

In 1092 there were three main contestants for power. One son, Maḥmūd, was at once proclaimed sultan by the vizier who had succeeded Niẓām-al-mulk in league with his own mother. The partisans of Niẓām-al-mulk, however, supported the eldest son, Barkiyāruq; while their uncle Tutush, already in power in Syria, decided to make a bid for the sultanate. Maḥmūd was quickly eliminated. Barkiyāruq entered Baghdad and was nominated by the caliph in February 1094, and a year later defeated and killed Tutush, but was unable to dislodge the latter's sons from Damascus and Aleppo. In other areas the claims of Barkiyāruq were disputed by his two half-brothers, Muḥammad and Sanjar. At various dates between 1099 and 1102 it was Muḥammad and not Barkiyāruq who was mentioned in the official Friday prayers in Baghdad. This really depended on which brother's influence was stronger in Baghdad for the time being. Barkiyāruq was still nominally supreme sultan at the time of his death (probably 1 January 1105), but before long the Atābeg of his four-year-old son was killed, and his brother Muḥammad was recognized in Baghdad. The other brother, Sanjar, who was mostly on good terms with Muḥammad, had been ruling Khurasan and the eastern provinces since 1097 and was recognized as supreme sultan on Muḥammad's death in 1118, but had only partial control of his own provinces and virtually no authority in Iraq and western Persia. With his death in 1157 in an insurrection, Seljūq rule in the east came to an end, though it continued in Iraq until 1194.

The caliph al-Muqtadī died suddenly in Baghdad one day (or five days) after he had named Barkiyāruq with himself in the official prayers (February 1094). This may have been another in the series of political murders, but the succession passed without incident to his son, al-Mustaẓhir. The rivalry of the various Seljūq emirs enabled the caliph to recover a little power.

2

THE MEDITERRANEAN PROVINCES

The Seljūq 'empire' did not really touch the Mediterranean, though Aleppo and Antioch acknowledged Malik-Shāh for a time and Tutush and his sons also controlled that region. The fortunes of the Islamic states round the Mediterranean may therefore be considered independently of the Seljūqs.

Spain and North Africa

The important fact in the history of Islamic North Africa in the second half of the eleventh century was the rise of the Almoravid empire. Like many other Islamic states in Africa, this arose out of a religious movement. In 1039 some chiefs of the Berber tribal group of the Ṣanhāja, returning from a pilgrimage to Mecca, were greatly impressed by some of the scholars of Cairouan and took with them a young man called Ibn-Yāsīn who had been recommended to them. He was established in a *ribāṭ* – a combination of a house of retreat and a fortress – on the Senegal river, and there he taught the Mālikite form of Islamic law and gave a training in piety. He attracted large numbers of adherents, and these came to be known as al-Murābiṭūn, 'those of the *ribāṭ*', anglicized as Almoravids. By about 1055 the Almoravids had become an army and entered on a period of rapid expansion under military leaders who recognized the spiritual authority of Ibn-Yāsīn. By 1061 the territory they controlled was so vast that their lieutenant in the northern area was given a measure of independence. In 1162 he founded Marrakesh as his capital, and before long he had made himself ruler over the fertile areas of Morocco and the western half of modern Algeria.

Eastern Algeria and Tunisia at this period were in a chaotic condition. The governor left in Tunisia by the Fāṭimids when they moved to Egypt had extended his control over all the Mediterranean coastal areas and then made himself more or less independent. His descendants, known as the Zīrid dynasty, ruled in Tunisia and another branch of the family, the Ḥammādid dynasty, ruled in eastern Algeria. About the middle of the century, however, the Fāṭimids encouraged and facilitated the westward movement of Arab tribesmen of Hilāl and Sulaym, whom it had proved impossible to assimilate in Egypt. There may also have been an idea of punishing the Zīrids for acknowledging the ʿAbbāsid caliph. The wild tribesmen certainly created havoc wherever they went. The two dynasties lost most of the hinterland and were reduced to the ports of al-Mahdiyya and Bougie respectively, in which they developed sea-power and so maintained themselves. They were not sufficiently strong, however, to prevent the Norman conquest of Sicily, 1060–91.

The weakness of Islamic Spain under the 'party kings' enabled the Christian princes in the north to strengthen their position whenever they managed to stop quarrelling among themselves. At the end of the tenth century they had had to pay tribute to the Muslims, but by the middle of the eleventh century they were able to demand tribute from some of the petty Muslim rulers. The Christian frontier was pushed gradually southwards, the most notable event being that in 1085 the weak ruler of Toledo was unable any longer to resist the pressure of the king of Castile and handed over the city to him. Toledo had an admirable defensive position, being surrounded on three sides by the Tagus, and was never recaptured by the Muslims. Many Muslims and Jewish scholars continued to live there, and it became the chief centre for the transmission of the Islamic intellectual heritage to western Europe.

The strongest remaining Muslim ruler in Spain was al-Muʿtamid of Seville, though he was also paying tribute to the king of Castile. Alarmed at the threatening turn of events after 1085, al-Muʿtamid invited the Almoravid leader, Yūsuf ibn-Tāshufīn, to come to the aid of the Spanish Muslims. Yūsuf brought an army to Spain in 1086 and severely defeated the king of Castile at Zallāqa near Badajoz. This ended Muslims paying tribute to the Christians, but the latter began to fight back, and Yūsuf was asked to return in 1088. He found the petty Muslim rulers so given to intrigue that he decided to dethrone them all and to attempt himself to retrieve the fortunes of the Muslims. He returned at the end of 1090 and set about this task. In less than a year he was in control of most of the south. Badajoz fell to him in 1094, Valencia in 1102 and Saragossa to his son and successor in 1110. Almoravid power seemed well established in Spain, but it soon began to decline and disappeared in rebellions in 1144 and 1145. In 1147 their rule in North Africa was ended by the capture of Marrakesh by a rival Berber Muslim empire, that of the Almohads or al-Muwaḥḥidūn.

The Fāṭimids

By the middle of the eleventh century the Fāṭimids were beginning to be baffled by the problem which various eastern dynasties had failed to solve – the problem of how to control the professional armies. Even in Egypt Turks predominated, though there were also Sudanese, Berbers and Armenians. There was intense rivalry between these groups which sometimes led to actual warfare. After 1058 power was virtually in the hands of military cliques, who had little idea of the real needs of the country. This led to an administrative and economic breakdown, and famine was frequent. After a severe famine lasting from 1065 to 1072 the caliph al-Mustanṣir (reigned 1035–94) appealed to a general of Armenian race called Badr al-Jamālī, then governor of Acre. This man at once set sail for Egypt with his Armenian bodyguard and a loyal army. Before the nature of his commission from al-Mustanṣir was realized he had seized and executed the Turkish generals and Egyptian officials likely to give trouble. By other energetic measures and by firm rule he restored a measure of prosperity. He was usually known as 'emir of the armies' (*amīr al-juyūsh*), though he was also in charge of the administration and the *da'wa* or religio-political propaganda. In 1094 his son al-Afḍal, or al-Malik al-Afḍal, succeeded to his position and maintained the prosperity of the country until his death in 1121. After that the situation rapidly deteriorated, and in 1171 the Fāṭimids were replaced by Saladin and the Ayyūbids.

Almost the first act of al-Afḍal was to arrange the succession to al-Mustanṣir, who died at the end of 1094. The latter had named his son Nizār as successor, but al-Afḍal quickly proclaimed instead a younger son, al-Mustaʿlī, and induced most of the senior officials to accept this. He probably feared that Nizār would take away his appointment, whereas he would be able to manage al-Mustaʿlī. Nizār fled to Alexandria, but eventually had to surrender. Though promised his safety, he completely disappeared. This led to schism in the Ismāʿīlite movement. The Fāṭimids had long had a network of missionaries or propagandists in the lands acknowledging the ʿAbbāsid caliph. Discontented groups in various regions had been attracted by the prospect of a revolution with military support from the Fāṭimids. Time passed, however, and nothing happened. At length in 1090, apparently despairing of Fāṭimid help, the Ismāʿīlites of the Seljūq domains led by Ḥasan-i Ṣabbāḥ (al-Ḥasan ibn-aṣ-Ṣabbāḥ) seized the stronghold of Alamūt (north of Qazvin in northern Persia) and several other fortresses. After the events of 1094 these people continued to profess allegiance to Nizār. When he disappeared, he was held to be in hiding, and Ḥasan-i Ṣabbāḥ was accepted as *ḥujja* or 'proof'. At first there was doubtless genuine belief in Nizār's right, as well as suspicion of the power of the 'emir of the armies' over the caliph. In time, however, Ḥasan-i Ṣabbāh must have known that he had lost contact with Nizār, but probably also realized that to recognize Nizār was an excellent method of making himself absolute head of the movement in the east and independent of Egypt.

The rest of the history of Ismāʿīlism is beyond the limits of the present study. The followers of Ḥasan-i Ṣabbāḥ are of course also known as the Assassins, who made political murder an instrument of policy and so gave the word its contemporary meaning. The name is a European corruption of the local Syrian name of *Ḥashīshiyyīn*, 'the grass [*ḥashīsh*] people', whose meaning is obscure, though it may be asserted that there is no good foundation for the colourful stories of the use of hashish to drug young men. The Nizārians are today represented by the followers of the Aga Khan. The Mustaʿlians also exist in two sub-sects, both of which are found in India (as the Bohorās) and in the Yemen.

The Crusades

The significance of the Crusades for the Islamic world, which is all that concerns us here, was very different from their significance for western Europe. For the Muslims in general the Crusades were little more than a frontier incident – a continuation of the kind of fighting that had been going on in Syria and Palestine for the last half-century, whenever there was no overlord within reach who was able to keep the peace. For the Europeans, on the other hand, the Crusades were linked with a great religious revival, and indeed with more than that – with a vast movement of the spirit in which western Christendom attained a new awareness of its identity.

The occasion which led to the First Crusade was a speech by Pope Urban II at Clermont in 1095. The pope was in part moved by an appeal for help from the Byzantine emperor which he had just received and which was in response to the Muslim pressure on the empire since the battle of Manzikert in 1071. He was also aware of the Christian successes in Spain, culminating in the acquisition of Toledo, and of the Christian conquest of Sicily. Many other factors were, of course, involved.

The Crusaders were in Constantinople in 1097, and conquered Antioch and Jerusalem in June 1098 and July 1099 respectively. Five small Crusading states were established, and the rest of the Palestinian and Syrian coastline was eventually occupied.

From the standpoint of Islamic history the Crusades were an extremely foolhardy enterprise. They were relying above all on the great fighting power of a few heavily armed knights; but they had no idea of climatic or political conditions in the Holy Land or of the vast resources of the Islamic world. The amazing thing is that they won such a number of successes; but this occurred only because of the recent troubles of the region and the fact that it was divided into one or two major commands and several minor ones, so that each petty ruler was thinking only of his own interests and was ready to change alliances for a temporary advantage. As soon as the Atābeg of Mosul was able to consolidate his power by defeating his rivals, he was strong enough to expel the Crusaders from Edessa; and similarly Saladin, reaching a position of power in 1169, united Egypt and much of Syria under his rule, and was then able to inflict a number of defeats on the Franks and finally to recapture Jerusalem in 1187.

The only Muslims deeply involved were those within range of the fighting. The sultan Barkiyāruq issued a summons to the 'holy war' against the Franks early in 1098 before the fall of Antioch, but there was no effective response. After the fall of Jerusalem and the massacre there, many Muslims fled to Damascus and Iraq; and the authorities were aware of the presence of the refugees. The caliph al-Mustaẓhir got the ulema to urge emirs and princes to join in the 'holy war'; but nothing was done. A few verses relative to the Crusade have been preserved; but it is noteworthy that al-Ghazālī, who was in Jerusalem in 1096, and may have passed through again in 1097, has nowhere the slightest reference to the Crusaders.

For the Muslims, of course, there was nothing new in having to fight Christians. Muḥammad had been on good terms with some Christians, but latterly had met with hostility at both the intellectual and military levels. The Qur'ān therefore provides Muslims with a picture of Christianity which makes it easy for them to believe in the superiority of Islam. This attitude to Christians hardened during the first century or two of Islam with the appearance of additional material. Thus the Crusades did not require any change of attitude from the Muslims. For most western Christians, on the other hand, contacts with Muslims were a new experience, and they required guidance about the attitude to adopt. Thus from the twelfth to the fourteenth centuries western Christian scholars were providing their fellows with more information about Islam and Muslims but at the same time creating a distorted image of Islam to enable Christians to believe in their own superiority. There are still some vestigial traces of the medieval image in western European thinking.

3

THE INTELLECTUAL STRUGGLE

In the second half of the eleventh century no outstanding work of pure literature was written in Arabic. Through this period, however, lived al-Ḥarīrī of Basra (1054–1122), whose *Assemblies* have, since his own lifetime, 'been esteemed as, next to the Koran, the chief treasure of the Arabic tongue'; but it was not until 1101 that he composed the first *Assembly*. The appearance of the *Assemblies* in the early years of the twelfth century is significant and will not be lost sight of, but the absence of pure literature immediately before that justifies placing the main emphasis on the religious and indeed theological thinking of the time.

One general point to be noticed at the outset is that in this period statesmen paid increasing attention to theology; and this was not because it interested them personally (though it may have done so), but because they thought that theology had important political effects. The Seljūqs, following Maḥmūd of Ghazna, thought it advantageous to their cause to appear as the defenders of Sunnism; and the viziers al-Kundurī and Niẓām-al-mulk even selected the school of theology to be supported. These men had probably all some awareness of the successes of Fāṭimid propaganda, and saw that it could be effectively met only by some form of Sunnite propaganda.

The growth of Ḥanbalism

During the Buwayhid period the Ḥanbalites were in the forefront of the reaffirmation of Sunnism against Imāmism and other heretical doctrines. The creed first put forward by the caliph al-Qādir and formally read in public at various later dates was essentially a Ḥanbalite document. It is therefore not surprising to find that by the early Seljūq period the Ḥanbalites in Baghdad had a large popular following which had a prominent part in a number of riots.

One of the main objects of attack for the Ḥanbalites was Muʿtazilism and in particular a lecturer called Abū-ʿAlī ibn-al-Walīd. In 1063 he was attacked physically by a Ḥanbalite group known as 'the companions of ʿAbd-as-Samad' (a man who had died about 1007); and in 1068 the Ḥanbalite leader, the *sharīf* Abū-Jaʿfar al-Hāshimī (d. 1077), attacked him verbally in front of a huge crowd. On this occasion the Qādiriyya was reaffirmed and a work on theology by an anti-rationalist Shāfiʿite of the previous century was also read. Muʿtazilism was also involved in the criticism by Abū-Jaʿfar of a fellow-Ḥanbalite Ibn-ʿAqīl (1040–1119). He was accused of repeating some of the teaching of Abū-ʿAlī ibn-al-Walīd, whose lectures he had attended, and of being an admirer of the mystic al-Ḥallāj, put to death in 922. In 1072 he made a public retractation in which he repented of following Muʿtazilite doctrines and believed that al-Ḥallāj had been rightly condemned.

Another series of incidents began in 1077 shortly before the death of Abū-Jaʿfar. A man known as Ibn-al-Qushayrī, the son of a famous Shāfiʿite jurist and mystic, and himself also jurist and mystic as well as Ashʿarite theologian, came to preach in the Niẓāmiyya college at Baghdad with the permission of Niẓām-al-mulk. As well as expounding Ashʿarite views on the Qur'ān (which differed somewhat from the Ḥanbalite), he – a little unjustly – accused the Ḥanbalites of anthropomorphism. Naturally there was some rioting. The Ḥanbalite Abū-Jaʿfar had the support of the Shāfiʿite head of the Niẓāmiyya, Abū-Is'ḥāq ash-Shīrāzī, and of a well-known mystic, Abū-Saʿd, as well as that of the caliph al-Muqtadī; but other Shāfiʿite ulema took the side of Ibn-al-Qushayrī, while Niẓām-al-mulk thought that the Ḥanbalites were being unduly assertive of their views. The authorities smoothed things over by removing the chief participants, without condemning them, and by prohibiting all preaching for a time. In 1083 and again in 1101 there were somewhat similar incidents as a result of Ashʿarite sermons.

From the various stories it is clear that the Ḥanbalites had come to have a numerical predominance in Baghdad, as both the sultan Malik-Shāh and the vizier Niẓām-al-mulk seem to have explicitly admitted. The Imāmites, on the other hand, had all gone to Hilla or elsewhere; Abū-Jaʿfar aṭ-Ṭūsī (d. 1067) is spoken of as the last notable Imāmite scholar in Baghdad. In the last third of the eleventh century, then, it would seem that the main opponents of the Ḥanbalites were the Ashʿarites and the Muʿtazilites. The Ashʿarites will be mentioned presently; but who were the Muʿtazilites? To judge from the names given in the sources, they were not members of the Muʿtazilite theological school, but were primarily Traditionists or Ḥanafite or Shāfiʿite jurists. Perhaps 'Muʿtazilite' was applied to them as a nickname by Ḥanbalites to indicate an unsatisfactory belief about the Qur'ān. Certain of them were also suspected of Imāmite sympathies, which is not surprising since Muʿtazilite views had an attraction for most Imāmites. The safest conclusion is that the situation was fluid and that many men avoided definite commitments as far as possible. In this way some who, when Imāmism had had Buwayhid support, had been reckoned Imāmites, may now have rather been called Muʿtazilites. If this were so, the Muʿtazilites here might have been associated with the wealthy classes which had previously supported the Imāmites. The main Ḥanbalite support seems to have been from the ordinary people of Baghdad.

The Ashʿarites and al-Ghazālī

With al-Bāqillānī (as was seen in the previous chapter) Ashʿarite rational theology became an important part of the intellectual life of Baghdad in the early eleventh century and it also spread to some of the provinces, notably to Nishapur. In Nishapur in 1053, however, Ashʿarism was officially condemned from the pulpits along with Imāmism on the injunction of Ṭughril-Beg's vizier al-Kundurī. The reason for this treatment of Ashʿarism is not explained, but it is possibly due to the fact that as Ḥanafites in law the vizier and Ṭughril-Beg both regarded the Shāfiʿites as opponents. Because of the condemnation the leading Ashʿarite of Nishapur, al-Juwaynī

(d. 1085), spent several years in Mecca and Medina, and in consequence came to be known as Imām al-Ḥaramayn, 'the imam of the two sanctuaries'. The death of Ṭughril-Beg and the accession of Alp-Arslān led to the replacement of al-Kundurī by Niẓām-al-mulk as vizier. The latter was a Shāfiʿite and Ashʿarite, and was further convinced that Ashʿarism was best suited to be the basis of Seljūq rule in its struggle against Fāṭimid propaganda. He therefore gradually founded about a dozen colleges, each known as the Niẓāmiyya, in Nishapur, Baghdad and various provincial centres in the east. Staff and students were well provided for by endowments, and the aim was to provide teaching of a high quality in Shāfiʿite jurisprudence and, in some cases, in Ashʿarite theology. Al-Juwaynī became first head of the Niẓāmiyya in Nishapur.

About 1077 a young scholar of nineteen went to Nishapur from neighbouring Ṭūs to study under al-Juwaynī. This was al-Ghazālī (Abu-Ḥāmid Muḥammad ibn-Muḥammad ibn-Muḥammad), one of the greatest of Muslim thinkers, though perhaps overesteemed in the West, since he is one of the Muslims towards whom westerners find it easiest to feel sympathetic. This again is largely due to the charm of his autobiographical *apologia pro vita sua*, entitled *Deliverance from Error*, which he completed two or three years before his death in December 1111. To fill out our understanding of the Islamic world up to 1100 it is well worth looking more closely at al-Ghazālī.

He was born at Ṭūs (near modern Meshhed) in 1058, and was educated there, at Jurjan and finally at Nishapur. Jurisprudence was the core of his education, and to this al-Juwaynī added Ashʿarite theology. On the death of al-Juwaynī in 1085 he was invited to join other scholars at the mobile camp and court of Niẓām-al-mulk. Here he so distinguished himself in intellectual debates that in 1091 he was appointed chief professor in the Niẓāmiyya college in Baghdad, at the age of thirty-three. His primary duty would be to lecture on jurisprudence; and he tells us that three hundred students attended his lectures. In 1095, however, he passed through an inner crisis, and also developed an impediment in his speech which prevented him from lecturing. The outcome of the crisis was a decision to abandon his professorship and adopt the life of a wandering ascetic. He slipped away from Baghdad in November 1095, ostensibly to make the pilgrimage to Mecca, but spent a year in retreat in Damascus and Jerusalem before actually doing so. Then, with one or two short halts, he seems to have made his way back to Ṭūs, where along with some young disciples he adopted a kind of monastic existence. In July 1106 he was persuaded by the son of Niẓām-al-mulk to take up the professorship at the Niẓāmiyya of Nishapur. Though still only in his early fifties, he retired from this post about 1110, perhaps because of ill health, and died at Ṭūs at the end of 1111.

In *Deliverance from Error* he relates how, after a period of scepticism he resolved to make an active search for ultimate (religious) truth in the four places in which it was most likely to be found: among the rational theologians, the philosophers, the Bāṭinites (that is, Ismāʿīlites) and the Ṣūfīs or mystics. He then describes his investigations as four chronological stages, though in his actual experience there was probably no strict separation of the various fields. His criticism of the rational theologians was that they operated within certain presuppositions which they refused to question, whereas he was interested precisely in the justification of these presuppositions. When he examined the disciplines of the philosophers (which included mathematics and natural science), he considered primarily how far they were compatible with Islamic dostrine. The Ismāʿīlites he was chiefly concerned to refute. Finally he decided that the truth of the Ṣūfīs could not be acquired by purely academic study, but only by sharing in their life; and this line of thought led to his departure from Baghdad.

Many other points could be discussed. Other factors which might underlie the decision to leave Baghdad include disgust at the worldliness of his colleagues, and fear of succumbing to political intrigue – a fear which could be based on the fact that he, a man in a prominent position, had for a time supported Tutush against Barkiyāruq, the ultimate victor. In general he seems to have been moved by a deep desire for 'the revival of the religious disciplines' in his own day, and this is in fact the title of his chief work.

Al-Ghazālī's achievements can be summed up under three heads. First, he was mainly responsible for defining the attitude of Sunnite Islam to philosophy, by showing that some of the philosophical disciplines were to be entirely rejected, whereas others, such as logic, could be useful servants of theology. Second, he contributed to the intellectual defeat of Ismāʿīlism. Third, he made an important contribution to gaining for Ṣūfism *droit de cité* within Sunnite Islam; where some earlier mystics had tended to be heretical in belief and practice, he demonstrated, in *The Revival of the Religious Disciplines* and elsewhere, that the observance of the ordinary duties of Islam could be a helpful basis for the life of a ṣūfī. One might have expected him to do something about the tensions between Ḥanbalites and Ashʿarites which had led to so many disturbances in Baghdad, but he does not discuss the subject explicitly. He may have felt that the problem was restricted to Baghdad, and he himself spent only a little more than four years in Baghdad. Moreover, while he vigorously attacked clear heresies, within Sunnism his attitude was eirenic, and he warned his colleagues that they should not declare other scholars infidels because of some slight divergence of view. This was mainly directed to disputes among Sunnites. Finally, it may be noted that, while the above points are those which have interested European scholars and which al-Ghazālī himself mentions in *Deliverance from Error*, his chief influence on Muslim scholars of the next two centuries, to judge from references to him, was in the field of jurisprudence!

Assessment

The intellectual currents of the Islamic heartlands in the second half of the eleventh century seem to show a further phase of the struggle between the Arab outlook or mentality on the one hand and Persian, Greek and similar outlooks on the other. The Ḥanbalite movement is in some ways the most Arab of the various legal and theological schools and movements within Islam, and thus the growth of Ḥanbalism is a mark of further self-assertion by the Arabs, especially against Greek rationalism. The Ḥanbalites tried to base all individual social and political life on the Qur'ān and the Traditions – that is, in a very general sense, on intuition, on ideas not derived from reason – and to exclude all use of reason. It is therefore fully in keeping that roughly the same period as saw the growth of Ḥanbalism should also have witnessed the appearance of the greatest literary product of the Arab mentality – which non-Arabs have great difficulty in being enthusiastic about – the *Assemblies* of al-Ḥarīrī. These are similar to the *Assemblies* of Badīʿ-az-zamān al-Hamadhānī, but are executed with unsurpassable wit and verbal brilliance.

On the opposing side from the Ḥanbalites were those who in

varying degrees advocated the use of reason on the Greek model. Virtually nothing is now heard of the Persian opponents of Arabism, perhaps because since the time of Firdawsī they felt they had a significant role within Islamic society and because Persian literature was now developing – the vizier Niẓām-al-mulk wrote a book in Persian on the art of governing. The extreme representatives of the Greek outlook were the philosophers, but they, though they had an immense influence on western Europe, stood apart from the main stream of Islamic thought. Then there were the Muʿtazilites who at this date may have stood for a less wholehearted acceptance of the Qur'ān as the basis of all activity. The Ashʿarites were opposed by the Ḥanbalites because they allowed some use of reason, but even al-Ghazālī, despite his enthusiasm for some aspects of philosophy, made it very clear that these could be accepted only in strict subordination to the Qur'ān and the Traditions.

It should also be noted, however, that the non-rational ideas on which all activity was to be based were those which had been generally accepted by the community of Muslims. Ideas derived from the experiences of an individual, however profound, were still suspect. This seems to be the point of making Ibn-ʿAqīl retract his admiration for al-Ḥallāj. In some of his later works al-Ghazālī suggests that the 'intuitive' knowledge of the mystic, which he calls *dhawq* or 'taste', is above the rational knowledge of the scholar; but this conception of 'taste' is not taken up by later writers.

The struggle or tension between Semitic intuition and Greek reason is one that has not yet been settled or resolved. We westerners tend to admire Greek reason for we realize that it is the source of our amazing scientific achievements, though we are beginning to understand something of its limitations. We must certainly not despise Semitic intuition, since, in the form of the revealed scriptures of Judaism and Islam, it has been the basis of some of the most stable communities the world has known.

Epilogue

THE REPLACEMENT OF CHRISTIAN CULTURE BY ISLAMIC

The five chapters of this work have surveyed some four and a half centuries of the history of the Fertile Crescent and the surrounding lands. They have sketched the growth of one of the world's great cultures; they have spoken of the rise and fall of dynasties; they have presented glimpses of considerable human achievements, individual and corporate, and of immeasurable human suffering. All this has been part of that march of humanity which goes steadily onwards and, perhaps on the whole, upwards. Some of the events and processes here described have contributed to making us Europeans what we are, and most of them have been still more closely associated with the formation of those of our fellow human beings who are the present bearers of Islamic culture.

Besides the processes described, however, another process was going on, but it was so gradual and imperceptible that it was impossible to mention its progress in a survey that moved forward decade by decade and reign by reign. This process was the disappearance – or perhaps one should say fossilization – of most of the Christian culture of the region. There was nothing dramatic about what happened; it was a gentle death, a phasing out. Yet the result of the process was an important 'event' in world-history, which deserves more attention from historians, especially Christian historians, than it has hitherto received. It is very closely linked with what has here been called 'the self-assertion of the Arabs', and indeed might be regarded as the negative side of that.

Before the Arab conquest of the Fertile Crescent the chief bearers of culture were the Christians. In Egypt there was virtually no one else. In Syria there were also a few philosophically minded pagans, who came to be known to the Muslims as Ṣabians. In Iraq there were Zoroastrian clergy and scholars who in addition to their own literature possessed some Indian works in translation. The level of learning among the Christians of Iraq appears to have been higher than that elsewhere, for there were several colleges where Christian theology and Greek science were taught in the medium of Syriac. Once the disturbances of the wars of conquest had subsided, not much was changed for the ordinary Christians, including the scholars. Life continued to be tolerable or even enjoyable. In Baghdad round about the year 1000 Christian and Muslim philosophers had a joint discussion circle. In Egypt under the Fāṭimids there were still many Christians in prominent positions. Yet there were certain social pressures on Christians, especially the pressure which came from being a *dhimmī* or second-class citizen; and as a result there was a steady trickle of conversions from Christianity to Islam. The Christians tended to be confined socially within their own community, and as the community diminished it became more difficult to maintain the institutions of higher learning. In so far as the latter still existed they tended to become fossilized. Christian culture was no longer living and growing, and the number of its bearers was constantly becoming less.

In order to understand how Christian culture came to fade away and how Islamic culture came to burgeon in its place – though Islamic culture is much the same culture but in an Arabic dress – it is necessary to look beyond the purely religious questions. In particular it is necessary to look at the relation between the Greek outlook and mentality and the Semitic, or more generally non-Greek, outlook and mentality. As a result of the conquests of Alexander the Great in the fourth century B.C. Greek influences spread into Asia as far as India. Christianity came to birth in a Jewish society that had erected formidable social defences against the intrusion of Greek ideas and customs; but in the changed circumstances of the early Roman empire these defences were preventing Judaism from developing into a world religion. From this standpoint Christianity is seen as having removed most of the Jewish defences to become a universalized form of the religion of the Old Testament. The Roman empire, however, was deeply hellenized, and when Christianity spread in non-Jewish circles it also became deeply hellenized.

The two centuries immediately before the Arab conquests witnessed a revolt within Christianity against the dominance of Greek ideas. Since the adherents of Greek ideas had a majority in the Ecumenical Councils which decided such matters, those who revolted against Greek ideas were branded as heretics. Essentially, however, those with whom we are here concerned were insisting on the right of non-Greek linguistic and cultural minorities to express their Christian faith in a manner consonant with their special outlook and mentality. Such are the Copts of Egypt – the native Egyptian Christians – who are reckoned to have held the Monophysite heresy. One group of Syriac-speakers, usually known as Jacobites, were also reckoned Monophysites. The other main group of Syriac-speakers, holding almost diametrically opposed views, are known by the nickname of Nestorians. At a later period the Armenian-speakers came to be regarded as holding yet another heresy. In short, what from the standpoint of the academic theologian are heresies, from the standpoint of the historian are expressions of the self-assertion of cultural groups. Indeed, especially in the case of the Syriac-speakers, these are examples of the same struggle between Semitic (or non-Greek) intuition and Greek reason which we have been looking at within the Islamic world. In Christianity the Great Church had become over-identified with Greek culture, but there was also a movement against Greek culture.

Finally we may ask why the Arabs succeeded where the Syriac-speakers failed. One obvious point is that the Christian non-Greeks were divided among themselves. Had there been several centuries more before the Arab conquest, Copts, Jacobites, Nestorians and Armenians might conceivably have produced a new culture. Yet this outcome does not seem likely, since the movement against Greek culture was in a sense defensive. The Arabs, on the other hand, discovered Greek science and philosophy at a time when they were still in a phase of expansion. Too much should not be made of this point, however, since the Nestorians were still expanding eastwards long after the Muslim conquest. Perhaps, then, Arab success was due not so much to the expanding and missionary quality of Islamic religion as to the Arabs' intense belief in themselves. As has been explained above, the expansion was military and political, not religious; but the creation of an Arab empire, coupled with the self-confidence and self-assertion of the Arabs, gave a strong impulse towards cultural unity once many subjects of the empire came to be attracted by Islam as a religion. To become a Muslim one had to become an Arab at least by clientship; and in addition one had to learn Arabic, since for centuries all religious thinking was in Arabic.

The unity and homogeneity of the new Islamic culture based primarily on the Arabic language is an undoubted fact, but there are also certain divisions within this culture which should not be overlooked. The protests of the Persians against Arab cultural domination have been mentioned, and also the appearance of a new Persian literature which fostered the growth of a Persian 'national' consciousness within Islamic culture. More fundamental, however, was the split between Sunnite and Shī'ite, even though at the present time more than nine-tenths of all Muslims are Sunnites. If anyone wants to pursue further this line of thought, he might consider whether there is any parallelism between the division among Syriac-speakers between Monophysite and Nestorian and the division among Muslims between Shī'ite and Sunnite. Nestorianism is not so far removed from Sunnism, and the Monophysite emphasis on the charismatic person has perhaps a slight resemblance to Shī'ism. If there is this parallelism, then the change from 'Christian' to Islamic culture is not so great as it seems, yet from the standpoint of organized religious communities the change is absolute.

Bibliography

The present work is an attempt to survey an extensive field of human affairs, though one which has been very unevenly cultivated by scholars. There is a vast amount of material available, and all that this bibliography can do is to mention the main works on the different aspects of the subject so as to enable the reader to begin to find his way about. Original sources are not included except in translation.

GENERAL WORKS

BIBLIOGRAPHIES AND OTHER ANCILLARY WORKS

There is an excellent critical bibliography, of which some forty or fifty pages are relevant to the period here studied: *Jean Sauvaget's Introduction to the History of the Muslim East*, Berkeley and Los Angeles, 1965. This is a translation with some expansion of *Introduction à l'histoire de l'orient musulman* by Jean Sauvaget, second edition revised by Claude Cahen, Paris, 1961. J. D. Pearson's *Index Islamicus 1906–55*, Cambridge, 1958, with *Supplements* covering five-yearly periods, lists without comment all relevant articles in a wide range of periodicals. The *Abstracta Islamica*, published annually since 1927 as part of the *Revue des Études Islamiques* (Paris), list books as well as the more important articles, sometimes with brief indications of the contents. The lists in both the *Index* and the *Abstracta* are classified.

On the chronology of the various caliphs, sultans and other rulers the fundamental work is: E. von Zambaur, *Manuel de genealogie et de chronologie pour l'histoire de l'Islam*, Hanover, 1927. The chief dates, with some slight revisions, are found in C. E. Bosworth, *The Islamic Dynasties*, Edinburgh, 1967. A useful geographical work for the provinces from Iraq to the Indian border is *The Lands of the Eastern Caliphate* by G. Le Strange, second impression, Cambridge, 1930.

An invaluable work of reference is the *Encyclopaedia of Islam*. The second edition (Leiden and London, 1960) now reaches to about the end of the letter I, and on several matters gives the fullest available account; some of the later articles of the first edition (Leiden, 1913–42) are still important. Historical and literary figures appear under their names, general topics under a (transliterated) Arabic caption. This work is cited below as *EI*².

GENERAL AND POLITICAL HISTORY

Brockelmann, Carl. *History of the Islamic Peoples*, London, 1949.
Hitti, Philip K. *History of the Arabs*, London, 1937.
Holt, Lambton and Lewis (eds.), *The Cambridge History of Islam*, two vols, Cambridge, 1970.
Laoust, Henri. *Les schismes dans l'Islam*, Paris, 1965.
Lewis, Bernard. *The Arabs in History*, London, 1950.
Mantran, Robert. *L'expansion musulmane (VIIᵉ–XIᵉ siècles)*, Paris, 1969.
Sourdel, Dominique and Janine. *La civilisation de l'Islam classique*, Paris, 1968.
Spuler, Bertold. *The Muslim World: a Historical Survey*, Part I, 'The Age of the Caliphs', Leiden, 1960.
von Grunebaum, Gustav E. *Classical Islam, a History 600–1258*, London, 1970.

Becker, C. H. *Islamstudien*, vol. 1, Leipzig, 1924.
Gibb, Sir Hamilton. *Studies on the Civilization of Islam*, London, 1962.

These two works are collections of articles; that by Gibb entitled 'An Interpretation of Islamic History' is specially relevant.

CULTURAL AND INTELLECTUAL HISTORY

Gardet, Louis and Anawati, M.-M. *Introduction à la theologie musulmane*, Paris, 1948.
Gibb, Sir Hamilton. *Mohammedanism, an Historical Survey*, London, 1949, etc.
Goldziher, Ignaz. *Vorlesungen über den Islam*, second edition, Heidelberg, 1925.
——, *Muslim Studies*, two vols, London, 1967, 1971. (English translation of a work which first appeared in German 1888–90.)
von Grunebaum, G. E. *Medieval Islam, a Study in Cultural Orientation*, Chicago, 1946.
——, *Islam: Essays in the Nature and Growth of a Cultural Tradition*, Menasha, 1955.
Watt, W. Montgomery. *Islamic Philosophy and Theology*, Edinburgh, 1962.
——, *Islamic Political Thought, the Basic Concepts*, Edinburgh, 1968.
——, *The Formative Period of Islamic Thought*, Edinburgh, 1973. (Contains the detailed justification of several of the views expressed in the present work.)
Wensinck, Arent Jan. *The Muslim Creed*, Cambridge, 1932.

LITERARY HISTORY

Blachère, Régis. *Histoire de la litterature arabe*, vols 1–3, Paris, 1952–66.
Brockelmann, Carl. *Geschichte der arabischen Litteratur*, two vols, second edition, Leiden, 1943–9; three Supplement-bänder, Leiden, 1937–42. (Mainly a list of manuscripts and printed editions, with brief biographical details.)
Dunlop, D. M. *Arab Civilization to AD 1500*, London 1971. (Also contains information about philosophy and science.)
Gibb, Sir Hamilton. *Arabic Literature*, second edition, Oxford, 1963. (The basis of many of the judgements in the present work.)
Ibn Khallikan's Biographical Dictionary, translated by Baron MacGuckin de Slane, reprinted New York, 1961. (The main emphasis is on writers and scholars, but there are notices of some rulers and statesmen.)
Kritzeck, James. (ed.), *Anthology of Islamic Literature*, Harmondsworth, 1964.

Nicholson, Reynold A. *A Literary History of the Arabs*, new impression, Cambridge, 1930, etc.
Sezgin, Fuat. *Geschichte des arabischen Schrifttums*, several vols, Leiden, 1967. (An enlarged form of Brockelmann, above, more from a Muslim standpoint.)
Williams, John Alden (ed.). *Islam*, New York, 1961. (Texts of religious interest in translation.)

JURISPRUDENCE

Coulson, Noel J. *A History of Islamic Law*, Edinburgh, 1964.
——, *Conflicts and Tensions in Islamic Jurisprudence*, Chicago, 1969.
Schacht, Joseph. *The Origins of Muhammadan Jurisprudence*, Oxford, 1950.
——, *An Introduction to Islamic Law*, Oxford, 1964.

I: THE UMAYYAD PERIOD

GENERAL

Al-Balādhurī, *The Origins of the Islamic State* (Eng. tr.), New York, 1916. (Chiefly an account of the early conquests.)
Al-Masʿūdī, *Les prairies d'or* (French tr.), nine vols, Paris, 1861–77.
Dennett, D. C. *Conversion and the Poll-tax in Early Islam*, Cambridge (Mass.), 1950.
Gabrieli, Francesco. *Muhammad and the Conquests of Islam*, London, 1968.
Løkkegaard, F. *Islamic Taxation in the Classic Period*, Copenhagen, 1950.
Shaban, M. A. *The ʿAbbāsid Revolution*, Cambridge, 1970.
Wellhausen, Julius. *The Arab Kingdom and its Fall* (Eng. tr.), Calcutta, 1927.

SPAIN

Palencia, A. González. *Historia de la España musulmana*, fourth edition, Barcelona, 1945.
Lévi-Provençal, E. *Histoire de l'Espagne musulmane*, three vols, Paris, 1940–7. (Reaches only to 1031.)
Terrasse, Henri. *Islam d'Espagne*, Paris, 1958.
Watt, W. Montgomery and Cachia, Pierre. *Islamic Spain*, Edinburgh, 1965.

'FORMS OF GOVERNMENT'

The following articles in *EI*² are relevant:
ʿAṭāʾ (Cl. Cahen) – stipends or pensions;
ʿArīf (S. A. el-Ali, Cl. Cahen) – military officials responsible for distributing stipends;
Dhimma (Cl. Cahen) – deals with 'protected minorities';
Dīwān (A. A. Duri) – Dīwān of ʿUmar; governmental bureaux;
Djaysh (Cl. Cahen) – the army;
Djund (D. Sourdel) – the military settlements in Syria.

II: THE FIRST ʿABBĀSID CENTURY

GENERAL

Abusaq, M. O. *The Politics of the Miḥna under al-Maʾmūn and his Successors*, Leiden (forthcoming).
Donaldson, D. M. *The Shiʾite Religion*, London, 1933.

Patton, W. M. *Aḥmed b. Ḥanbal and the Miḥna*, Leiden, 1897.
Sourdel, Dominique. *Le vizirat 'abbāside de 749 à 936*, two vols, Damascus, 1959–60.

LAW AND TRADITIONS

Al-Bukhārī, *Les traditions islamiques* (French tr.), four vols, Paris, 1903–14.
Guillaume, Alfred. *The Traditions of Islam*, Oxford, 1924. (Follows Goldziher, *Muslim Studies*, ii.)
Majid Khadduri, *Islamic Jurisprudence: Shāfi'ī's Risāla*, Baltimore, 1961.
Mishkāt al-maṣābīḥ, Eng. tr. by J. Robson, four vols, Lahore, 1963–5.

III: THE 'ABBĀSID DECLINE

GENERAL (in addition to works already mentioned)

Bowen, H. A. *The Life and Times of 'Alī ibn 'Isā, the good Vizier*, Cambridge, 1928.
Ivanow, W. *Ismaili Tradition concerning the Rise of the Fatimids*, London, 1942.
Lewis, Bernard. *The Origins of Ismā'īlism*, Cambridge, 1940.
Miskawaih, *The Experiences of the Nations* (Eng. tr. by D. S. Margoliouth), three vols, Oxford, 1921.
Articles in *EI*²: 'Abbāsids, Buwayhids, Fāṭimids, Ḥamdānids, al-Barīdī, Badjkam, Ibn Rā'iḳ.

LITERATURE AND THEOLOGY

Ibn Qutayba, *Le traité des divergences du ḥadīt* (French tr. by G. Lecomte), Damascus, 1962.
Laoust, Henri. *La profession de foi d'Ibn Baṭṭa*, Damascus, 1958. (Has a long introduction on the development of Ḥanbalism.)
Lecomte, Gérard. *Ibn Qutayba, l'homme, son œuvre, ses idées*, Damascus, 1965.
McCarthy, Richard J. *The Theology of al-Ash'arī*, Beirut, 1953. (Mainly translations.)
Madelung, Wilfred. *Der Imam al-Qāsim ibn Ibrāhīm*, Berlin, 1965. (Authority for the Zaydites of the Yemen.)
Pellat, Charles. *Le milieu baṣrien et la formation de Ǧāḥiẓ*, Paris, 1953.
——, *The Life and Works of Jāḥiẓ* (Eng. tr.), London, 1969. (Chiefly translations from Jāḥiẓ himself.)
——, art. Djāḥiẓ in *EI*².

WORKS ON ṢŪFISM

Anawati, G. C. and Gardet, Louis, *Mystique musulmane*, Paris, 1961.
Arberry, A. J. *The Doctrine of the Ṣūfīs*, Cambridge, 1935. (Translation of a work by al-Kalābādhī, d. *c.*995.)
——, *The Book of Truthfulness*, London, 1937. (Text and translation of a book by al-Kharrāz, d. *c.*900.)
——, *Sufism*, London, 1950.
Massignon, Louis. *La passion d'al-Hallaj, martyr mystique de l'Islam*, two vols, Paris, 1922. (Important for the whole intellectual history of early Islam; a second edition and English translation are in preparation.)
——, *Essai sur les origines du lexique technique de la mystique musulmane*, second edition, Paris, 1954. (Also deals with the history of ṣūfism before al-Ḥallāj.)
Nicholson, R. A. *The Kashf al-Mahjūb of al-Hujwīrī* (Eng. tr.), London, 1911. (Deals with the early history of ṣūfism.)
——, *The Idea of Personality in Ṣūfim*, Cambridge, 1923.

Smith, Margaret. *Rābi'a the Mystic and her Fellow-Saints in Islam*, Cambridge, 1928.
——, *An Early Mystic of Baghdad*, London, 1935. (A study of al-Muḥāsibī, d. 857.)
van Ess, Josef. *Die Gedankenwelt des Ḥāriṯ al-Muḥāsibī*, Bonn, 1961.

IV: THE BUWAYHID PERIOD

GENERAL

Bosworth, C. E. *The Ghaznavids: their Empire in Afghanistan and Eastern Iran, 994–1040*, Edinburgh, 1963.
Canard, M. *Histoire de la dynastie des H'amdanides de Jazīra et de Syrie*, Paris, 1953.
Kabir, Mafizullah. *The Buwayhid Dynasty of Baghdad*, Calcutta, 1964.
Mez, Adam. *The Renaissance of Islam* (Eng. tr.), Patna, 1937. (Describes many different aspects of the civilization of Islam during the tenth century.)
*EI*², art. 'Imād al-Dawla (Cl. Cahen). (Has additional bibliography for the Buwayhids in general.)

SCIENCE AND PHILOSOPHY

Dunlop, D. M. *Arabic Science in the West*, Karachi, n.d. (Based on four lectures given in Cambridge in 1953; see also his *Arab Civilization*.)
Miele, Aldo. *La science arabe et son rôle dans l'évolution scientifique mondiale*, revised edition, Leiden, 1966. (A valuable guide with extensive references.)
Ullman, Manfred. *Die Medizin im Islam*, Leiden, 1970. (An exhaustive account; part of the *Handbuch der Orientalistik*, which will also contain volumes on the other sciences and philosophy.)
van Ess, Josef. 'Ḍirār b. 'Amr und die "Cahmīya"; Biographie einer vergessenen Schule', *Der Islam*, xliii (1967), 241–79; xliv (1968), 1–70, 318–20. (Important for the earliest study of Greek ideas.)
Walzer, Richard. *Greek into Arabic*, Oxford, 1962. (Articles reprinted, of which the first is a sketch of Islamic philosophy.)
——, 'L'éveil de la philosophie islamique', *Revue des Études Islamiques*, xxxviii (1970), 7–42, 207–42.
Watt, W. Montgomery. *The Influence of Islam on Medieval Europe*, Edinburgh, 1972. (Pp. 30–43 deal with 'Arab Achievements in Science and Philosophy', with bibliographical notes, 98–101.)
Wickens, G. M. (ed.). *Avicenna: Scientist and Philosopher*, London, 1952.

LITERATURE

Nicholson, R.A. *Studies in Islamic Poetry*, Cambridge, 1921. (Mainly about the *Meditations* of al-Ma'arrī, with translations.)

V: THE EARLIER SELJŪQ PERIOD

GENERAL

Cahen, Claude. *Pre-Ottoman Turkey*, London. 1968.
Laoust, Henri. *La politique de Ġazālī*, Paris, 1970.
Lewis, Bernard. *The Assassins*, London, 1967.
*EI*²: arts. al-Basāsīrī; Alp- Arslān.

LITERARY AND INTELLECTUAL

al-Ghazālī. *The Revival of the Religious Disciplines* (*Iḥyā'*); the following separate books have been translated into English: i (Knowledge), ii (The Creed), iii

(Purity), by N. A. Faris, Lahore, 1962, 1963, 1966; iv (Worship) by E. E. Calverley, Madras, 1925; v (Almsgiving) by Faris, Beirut, 1966; xviii (Music and Feeling) by D. B. Macdonald in *Journal of the Royal Asiatic Society*, 1901, 1902; xx (Muḥammad's Example) by L. Zolondek, Leiden, 1963; xxxiii (Fear and Hope) by W. McKane, Leiden, 1962.

al-Ḥarīrī. *The Assemblies* (Eng. tr. by T. Chenery and F. Steingass), two vols, London, 1867, 1898.

Ibn Ḥazm. *The Ring of the Dove* (Eng. tr. by A. J. Arberry), London, 1953.

Makdisi, George. *Ibn 'Aqīl et la résurgence de l'Islam traditionaliste au XIe siècle*, Damascus, 1963.

Niẓām-al-mulk. *The Book of Government* (Eng. tr. by H. Darke), London, 1960.

Watt, W. Montgomery. *The Faith and Practice of al-Ghazālī*, London, 1953. (Translations of *Deliverance from Error* and *The Beginning of Guidance.*)

——, *Muslim Intellectual: a Study of al-Ghazali*, Edinburgh, 1963.

EPILOGUE (and Muslim–Christian relations)

'Alī aṭ-Ṭabarī. *The Book of Religion and Empire* (Eng. tr. by Mingana), Manchester, 1922.

The Apology of Timothy, in A. Mingana, *Woodbrooke Studies*, vol. 2, Cambridge, 1928.

Browne, Laurence E. *The Eclipse of Christianity in Asia*, Cambridge, 1933.

Fritsch, E. *Islam und Christentum im Mittelalter*, Breslau, 1930.

Watt, W. Montgomery. 'The Attitude of Islam to Christianity' in *Islam and the Integration of Society*, London, 1961, 258–77.

Appendix

1: *Note on Arabic Names*

The full name of an Arab and of many non-Arab Muslims may consist of as many as five elements, some of which may be multiple.

1. The name proper (*ism*); e.g. Muḥammad, Ibrāhīm, Hishām; also compounds such as: ʿAbd-Allāh ('servant of God'), ʿAbd-ar-Raḥmān ('servant of the Merciful'). Some non-Arabs may have both an Arabic and, for example, a Turkish name.

2. The 'father-name' (*kunya*), that is, 'father of . . .'; e.g. Abū-Ḥanīfa ('father of Ḥanīfa'). Originally this was bestowed after the birth of a male child (sometimes, especially in pre-Islamic times, of a female), but it could also be given as a mark of honour or in anticipation. Muḥammad's childless wife ʿĀ'isha was given the *kunya* Umm-ʿAbd-Allāh in respect of a nephew.

3. The filiation or genealogy, in the form 'ibn-X (or bint-X) ibn-Y ibn-Z . . .', that is, 'son (or daughter) of X, who was the son of Y who was son of Z . . .'. Some men are commonly known by such a name, e.g. Ibn-Hishām. Aḥmad ibn-Ḥanbal is properly Aḥmad ibn-Muḥammad ibn-Ḥanbal.

4. The relative or adjectival name (*nisba*), which may be formed from a town, a tribe, a distinguished ancestor, etc.; e.g. al-Baghdādī, al-Hāshimī, al-Fāṭimī.

5. The *laqab*, which may be either a nickname, like al-Jāḥiẓ ('the goggle-eyed'), al-Ḥallāj ('the carder'), or a name of honour, like Rukn-ad-dawla ('support of the state'). The 'throne-names' of the

ʿAbbāsids and others, such as al-Manṣūr ('the one made victorious', sc. by God), are a form of *laqab*.

The use of names has always been to some extent a matter of fashion. It has mostly been the practice for a man's friends and disciples to address him by his *kunya*, and this is often followed in books by disciples. Historians may use different parts of the name in different contexts. In the Buwayhid period names of honour (conferred by the caliph) began to proliferate. What is important is that a short but distinctive form should be used; it is presumably for this reason that the jurist mentioned is known as Aḥmad ibn-Ḥanbal. In the present work a single form has usually been adhered to. Use has been made of hyphens to indicate groups of words which constitute a single unit and may not be split up or shortened; e.g. Ibn-Hishām, ʿAbd-ar-Raḥmān, Rukn-ad-dawla. The journalistic contraction of Gamāl ʿAbd-an-Nāṣir, the late ruler of Egypt, to 'Nasser' is a blasphemous solecism, for it means that instead of being 'servant of the Victory-giver' he becomes 'the Victory-giver', that is God!

The *kunya* usually comes before the name proper, and an honorific *laqab* comes first of all. The *nisba* is usually last.

2: *Note on Islamic Dates*

In the present work the dates have all been given according to the Christian era. In the sources, however, they are all given according to the Islamic era, the era of the Hijra. This is considered to have begun on 16 July, A.D. 622, the first day of the old Arab year in the course of which Muḥammad made his Hijra or migration from Mecca to Medina. Unfortunately the calculation of equivalent Christian dates is a complex matter, since the Islamic year consists of twelve lunar months or 354 days. This means that the Islamic year may begin at any point in the solar year, and that 100 Islamic years equal about 97 solar years. Relatively simple conversion tables are given in G. S. P. Freeman-Grenville, *The Muslim and Christian Calendars*, London, 1963. The fundamental work is: *Wüstenfeld-Mahler'sche Vergleichungs-Tabellen zur muslimischen und iranischen Zeitrechnung*, third edition (edited by Bertold Spuler), Wiesbaden, 1961; this gives the Christian date for the first day of each Islamic month, and much other information.

The chief point to be noted in connection with the present work is that, where only the Islamic year is given for a birth, death or other event, it is generally impossible to say in which of two Christian years this took place. Some authors give both Christian years, e.g. 286 A.H./899–900 A.D.; but this is not as precise as it appears to be since 899–900 here means from 17 January 899 to 6 January 900, whereas 901–2 (for 289 A.H.) means from 16 December 901 to 4 December 902. In the present work the convention has been followed that, where only the Islamic year is known, the Christian year *in which it begins* has been treated as the equivalent. Where the Islamic month is known the precise Christian year can be given except in those cases where the month falls between two Christian years.

Index

In the alphabetical order the Arabic article (al-, an-, etc.) is neglected